The Taxing Power

Recent Titles in
Reference Guides to the United States Constitution
Jack Stark, Series Editor

The Right to the Assistance of Counsel
James J. Tomkovicz

Prohibited Government Acts
Jack Stark

State Sovereign Immunity
Melvyn R. Durchslag

Constitutional Remedies
Michael Wells and Thomas A. Eaton

Privileges and Immunities
David Skillen Bogen

Searches, Seizures, and Warrants
Robert M. Bloom

The Supremacy Clause
Christopher R. Drahozal

Procedural Due Process
Rhonda Wasserman

Double Jeopardy
David S. Rudstein

Freedom of the Press
Lyrissa Barnett Lidsky and R. George Wright

The Taxing Power

A Reference Guide to the United States Constitution

Erik M. Jensen

Foreword by Henry P. Monaghan

REFERENCE GUIDES TO THE
UNITED STATES CONSTITUTION, NUMBER 11
Jack Stark, *Series Editor*

PRAEGER

Westport, Connecticut
London

Library of Congress Cataloging-in-Publication Data

Jensen, Erik M.
The taxing power : a reference guide to the United States Constitution / Erik M. Jensen; foreword by Henry P. Monaghan.
p. cm.—(Reference guides to the United States Constitution, ISSN 1539-8986; no. 11)
Includes bibliographical references and index.
ISBN 0-313-31229-X (alk. paper)
1. Taxation—Law and legislation—United States.
2. Taxing power—United States. I. Title. II. Series.
KF6289.J46 2005
343.7304—dc22 2004017543

British Library Cataloguing in Publication Data is available.

Library of Congress Catalog Card Number: 2004017543
ISBN: 0-313-31299-X
ISSN: 1539-8986

First published in 2005

Praeger Publishers, 88 Post Road West, Westport, CT 06881
An imprint of Greenwood Publishing Group, Inc.
www.praeger.com

Printed in the United States of America

The paper used in this book complies with the Permanent Paper Standard issued by the National Information Standards Organization (Z39.48-1984)

10 9 8 7 6 5 4 3 2 1

Contents

Series Foreword

JACK STARK

One can conceive of the United States Constitution in many ways. For example, noting the reverence in which it has been held, one can think of it as equivalent to a sacred text. Unfortunately, most of its devotees have had less knowledge and even less understanding of the document than they have had reverence for it. Sometimes it is treated as primarily a political document and on that basis has been subjected to analysis, such as Charles Beard's *An Economic Interpretation of the Constitution of the United States*. One can plausibly argue that the Constitution seems most astounding when it is seen in the light of the intellectual effort that has been associated with it. Three brief but highly intense bursts of intellectual energy produced, and established as organic law, most of the Constitution as it now exists. Two of these efforts, sustained over a long period of time, have enabled us better to understand that document.

The first burst of energy occurred at the Constitutional Convention. Although some of the delegates' business, such as the struggle between populous and nonpopulous states about their representation in Congress, was political, much of it was about fundamental issues of political theory. A few of the delegates had or later achieved international eminence for their intellects. Among them were Benjamin Franklin, Alexander Hamilton, and James Madison. Others, although less well known, had first-rate minds. That group includes George Mason and George Wythe. Many of the delegates contributed intelligently. Although the Convention's records are less than satisfactory, they indicate clearly enough that the delegates worked mightily to constitute not merely a polity but a rational polity—one that would rise to the standards envisioned by the delegates' intellectual ancestors. Their product, though brief, is amazing. William Gladstone called it "the most wonderful work ever struck off."

Despite the delegates' eminence and the Constitution's excellence as seen from our place in history, its ratification was far from certain. That state of affairs necessitated the second burst of intellectual energy associated with that document: the debate over ratification. Soon after the Convention adjourned, articles and speeches—some supporting the Constitution and some attacking it—began to proliferate. A national debate commenced, not only about the document itself, but also about the nature of the polity that ought to exist in this country. Both sides included many writers and speakers who were verbally adroit and steeped in the relevant political and philosophical literature. The result was an accumulation of material that is remarkable for both its quantity and its quality. At its apex is *The Federalist Papers,* a production of Alexander Hamilton, James Madison, and John Jay that deserves a place among the great books of Western culture.

Another burst, not as impressive as the first two but highly respectable, occurred when the Bill of Rights was proposed. Some delegates to the Constitutional Convention had vigorously asserted that such guarantees should be included in the original document. George Mason, the principal drafter of the Virginia Declaration of Rights, so held, and he walked out of the Convention when he failed to achieve his purpose. Even those who had argued that the rights in question were implicit recognized the value of adding protection of them to the Constitution. The debate was thus focused on the rights that were to be explicitly granted, not on whether any rights *ought* to be explicitly granted. Again many writers and speakers entered the fray, and again the debate was solidly grounded in theory and was conducted on a high intellectual level.

Thus, within a few years a statement of organic law and a vital coda to it had been produced. However, the meaning and effect of many of that document's provisions were far from certain; the debates on ratification of the Constitution and the Bill of Rights had demonstrated that. In addition, the document existed in a vacuum, because statutes and actions had not been assessed by its standards. The attempt to resolve these problems began after Chief Justice John Marshall, in Marbury v. Madison, asserted the right of the U.S. Supreme Court to interpret and apply the Constitution. Judicial interpretation and application of the Constitution, beginning with the first constitutional case and persisting until the most recent, is one of the sustained exertions of intellectual energy associated with the Constitution. The framers would be surprised by some of the results of those activities. References in the document to "due process," which seems to refer only to procedures, have been held also to have a substantive dimension. A right to privacy has been found lurking among the penumbras of various parts of the text. A requirement that states grant the same "privileges and immunities" to citizens of other states that they granted to their own citizens, which seemed to guarantee important rights, was held not to be particularly important. The corpus of judicial interpretations of the Constitution is now as voluminous as that document is terse.

As the judicial interpretations multiplied, another layer—interpretations of interpretations—appeared, and also multiplied. This layer, the other sustained intellectual effort associated with the Constitution, consists of articles, most of them published in law reviews, and books on the Constitution. This material varies in quality and significance. Some of these works of scholarship result from meticulous examination and incisive thought. Others repeat earlier work, or apply a fine-tooth comb to matters that are too minute even for such a comb. Somewhere in that welter of tertiary material is the answer to almost every question that one could ask about constitutional law. The problem is finding the answer that one wants. The difficulty of locating useful guidance is exacerbated by the bifurcation of most constitutional scholarship into two kinds. In "Two Styles of Social Science Research," C. Wright Mills delineates macroscopic and molecular research. The former deals with huge issues, the latter with tiny issues. Virtually all of the scholarship on the Constitution is of one of those two types. Little of it is macroscopic, but that category does include some first-rate syntheses such as Jack Rakove's *Original Meanings*. Most constitutional scholarship is molecular and, again, some fine work is included in that category.

In his essay, Mills bemoans the inability of social scientists to combine the two kinds of research that he describes to create a third category that will be more generally useful. This series of books is an attempt to do for constitutional law the intellectual work that Mills proposed for social science. The author of each book has dealt carefully and at reasonable length with a topic that lies in the middle range of generality. Upon completion, this series will consist of thirty-seven books, each on a constitutional law topic. Some of the books, such as the book on freedom of the press, explicate one portion of the Constitution's text. Others, such as the volume on federalism, treat a topic that has several anchors in the Constitution. The books on constitutional history and constitutional interpretation range over the entire document, but each does so from one perspective. Except for a very few of the books, for which special circumstances dictate minor changes in format, each book includes the same components: a brief history of the topic, a lengthy and sophisticated analysis of the current state of the law on that topic, a bibliographical essay that organizes and evaluates scholarly material in order to facilitate further research, a table of cases, and an index. The books are intellectually rigorous—in fact, authorities have written them—but, due to their clarity and to brief definitions of terms that are unfamiliar to laypersons, each is comprehensible and useful to a wide audience, one that ranges from other experts on the book's subject to intelligent non-lawyers.

In short, this series provides an extremely valuable service to the legal community and to others who are interested in constitutional law, as every citizen should be. Each book is a map of part of the U.S. Constitution. Together they map all of that document's territory that is worth mapping. When this series is complete, each book will be a third kind of scholarly work that combines the macroscopic and the molecular. Together they will explicate all of the important constitutional topics. Anyone who wants assistance in understanding either a topic in constitutional law or the Constitution as a whole can easily find it in these books.

Foreword

HENRY P. MONAGHAN
HARLAN FISKE STONE PROFESSOR OF CONSTITUTIONAL LAW, COLUMBIA UNIVERSITY

Many academic subjects have seldom-studied backwaters and eddies. Federal taxation provides one such example. Federal taxation is, of course, a hugely important topic on many levels, and the Internal Revenue Code and its implementing regulations are studied assiduously. But the constitutional underpinnings of federal taxation are not. Entrenched wisdom has it that the relevant constitutional provisions impose no meaningful internal limits on the national taxing power, certainly not after ratification of the Sixteenth Amendment. Accordingly, constitutional law casebooks treat federal taxation not as an independent topic, but as an aspect of some other subject, such as use of the taxing power to achieve regulatory ends not achievable under the commerce clause.

Serious study of the taxing power as an independent topic seems to have peaked during the late nineteenth century, and it ended with the ratification of the Sixteenth Amendment. Perhaps constitutional law scholars would have paid more heed to the subject had the Supreme Court done so, but seemingly the Court decides a noteworthy case in this area only about once a century. In its first tax case, Hylton v. United States (1796), which did attract considerable attention, the Court upheld a tax on carriages (a tax that James Madison believed was unconstitutional)—with the various justices making some strong statements about the scope of the taxing power. A century later, in Pollock v. Farmers' Loan and Trust Co. (1895), the Court invalidated aspects of an income tax in a decision that was front page news at the time. Because the tax was politically popular and because *Pollock* seemed to have rejected longstanding precedent (including *Hylton*), the decision was widely condemned (and in practical effect was overturned fairly quickly by the Sixteenth Amendment).

Pollock was the last publicly visible Supreme Court tax case. Now, after yet another century has elapsed, the topic shows modest signs of a revival. In United States v. International Business Machines Corp. (1996) and United States v. United States Shoe Corp. (1998), the Court determined that the application of two tax statutes violated the Export Clause of the constitution. In their technical details, *IBM* and *U.S. Shoe* are of limited practical importance: the relevant clause forbids only certain levies on "articles exported"; it says nothing about taxes of general application. Nevertheless, the cases are noteworthy because they reinvigorate the long dormant idea that the constitution does impose some internal limits on the taxing power.

One of the virtues of *The Taxing Power* is that Erik Jensen shows how much more has been going on judicially than my simplified historical summary suggests. In the process, he challenges deeply ingrained scholarly and judicial consensus that the constitution *should not* (and therefore *does not*) contain any significant internal constraints on the taxing power. *The Taxing Power* should help modify the conventional wisdom. The relationship between the constitution and taxation is, in fact, a fascinating and complex one, as Professor Jensen demonstrates. To be sure, the constitution dramatically increased the nation's power to raise revenue—no one (and certainly not Professor Jensen) seriously questions that proposition. It is, therefore, easy to forget that the document also built internal checks into the taxing power. Limiting congressional power to tax is the explicit aim of several constitutional provisions—the Uniformity Clause, the direct-tax apportionment clauses, and the Export Clause—and other doctrines have developed that, in some circumstances, have constrained congressional power.

No scholar in recent times had brought together the learning on these various constitutional provisions and doctrines. Professor Jensen has now done just that, in a comprehensive and satisfying manner, and he has done so in lucid and sparkling prose. Jensen is part of a small group of legal scholars whose studies of taxation and the constitution are now attracting attention throughout the legal academy. Some of these scholars approach the subject from the perspective of constitutional lawyers and others with the outlook of tax lawyers, Jensen's area of substantive expertise. Some adhere to the traditional view that the taxing power is largely unconstrained; others, like Jensen, see the Constitution as significantly limiting that power.

The goal of this new scholarship is not necessarily to change the law's direction. Some of the taxing clauses and doctrines are of largely historical interest, and, although Jensen attempts to find contemporary significance for nearly all of them, not everyone will be persuaded by that effort. But whether he is persuasive on an item-by-item basis is beside the point. Jensen presents the interpretive disputes fairly, and he convincingly argues that the constitutional limitations on the taxing power are interesting, potentially important, and surely worth study. Whatever the immediate doctrinal effects, *The Taxing Power* should help to invigorate the study of the constitution's place in federal taxation, and that by itself is a reason to welcome this book. And if Professor Jensen is right on the merits and some of the limitations turn out to be more important than scholarly commentators have assumed to this point—if, for example, the Direct-Tax Clauses really do matter even today—that's all the more reason to be grateful (or is it?) for this thoroughly engaging book.

Acknowledgments

This book is the culmination of several years' study of constitutional limitations on the taxing power. Along the way I have been encouraged by many different colleagues at Case Western Reserve University and elsewhere. I am particularly indebted to Professor Jonathan L. Entin, who has read earlier versions of several chunks of the material in this book and who co-authored articles with me on requisitions and the relationship between the taxing power and the Compensation Clause. To avoid inadvertently omitting anybody else important, I will list no other names. But you know who you are, and I thank you.

I also thank Laura Gorjanc, of the Case School of Law class of 2004, who taught me almost everything I know about intergovernmental tax immunity.

Erik Jensen
Cleveland, Ohio
November 2004

1

Introduction

The Congress shall have Power To lay and collect Taxes, Duties, Imposts and Excises, to pay the Debts and provide for the common Defense and general Welfare of the United States; but all Duties, Imposts and Excises shall be uniform throughout the United States.—Article I, section 8, clause 1

Taxation may seem like a dry-as-dust subject, and it does not ordinarily attract much attention from constitutional scholars. But in 1787, invigorating the revenue system was one of the primary reasons for a new constitution. It was no accident that the Taxing Clause begins the list of congressional powers in Article I, section 8.

By any standard, the national government formed under the Articles of Confederation had little power. As its name suggests, the Articles created a confederation of states, rather than a modern government with power over individuals. Under the Articles, the Continental Congress could not impose taxes of any sort—no duties on imports, no excises, no real-estate taxes, and certainly nothing like a personal income tax (a concept that was, in any event, largely unknown at the time of the founding).

With no real taxing power over individuals available to it, the Continental Congress had three mechanisms to fund the Revolutionary War effort. Pursuant to a provision in the Articles, it could and did print paper money. In cranking up the printing presses, Congress was obviously doing what it felt it had to do to survive, but this was an act of desperation for a fiscally suspect government, not a policy to be followed by a stable regime during peacetime.

The Articles also specifically granted the Continental Congress power to borrow funds, but borrowing was easier said than done. Since repayment was dependent on the cooperation of the often recalcitrant states—money to repay any loans would ultimately have to come from the states through the requisitions process described in the following section—the national government was not a particularly creditworthy institution. Benjamin Franklin had some success arranging wartime loans from the French government, but Franklin's success depended in large part on his special relationship with the *ancien régime*, something the United States obviously could not depend on forever.

That left requisitions as the primary source of revenue provided for in the Articles. Congress could requisition funds from the states and leave it up to the states to determine where the funds would come from. That was fine if the states complied, and sometimes they did. But if a state ignored a requisition, the national government could do nothing about it.

As a result, in practice requisitions turned out to be little more than requests for contributions—occasionally honored, but often not (hence the national government's difficulty in borrowing). Even the strongest skeptics of national power, of which there were many at the founding, understood that the taxing power had to be enhanced if there was to be a really *United* States of America. A government without a dependable way of raising revenue would be unable to function.

Something had to change, and change it did. As Roger Brown has put it, "The experience with the breakdown of taxation . . . drove the constitutional Revolution in 1787."[1] After ratification of the Constitution, the United States was, for the first time, able to levy taxes that would operate directly on American citizens and residents, without the states serving as intermediaries. The creation of a true national taxing power was an enormous step—indeed, one might argue, an essential step in the creation of a nation. The nature of that taxing power (with, along the way, some discussion of the related borrowing power) is the subject of this book.

The conventional wisdom these days is that Congress is basically unconstrained in what it can do in the tax area. For example, Professor Bruce Ackerman has posited that "there are no significant limits on the national governments's taxing, spending, and regulatory power where the economy is concerned—other than the requirement that government compensate owners if their property is taken for public purposes."[2] If that is so, then there is little interesting to say about the taxing power, other than describing the history of how we got to where we are. The history is in fact interesting in itself, but in this introduction I shall begin defending the proposition that the nature of the taxing power today—and, in particular, the limitations on that power—is a subject worthy of serious discussion in its own right.

IS THE TAXING POWER PLENARY?

With a Constitution unquestionably intended to make it possible for the national government to raise revenue, it is perhaps not surprising that commentators today, with few exceptions, emphasize the broadness of the taxing power. The Constitution has been referred to as a *pro-tax* document, and the taxing power is often characterized as *plenary*, used in this context to mean without significant limits. Historian Loren Beth, for example, has described the taxing clause in Article I, section 8 as "so sweeping that it has seldom been construed as an interference with any tax measure."[3]

If the taxing power were really that broad and unconstrained, this book could have been *very* short, as I suggested earlier. Following a chapter or two of history, the analysis section could have been one sentence long: Congress can do whatever it wants in taxation. The end.

So one might reasonably ask about the importance of this subject. Is this book on the taxing power thrown into an important series on the Constitution merely for the sake of completeness? (There will probably be discussion somewhere on "Title[s] of Nobility" and "Letters of Marque," too, but not a whole book on those dated topics!)

Things cannot be that easy and, as a result, the book cannot be that short. To be sure, one can find support for a plenary-power conception in snippets from the constitutional text, founding-era documents, and the case law interpreting the constitutional text. The first clause in Article I, section 8 quoted above—"The Congress shall have Power To lay and collect Taxes, Duties, Imposts and Excises"—is by itself far-reaching in its implications. Add the commonly held idea that the powers granted the national government under the Constitution are necessarily broader than the specifics enumerated in Article I, section 8, and the mixture is a potent one indeed. The latter idea—that congressional power is broader than the powers enumerated in Article I, section 8—is grounded either in the proposition that the General-Welfare Clause ("The Congress shall have Power To lay and collect Taxes . . . and *provide for the . . . general Welfare of the United States*") is an independent grant of congressional power or in the extra-constitutional proposition that a government must have the revenue power to do whatever needs to be done.

For example, Alexander Hamilton argued in Federalist 23 that "it is both unwise and dangerous to deny the federal government an unconfined authority in respect to all those objects which are intrusted to its management,"[4] and taxation was one of the powers needed for an "energetic government."[5] If the government needs to tax, and of course it does, the power "ought to exist without limitation, *because it is impossible to foresee or to define the extent and variety of national exigencies, and the correspondent extent and variety of the means which may be necessary to satisfy them.*"[6]

In Federalist 30, Hamilton insisted that the taxing power should be limited not by the terms of the Constitution but only by the "resources of the community":

> Money is, with propriety, considered as the vital principle of the body politic; as that which sustains its life and motion and enables it to perform its most essential functions. A complete power, therefore, to procure a regular and adequate supply of revenue, as far as the resources of the community will permit, may be regarded as an indispensable ingredient in every constitution.[7]

Hamilton's conception of an expansive taxing power found a receptive audience in the early Supreme Court. In Hylton v. United States (1796), the Court for the first time considered the nature of the taxing power. In upholding the constitutionality of a national tax on carriages, the justices—all Federalists sympathetic to the government's arguments presented by former Secretary of the Treasury Hamilton—viewed the power expansively. Justice Samuel Chase, for example, wrote that the "term taxes, is generical, and was made use of to vest in Congress plenary authority in all cases of taxation."[8]

Hylton was just the beginning. The Court has used the term *plenary power* or something similar often since 1796. As recently as Ptasysnki v. United States (1983), a case arising under the Uniformity Clause (the subject of Chapter 5), the Court characterized "Congress' power to tax [as] virtually without limitation."[9]

Those were strong words indeed, and contrasted with what had existed under the Articles of Confederation, the taxing power does seem to be all-encompassing. When the benchmark is no power at all—when the national government had previously been unable even to impose a duty on imports—it took little in the way of augmentation for the taxing power to seem extraordinary. The description of the Constitution as pro-tax fairly characterizes the historically important contrast between the Articles and the Constitution.

But the term *pro-tax*, like the term *plenary power*, can be misleading. It requires a leap of faith to conclude that the taxing power created by the Constitution, strengthened though that power unquestionably had been, was intended to be virtually unlimited. Such a characterization wrenches the Constitution out of its historical context, which, Professor Owen Fiss notes, was "defined by the desire to prevent abuses of the power of taxation."[10] Founders who had so recently been concerned about taxation without representation were unlikely to have intentionally created an unconstrained national taxing power.

The plenary-power conception also necessarily discounts (or totally ignores) several specific limitations on the taxing power in the Constitution. One explicit constraint is included in the language of the first clause of Article I, section 8 quoted earlier, the requirement that "Duties, Imposts and Excises shall be uniform throughout the United States." One might be able to imagine reasons for having a geographically variable tax, say, but the Uniformity Clause prevents Congress from even trying such a strategy. Elsewhere in Article I, in sections 2 and 9, the Constitution provides that direct taxes must be apportioned among the states on the basis of respective state populations (the direct-tax apportionment rule), a requirement that certainly complicates (and thus makes more difficult) the enactment of direct taxes, whatever they are. Also in Article I, section 9, Congress is altogether precluded from imposing taxes or duties on "Articles exported from any State" (the Export Clause).

Sometimes form matters, and, in form, the Uniformity Clause, the Direct-Tax Clauses, and the Export Clause do not look like trivial limitations on congressional power. Furthermore, if the founding generation really thought that the General-Welfare Clause or some other abstract principle could trump all specific limitations on the taxing power, a great deal of energy in the ratification debates was devoted to a nonissue.

In fact, it was the anti-federalists who expressed concern about what they viewed as the open-endedness of the taxing power. Supporters of the Constitution, who understood the need to make the Constitution palatable to the American population, generally stressed the limits on that power. In Federalist 41, for example, James Madison responded to constitutional opponents who had asserted that the Taxing Clause in Article I, section 8, with its general-welfare provision, "amounts to an unlimited commission to exercise every power which may be alleged to be necessary for the common defense or general welfare." Nonsense, wrote Madison, "No stronger proof could be given of the distress under which these writers labor for objections, than their stooping to such a misconstruction."[11]

If the Constitution had listed only very general powers, Madison argued, the case for an expansive reading of the taxing power would have been stronger, although even then "it would have been difficult to find a reason for so awkward a form of describing an authority to legislate in all possible cases." In any event, that was not the way the Constitution was set up. Instead, Article I, section 8 includes a long list of specific congressional powers, and it is difficult to infer from such a list that Congress has the "authority to legislate in all possible cases." Madison explained, "[T]he idea of an enumeration of particulars which neither explain nor qualify the general meaning, and can have no other effect than to confound and mislead, is an absurdity."[12] Madison was clearly unsympathetic to reading the Constitution in a way that would have extended the taxing power beyond its terms, including the specific limitations on the taxing power.

Reading the introductory language of Article I, section 8 in isolation thus gives an incomplete conception of the taxing power. Congress without doubt has the "power to lay and collect Taxes, Duties, Imposts and Excises," but a discussion of the national taxing power is inevitably a discussion of the limitations on that power. Indeed, as will become clear throughout this book, one might say that it is the *limitations* on what Congress can do that define the taxing power, and it is only if the limitations are trivial that the taxing power can properly be characterized as *plenary* or *virtually without limitation*.

ARE THE LIMITATIONS TRIVIAL?

Plenary-power proponents have to concede that the Constitution contains specific limitations on the taxing power—like them or not, the limitations are there—but some proponents nevertheless maintain that the limitations are trivial. The limitations deal only with mechanics, or so the argument goes. They have little effect on the grand constitutional scheme, which provides for a taxing power that can reasonably be characterized as *plenary*.

The argument is this: with one exception (in the Export Clause), the limitations do not prohibit Congress from enacting any particular type of tax. As historian Dall Forsythe has written, the nationalist founders, "anxious that there be no limitations on the kind of taxes the general government could levy[,] were almost entirely successful, and (except for export duties) no single tax was altogether denied the new Congress."[13] With this understanding of the potential scope of congressional power (Congress can enact nearly any *kind* of tax), plenary-power proponents stress the insignificance of the specific limitations. From the proposition that the power over taxation is plenary in the sense that Congress has at least some authority over almost all areas of taxation, the inference is drawn that the power is nearly unlimited.

The Supreme Court itself has occasionally implied that the uniformity and direct-tax apportionment rules are little more than irritants. (As will be discussed later, until the late 1990s there was also reason to doubt that the Export Clause was on the Court's radar screen.) In Brushaber v. Union Pacific Railroad Co. (1916), for example, the Court suggested that these rules are compatible with an omnipotent taxing power—the rules "were not so much a limitation upon the complete and all embracing authority to tax, but in their essence were simply regulations concerning the mode in which the plenary power was to be exerted."[14]

Brushaber echoed the interpretation of the uniformity and apportionment rules expounded in Veazie Bank v. Fenno (1869), where the Court stated: "These are not strictly limitations of power. They are rules prescribing the mode in which it shall be exercised. It still extends to every object of taxation, except exports, and may be applied to every object of taxation, to which it extends, in such measure as Congress may determine." As a result,

> [t]he comprehensiveness of the power . . . given to Congress, may serve to explain, at least, the absence of any attempt by members of the Convention to define, even in debate, the terms of the grant. The words used certainly describe the whole power, and it was the intention of the Convention that the whole power should be conferred. The definition of particular words, therefore, became unimportant.[15]

"Simply regulations"? "Not strictly limitations of power"? "The definition of . . . words . . . became unimportant"? If these characterizations of the explicit limitations on the taxing power are accurate, and this was the United States Supreme Court, after all, then the term *plenary* might reasonably be applied to the taxing power. Detailed examination of the uniformity rule and the direct-tax apportionment rule will come later in this volume, but suffice it to say for now that this disparagement of two explicit limitations on the taxing power is not self-evidently correct. The technically accurate point—that the Constitution imposes almost no limits on the *kinds* of taxes Congress might impose—does not translate into no limits on the taxing power.

That the limitations can be serious even if they do not explicitly prohibit particular kinds of taxes can be illustrated by considering the effect that the direct-tax apportionment rule had on the modern income tax. The concept of an income tax was new in the late eighteenth century, and it was probably unknown to most of the founders. (England did not enact an income tax until 1799. Some founders became familiar with Adam Smith's *The Wealth of Nations*, in which Smith discussed income taxes, but it is not clear that Smith was read by many founders before the Constitution was ratified.) The founders thus had no reason to say anything one way or the other about income taxes at the Constitutional Convention or in the ratification debates.

As plenary-power proponents stress, the imposition of such a tax was within Congress's power "to lay . . . Taxes" once the Constitution was ratified. Whatever the Sixteenth Amendment did, the 1913 Amendment was not necessary to make an income tax possible—something the Supreme Court has noted several times, in *Brushaber* and its companion, Stanton v. Baltic Mining Co. (1916), for example.[16]

If Congress could have enacted an income tax in 1789, and almost no one disputes that proposition, is there any reason to care about the original limitations on the taxing power? Of course there is. Congress has always had the power to enact an income tax, but until the Sixteenth Amendment was ratified, Congress did not clearly have the power to enact anything like the modern income tax.

The Sixteenth Amendment was critical because, in Pollock v. Farmers' Loan & Trust Co. (1895), a case that will be discussed in detail in Chapter 4, the Court concluded that the direct-tax apportionment rule was more than a simple "regulation." In *Pollock*, the Court struck down an 1894 income tax on the ground that it was a direct tax that had not been properly apportioned among the states on the basis of population.

The significance of that determination cannot be overstated. Regardless of *Pollock*, an *apportioned* income tax would have been constitutionally acceptable, but Congress had not enacted an apportioned income tax, and for very good reasons. Apportioning an income tax among the states on the basis of respective state populations would probably have required different tax rates in different states (or some other rickety structure). Furthermore, to make apportionment come out right, citizens of higher-income states would probably have been subject to tax at *lower* rates than those in lower-income states. Apportionment of that sort could have been handled technically (congressional staffers can do the math to get the numbers right), but such a step would have been almost impossible politically.

The practical result of *Pollock*, taken seriously, was that the income tax as we have come to know it was impossible without a constitutional amendment. That Congress had had the power since 1789 to enact an apportioned income tax was technically true but largely irrelevant. The Supreme Court can call a rule that effectively precludes an unapportioned income tax simply a *regulation* if it wishes, or it may say that the rule is "not strictly [a] limitation of power," but to casual observers, the direct-tax apportionment rule, as interpreted in *Pollock*, was an absolute roadblock preventing Congress from doing what it wanted to do.

Most commentators today disparage *Pollock*, but, regardless of whether the case was clearly right, it was on the books and Congress had to deal with it. Indeed, it is because the apportionment rule was so important that the Sixteenth Amendment was critical in the development of American taxation. By exempting "taxes on incomes" from the apportionment rule, the Amendment made it possible for Congress to enact an *unapportioned* tax on incomes—with the same rates across the country and higher collections *per capita* from the states with higher-income populations. The Amendment made the modern income tax possible in the United States.

This brief history of the income tax illustrates that the limitations on the national taxing power in the Constitution have in fact had significant effect across the centuries. That should not be a surprise; the founders intended the limitations to have effect. Even staunch proponents of a strong national taxing power in the founding era understood this. Despite the bombastic language quoted above from two numbers of *The Federalist*, Alexander Hamilton, that most nationalistic of nationalists, recognized that serious limits on the taxing power were built into the Constitution. In discussing the direct-tax apportionment rule in Federalist 36, for example, Hamilton emphasized that "[t]he abuse of this power of [real-estate] taxation seems to have been provided against with guarded circumspection."[17] The apportionment rule had a purpose, to prevent abusive taxation of a particular sort, and the rule was structured to effectuate that purpose.

Hamilton presumably would have interpreted the apportionment rule and the other limitations on the taxing power narrowly, and he probably wished that they were not in the Constitution to begin with. But he conceded their existence and effect, as he had to—if only for political reasons. He wanted the Constitution to be ratified, and stressing an unlimited taxing power would almost certainly have doomed the ratification of that document.

THE CONTEMPORARY RELEVANCE OF THE LIMITATIONS ON THE TAXING POWER

All of the discussion to this point has been relevant to the general proposition that the limitations in the Constitution on the taxing power matter and are thus worth serious consideration. Toward that same general end, one more argument made by plenary-power proponents is worth introductory attention: that whatever the historical importance of the limitations, little or nothing of this matters today, except to students of American history. Times have changed, it is often argued, passing the limitations by.

One important way in which times have arguably changed is that the judiciary has generally been reluctant since the 1920s (and maybe even earlier) to take the limitations seriously. Judges tend to see tax statutes as valid unless the statutes have clear constitutional flaws, and tax statutes hardly ever have clear constitutional flaws. This inclination to defer to Congress characterizes the judiciary in most areas of taxation. For example, in *Ptasysnki*, the Uniformity Clause case decided in 1983, the Supreme Court wrote that "[w]here . . . Congress has exercised its considered judgment with respect to an enormously complex problem, we are reluctant to disturb its determination."[18] Indeed, with the exception of two

Supreme Court cases interpreting the Export Clause in the 1990s, United States v. International Business Machines Corp. (1996) and United States v. United States Shoe Corp. (1998), the Supreme Court has struck down no taxing statutes on constitutional grounds since the 1920s.

Furthermore, the longer the Court maintains a hands-off posture, the greater the likelihood of future deference to congressional enactments. Because so little attention was paid to the Constitution in twentieth-century taxation, it would be difficult, and maybe even impossible, to get the tax system of the twenty-first century back into conformity with old-fashioned constitutional constraints—assuming we could agree on what they are. The clock, say plenary-power proponents, cannot be turned back.

In any event, the old concepts (again assuming we could agree on what they are) might not work today. An obvious conceptual problem is how to apply centuries-old provisions (and a nearly century-old provision, the Sixteenth Amendment) to the analysis of tax systems that could not possibly have been contemplated at the time those provisions were adopted. Few modern forms of taxation were known to the founders, and some of the forms that were discussed at the Constitutional Convention, such as capitation taxes or national taxes on real estate, have either not been attempted at all by Congress (the capitation tax) or have not been used for more than a century. (The last national real estate tax was enacted in 1861.) Furthermore, the Constitution is silent (for which we can all be grateful) about the taxation of business entities: not a mention of the taxation of partnerships, limited liability companies, trusts, and corporations—the meat and potatoes of many tax lawyers.

Giving Congress a free hand in taxation is thus inevitable to deal with changing conditions in society, or so plenary-power proponents argue. And, if the Supreme Court defers to Congress, acting as if the taxing power is limitless, then, as a practical matter, the taxing power may be limitless. Professor Richard Epstein (not a plenary-power proponent by any means) has made the point this way:

> It seems clear that our own original constitutional structure did purport to impose explicit limitations upon the power to tax . . . . Yet . . . where suspect classes and fundamental rights (as defined by the current jurisprudence) are not at issue, these limitations have all eroded with time; so today, over vast spheres of economic activity, the power to tax is plenary.[19]

Similarly, in discussing the income tax, Professor Boris Bittker has explained how a once restricted power may have become all-encompassing: "[T]he federal power to tax income is not free-floating or 'plenary' in nature, but is instead subject to numerous constitutional provisions . . . . [But] these constitutional restraints seldom create any serious problems in the day-to-day application of the federal income tax."[20]

If all of that is not convincing enough, a plenary-power proponent can throw in the apparent clincher: the founding period is no longer the benchmark for analysis. The ratification of the Sixteenth Amendment in 1913, exempting "taxes on incomes" from the direct-tax apportionment rule, changed everything: regardless of whether the old rules ever mattered much, they do not matter now because the Amendment so dramatically extended congressional power.

In 1895, when the Supreme Court invalidated an income tax on the ground that it was a direct tax that had not been properly apportioned (Pollock v. Farmers' Loan & Trust Co., 1895), students of the Constitution had reason to care about the meaning of the term "direct taxes." However, whatever the appropriate characterization of an income tax under the terms of the original Constitution, such a tax today need not be apportioned. Furthermore, with the income tax's having assumed so much importance in the American revenue system, constraining national taxing power in other respects is beside the point. Professor Michael Graetz has written that, "[a]fter the constitutional validity of the income tax was settled by the ratification of the Sixteenth Amendment in 1913, the authority of the Congress in the field of taxation has not been seriously challenged,"[21] presumably because there would be little or no point to such a challenge. With the unapportioned income tax available for revenue, who cares whether Congress can enact an unapportioned national tax on real estate?

Those arguments are not without merit. Although a legal author hates to admit it, relatively little of the doctrine discussed in this book is likely to have immediate, practical consequences in dispute resolution. It will continue to be the case that the overwhelming majority of tax cases that raise constitutional issues will be brought by tax protesters—the sorts of folks who raise frivolous constitutional claims (that the Sixteenth Amendment was not properly ratified, for example), not serious issues about limits on the national taxing power.

Nevertheless, it is one of the purposes of this book to demonstrate that the limitations on the national taxing power are important even if understood in their most limited ways, and that, understood as the founders knew them, the limitations could have even more far-reaching effect today. Among the conclusions that might be drawn from this book is that, if its provisions are taken seriously, the Constitution would constrain taxation to a much greater extent than is generally understood. Except for the Sixteenth Amendment's important effect on the direct-tax apportionment rule, that rule, the uniformity rule, and the Export Clause remain on the books. Unless those restrictions mean nothing, or almost nothing, it is inaccurate to characterize the taxing power as "virtually without limitation."

The judicial focus of so much constitutional inquiry and the paucity of litigation on most of these issues mask another respect in which constitutional limitations on the taxing power might be important. Judicial deference to Congress has been great in taxation, to be sure. But since Congress also must follow the Constitution, a rule of deference is not the same as no restrictions at all. Even if the legitimacy of a newly enacted tax is never tested in the courts, one should expect *Congress* to be paying attention to constitutional dictates.

For example, no one would suggest that federal estate tax rates could vary from state to state. The Uniformity Clause, discussed in Chapter 5, requires geographical uniformity, if nothing else, and that core meaning of the Clause is beyond dispute. The lack of serious contemporary litigation about uniformity is evidence of the strength of the rule, not its weakness. Perhaps "uniformity" could have been interpreted in a still broader way, but the rule has not been eviscerated.

Similarly, while the direct-tax apportionment rule may be moribund for many purposes, certain types of taxes may not have been enacted, at least in part, because of the rule's existence. Since 1861, we have not seen a federal tax on real estate, a fact that may be partly attributable to a congressional sense (based on settled doctrine) that such a tax would have to satisfy the apportionment rule. Indeed, between 1798 and 1861 Congress carefully provided for apportionment in several national taxes on real estate. Who cares today whether Congress can enact an unapportioned tax on real estate? Because founding-era taxes on real estate were the wealth taxes of the day, one quick, easy answer to that question is that those who propose a national tax on wealth care deeply.[22]

Finally, when we think about the contemporary importance of constitutional limitations on the taxing power, we should not forget the Export Clause, the sudden new star of constitutional tax litigation. When the Supreme Court referred to the taxing power as "virtually without limitation" in 1983, the Court's language was hyperbolic even by the standards of the time, and the hyperbolic language did not guide the Court in subsequent decisions. Twice in the 1990s, the Court enforced the Export Clause, striking down the application of taxing statutes under the authority of the Clause. United States v. International Business Machines Corp. (1996); United States v. United Shoe Corp. (1998).

By reinvigorating the Export Clause, the Court at a minimum forced renewed interest in export taxation, an area that the Court had ignored since 1923, and, by acting so forcefully twice within a short period of time, the Court may have done even more. Although the opinions in the Export Clause cases limit the holdings and analysis to the particulars of that Clause and the specific facts involved, it is difficult not to wonder whether the Court has a renewed interest in policing the taxing power. Chapter 9, dealing with the Export Clause, considers whether the logic of the Court's decisions in *IBM* and *United Shoe* may have implications for the interpretation of other limitations on the taxing power as well.

It is enough for present purposes if the reader entertains the following narrow propositions: the textual limitations on the taxing power mean something, and the power to tax is not so great that specific textual limitations on the taxing power can be ignored. Those limitations should be reexamined in light of the possibility of a less-than-plenary taxing power. And, to give immediacy to our study, we should remember that the Supreme Court has been taking all sorts of constitutional limitations much more seriously in recent years.[23]

WHAT THE BOOK WILL COVER

Much of this book will focus on the history and the meaning of the explicit limitations on the taxing power—the Uniformity Clause, the Direct-Tax Clauses, and the Export Clause—and the history and meaning of the Sixteenth Amendment. The book will also examine some other, once important restrictions on the national taxing power that were derived from the constitutional structure or from specific constitutional provisions that are silent about taxation. For example, at one time, congressional power to tax almost anything associated with states or municipalities was understood to be forbidden by the doctrine of intergovernmental immunity. The impact of that doctrine has been substantially diminished by judicial developments, but it may retain a modicum of importance.

As is generally true with books in this series, the discussion is divided into history and analysis, but a clear-cut distinction will not be possible in this volume. For example, the meaning of the Direct-Tax Clauses today is dependent, in some important respects, on what the Supreme Court said about those Clauses in the seminal case of Hylton v. United States (1796) and what a very different Court said, a century later, in Pollock v. Farmers' Loan & Trust Co. (1895). Both of those cases purport to define the meaning of the Clauses as originally understood at the Constitutional Convention and in the ratification debates. Are *Hylton* and *Pollock* "history" or are they part of the analysis? They are both. One cannot understand the historical development of constitutional concepts affecting taxation without understanding both cases, but one will also have difficulty in understanding the state of the law now without an adequate grounding in those older decisions.

With the caveat in mind that a clear demarcation between history and analysis is impossible in this area, Part I discusses the history of the taxing power generally; several specific limitations contained in the original document (Uniformity Clause, Direct-Tax Clauses, and Export Clause); and the Sixteenth Amendment, ratified in 1913, which modified the Direct-Tax Clauses.

Part II discusses the nature of the taxing power today, and it does so primarily by analyzing the various limitations on the power. Chapter 5 discusses the uniformity rule, and Chapter 6 details the Direct-Tax Clauses. Chapter 7 considers the meaning of the Sixteenth Amendment and the changes the Amendment made to the Direct-Tax Clauses. Chapter 8 then discusses what levies, if any, remain subject to the direct-tax apportionment rule after the Sixteenth Amendment. Chapter 9 explicates the Export Clause, the one limitation on the taxing power that has attracted Supreme Court attention in the last decade. Finally, Chapter 10 discusses a number of miscellaneous provisions, rules, and doctrines that have affected, and in some cases continue to affect, the taxing power, such as the intergovernmental immunity doctrine.

NOTES

1. Roger H. Brown, *Redeeming the Republic: Federalists, Taxation, and the Origins of the Constitution* (Baltimore: Johns Hopkins University Press, 1993): p. 3.
2. Bruce Ackerman, "Taxation and the Constitution," *Columbia Law Review* 99 (1999): 1, 3.
3. Loren P. Beth, *The Development of the American Constitution 1877–1917* (Henry S. Commager & Richard B. Morris eds., New York: Harper & Row, 1971): p. 154.
4. *The Federalist No. 23*, at 156 (Alexander Hamilton) (Clinton Rossiter ed., New York: Mentor Books, 1961).
5. *The Federalist No. 23*, at 157.
6. *The Federalist No. 23*, at 153.
7. *The Federalist No. 30*, at 188 (Alexander Hamilton) (Clinton Rossiter ed., New York: Mentor Books, 1961).
8. *Hylton*, 3 U.S. (3 Dall.) at 176.
9. *Ptasynski*, 462 U.S. at 79.
10. Owen M. Fiss, *History of the Supreme Court of the United States: Troubled Beginnings of the Modern State, 1888–1910* (New York: Macmillan, 1993): pp. 88–89.
11. *The Federalist No. 41*, at 262 (James Madison) (Clinton Rossiter ed., New York: Mentor Books, 1961).
12. *The Federalist No. 41*, at 263.
13. Dall W. Forsythe, *Taxation and Political Change in the Young Nation 1781–1833* (New York: Columbia University Press, 1977): p. 21.
14. *Brushaber*, 240 U.S. at 13.
15. *Veazie Bank*, 75 U.S. (8 Wall.) at 541.
16. *Brushaber*, 240 U.S. at 17–18; *Stanton*, 240 U.S. at 112.
17. *The Federalist No. 36*, at 220 (Alexander Hamilton) (Clinton Rossiter ed., New York: Mentor Books, 1961).
18. *Ptasynski*, 462 U.S. at 86.
19. Richard A. Epstein, "Taxation in a Lockean World," *Social Philosophy & Policy* 4 (1986) (footnotes omitted): 49, 71.
20. Boris I. Bittker, "Constitutional Limits on the Taxing Power of the Federal Government," 41 *Tax Lawyer* (1987): 3, 9.
21. Michael J. Graetz, *The Decline (and Fall?) of the Income Tax* (New York: W. W. Norton, 1997): p. 285.
22. *See, e.g.*, Bruce A. Ackerman & Anne Alstott, *The Stakeholder Society* (New Haven: Yale University Press, 1999).
23. *See, e.g.*, Printz v. United States (1997) (Tenth Amendment); Seminole Tribe v. Florida (1996) (Eleventh Amendment); United States v. Lopez (1995) (Commerce Clause).

PART I

History

2

The Founding and Taxation

The history of the taxing power has two distinct but obviously related strains: the Constitution was intended to make it possible for the national government to raise revenue, but it was also intended to make it difficult for the national government to abuse the revenue power. After the disastrous experience under the Articles of Confederation, almost everyone understood that, if there was going to be a *United* States of America, it was necessary for the national government to have the power to tax individuals. That meant replacing or at least augmenting the requisitions system that existed under the Articles. For a generation that had fought a war with England about taxation, however, it was equally important that any taxing power be constrained.

THE SYSTEM OF REQUISITIONS

Under the Articles of Confederation, the Continental Congress had no power to tax individuals directly; Congress's power to raise revenue, such as it was, was directed at the states. When revenue was needed, the states would be sent "requisitions," and the states could raise the requisitioned funds however they wished within a prescribed period. Article VIII of the Articles provided that

> [a]ll charges of war, and all other expenses that shall be incurred for the common defence or general welfare, and allowed by the United States in Congress assembled, shall be defrayed out of a common treasury, which shall be supplied by the several States, in proportion to the value of all land within each State, granted to or surveyed for any person, as such land and the buildings and improvements thereon shall be estimated according to such mode as the United States in Congress assembled, shall from time to time direct and appoint.
>
> The taxes for paying that proportion shall be laid and levied by the authority and direction of the Legislatures of the several States within the time agreed upon by the United States in Congress assembled.

Consistent with the idea of the government as a confederation, the state governments were effectively interposed between the national government and the citizens and other residents of each state.

In the early days of the Constitutional Convention, the debate on the revenue power was part of the larger debate about the relative merits of the New Jersey and Virginia Plans, which were introduced by the delegations from those two states. The New Jersey Plan saw the national government operating directly on state governments, as was true under the Articles of Confederation; the Virginia Plan rejected the structure of the Articles and saw the national government necessarily operating directly on individuals.

It was probably a foregone conclusion that, unless the Convention was going to implode, the Virginia Plan would prevail. The Articles of Confederation had failed in significant ways, and a different form of constitution was necessary if the United States was going to continue. Nevertheless, concluding that the national government should have some taxing power over individuals was just the first step in the deliberations. Defining the scope of that power was the real issue.

The scope of a revenue power directed at individuals was a concern for at least two reasons—excessive taxation could have unhappy effects on the individuals themselves, of course, and, perhaps more important, excessive taxation could have potentially disastrous effects on the states. The states were interested parties because, if the national government overdid a particular form of taxation, it could decimate the tax bases of the states. Anti-federalist Brutus, writing in the *New York Journal* shortly after the Constitutional Convention had concluded, argued that, "if the foederal [*sic*] government begins to exercise the right of taxation in all its parts, the legislatures of the several states will find it impossible to raise monies to support their governments."[1] Another concern of the states, expressed most vigorously by southern delegates to the Convention, was that without adequate protection in the Constitution, the national government could use its taxing power to cripple one section of the country. That theme will reappear in the discussion of several of the constitutional clauses dealing with taxation.

The requisitions system had been safe on all counts. There was no possibility that the national government might abuse individual citizens because the states tempered the national power. (If any abuse of individual taxpayers occurred with requisitions, it had to be attributable to the mechanisms used by a particular *state* to raise revenue to forward to the United States.) The states' tax bases were not in danger because the states decided how to raise the revenue for national purposes. By tying the amounts requisitioned to land value (which in an agrarian society was assumed to be the primary measure of a state's wealth), the system also seemed to provide for a geographically fair distribution of the tax burden. With requisitions fairly apportioned, no one section of the country could gouge another section.

If anything, however, the requisitions system turned out to be *too* safe. The system could not guarantee a predictable stream of revenue for the national government. Part of the problem was that Congress had difficulty apportioning tax liability among the states. The value of land in the various states was to be used in the allocation process, but few, if any, states had valued their lands.[2] As Alexander Hamilton explained in Federalist 21, "In every country it is an herculean task to obtain a valuation of the land; in a country imperfectly settled and progressive in improvement, the difficulties are increased almost to impracticability."[3] Finally, in 1783, the Continental Congress moved to use respective state populations to apportion requisitions (on the understanding that population was a good-enough proxy for real-estate value), and it was here that the three fifths rule for counting slaves first appeared in American history—an attempt to provide rough equality between the North and the South.[4]

As hard as it was to come up with a workable method of apportioning requisitions, the even more serious defects of requisitions were the recalcitrance of the states and the powerlessness of the national government to do anything about that recalcitrance. A state might honor its obligation to send requisitioned funds, but it also might refuse. What was the national government going to do in that case? Sending troops would probably have been politically impossible in any event, and with a battle for independence going on, using troops was out of the question.

The requisitions system was not a complete failure; Roger Brown has calculated a compliance rate of about 37 percent for the period between October 1781 and August 1786.[5] That was clearly not good enough for a functioning government, however, particularly during wartime, and modifying the Articles of Confederation to provide for a stronger revenue power was a practical impossibility. Under Article XIII, doing so would have required unanimous approval of the states.

A fundamental change was therefore necessary if the national government was going to satisfy its basic financial needs. Alexander Hamilton was emphatic in Federalist 30: "What remedy can there be for this situation, but in a change of the system which has produced it—in a change in the fallacious and delusive system of quotas and requisitions?"[6] Or, as he put it at the New York ratifying convention in June 1788, "What, sir, is the cure for this great evil? Nothing, but to enable the national laws to operate on individuals, in the same manner as those of the states do."[7] Rufus King echoed those sentiments at the Massachusetts ratifying convention: "Laws, to be effective, . . . must not be laid on states, but upon individuals."[8]

And that is what happened. The Virginia Plan generally prevailed, in taxation and otherwise. As Justice O'Connor wrote in New York v. United States (1992), "[T]he Convention opted for a Constitution in which Congress would exercise its legislative authority directly over individuals rather than over States."[9]

The system had to be changed to make it possible to reach the pocketbooks of individuals, but an American generation that had fought British imperialism was not indifferent to the potential for abusive taxation. Few founders were willing to give the new government unlimited taxing power, and hardly anyone was willing to admit that an unconstrained taxing power was what he wanted. Providing for such a power would have doomed the Constitution in most, if not all, of the state ratifying conventions.

If taxes were to be levied on individuals, it was therefore thought necessary to have protections against governmental abuse built into the system—to protect individuals, who would no longer be shielded by states interposed between them and the national government, and to protect the states themselves. The idea that any national tax burden on individuals should be distributed in a geographically fair way was reflected in the Uniformity Clause (requiring that "Duties, Imposts and Excises . . . shall be uniform throughout the United States"); the Direct-Tax Clauses (requiring that direct taxes, a category that at a minimum included land and capitation taxes, be apportioned among the states on the basis of respective state populations); and the Export Clause (prohibiting taxation of exported articles), all of which will be discussed in detail presently.

But, before examination of the particular clauses, it is worth noting that, in the minds of some founders, providing for taxation of individuals did not necessarily mean that the system of requisitions should disappear. Indeed, the anti-federalists, who particularly feared the direct taxing power, tried to combine the two processes, with requisitions having primacy. The anti-federalists thought the apportionment requirement for direct taxes was a step in the right direction, but they also thought the rule did not sufficiently protect the states' citizens and the states' tax bases against this new, possibly massive national power. The anti-federalists therefore fought to retain the requisitions process in an adulterated form, to "make room in the system of revenue raising," as Professor Herbert Storing has put it, "for both the national and the federal principles."[10]

At the Constitutional Convention, on August 21, 1787, Luther Martin of Maryland proposed a provision that, if accepted, would have done just that. Requisitions would have been the normal first step in revenue-raising, with direct taxation available to the national government only as a backup. The requisitions process, that is, would have been used until a state was delinquent, at which point the national government could have taxed the states' citizens directly.[11] At the Maryland ratifying convention in 1788, Martin explained:

> Many of the members, and myself in the number, thought that the *States* were much *better judges* of the circumstances of their citizens, and what sum of money could be collected from them by *direct taxation*, and of the manner in which it could be raised, with the *greatest ease* and *convenience* to their citizens, than the *general government* could be; and that the general government *ought not* to have the power of laying direct taxes in any case, but in that of the *delinquency* of a State.[12]

The uniformity rule in the Constitution was not sufficient protection against governmental overreaching, argued Martin, because it did not prevent imposing duties, imposts, and excises in a way that was superficially uniform—the same tax rate applicable in all states, for instance—but that unfairly harmed states where certain types of properties were concentrated.[13] For example, a head tax on slaves could have been "uniform" (so many dollars per slave) but such a tax would obviously have primarily burdened the southern states. The direct-taxing power, tempered though it was by the apportionment rule, was also so draconian (the national government imposing its taxing power directly on landowners, say, without the interposition of the state governments) that it should be used only as a last resort.

Martin's proposal was not adopted at the Convention, but the issue of requisitions did not go away. In May 1788, a group that called itself *A Minority of the Maryland Ratifying Convention*, presumably reflecting Martin's influence, unsuccessfully asked that Maryland insist on the following constitutional amendment: "That, in every law of Congress imposing *direct* taxes, the *collection* thereof shall be *suspended* for a reasonable certain time therein limited, and on payment of the sum by any State, by the time appointed, such taxes shall not be collected."[14]

Virginia may have been the home of the Virginia Plan, but the Virginia ratifying convention in June 1788 was also a hotbed of pro-requisitions sentiment. Consistent with Luther Martin's position in Maryland, George Mason argued on June 4 that "[a]n indispensible amendment in this case, is, that Congress shall not exercise the power of raising direct taxes till the States shall have refused to comply with the requisitions of Congress."[15] And Patrick Henry, never shy and retiring, exclaimed on June 5: "I will never give up the power of direct taxation, but for a scourge: I am willing to give it conditionally; that is, after non-compliance with requisitions . . . ."[16]

Even after ratification of the Constitution, the push for requisitions continued. In 1789 the brand new House of Representatives considered a constitutional amendment that would have permitted direct taxes to be levied only "where the moneys arising from the duties, imposts, and excise, are insufficient for the public exigencies, nor then until Congress shall have made a requisition upon the States to assess, levy, and pay their respective proportions of such requisitions."[17]

But the opponents of requisitions prevailed; the Constitution was not amended to make requisitions the preferred method of raising revenue. Requisitions had not worked under the Articles, and there was serious concern about how they could ever be enforced. At the New York ratification convention in 1788, Alexander Hamilton stressed the futility of requisitions as the foundation of the national revenue system:

> But can we believe that one state will ever suffer itself to be used as an instrument of coercion? The thing is a dream; it is impossible. Then we are brought to this dilemma—either a federal standing army is to enforce the requisitions, or the federal treasury is to be left without supplies, and the government without support.[18]

Hamilton's criticisms were representative of legitimate fears: how could a requisition to a recalcitrant state be enforced without civil war? At the Virginia ratifying convention on June 5, 1788, Edmund Randolph stressed, "When gentlemen complain about the novelty [of direct taxes], they ought to advert to the singular one that must be the consequence of the requisitions—an army sent into your country to force you to comply."[19] On June 11, James Madison also warned about the consequences of requisitions: "I conceive that every requisition that will be made on my part of America will kindle a contention between the delinquent member and the general government."[20]

Requisitions as a primary source of national revenue thus fell by the wayside, and the Constitution makes no mention of them. One interesting question remains, however. Although requisitions were clearly rejected as the primary source of national revenue, are they impermissible today? This question is probably of only theoretical interest; it is hard to imagine a twenty-first century Congress thinking about levying requisitions. But if Atlantis were to rise and Congress were to requisition funds from the states, could a state properly ignore the requisition on the ground that it is unconstitutional? This question will be addressed in Chapter 10.

THE UNIFORMITY RULE (AND THE PORT-PREFERENCE CLAUSE)

[A]ll Duties, Imposts and Excises shall be uniform throughout the United States
—Article I, section 8, clause 1

If the Constitution was going to do away with requisitions as the primary revenue source for the national government, holding the national taxing power within acceptable limits was essential. Permitting the government to tax individuals, without the states' serving as intermediaries, represented an extraordinary increase in national power, requiring serious precautions against abuse.

One of those precautions was the Uniformity Clause appended to the first clause of Article I, section 8, requiring that "all Duties, Imposts and Excises . . . be uniform throughout the United States." The debates in the Constitutional Convention, as reported by James Madison and others, contain surprisingly little about the origins and purposes of the Uniformity Clause. The desire to maintain geographic fairness clearly played a role at an abstract level, but there was no detailed discussion in Philadelphia of how the Clause would apply in practice.

Although unavailable to the national government under the Articles of Confederation, the power to levy indirect taxes, by which, Alexander Hamilton explained in Federalist 36, "must be understood duties and excises on articles of consumption,"[21] was not radically new. The states had historically imposed such consumption taxes, and there had been a push under the Articles to grant the national government the power to levy imposts.[22] That move, however, was stifled by the unanimity rule required to change the Articles.

The Uniformity Clause began its life connected to what became the Port Preference Clause in Article I, section 9, clause 6. Quoting from Elliot's *Debates*, the Supreme Court, in Knowlton v. Moore (1900), described events on August 25, 1787, as follows:

> Mr. [Daniel] Carroll and Mr. [Luther] Martin [both of Maryland] expressed their apprehensions . . . that, under the power of regulating trade, the general legislature might favor the ports of particular States, by requiring vessels destined to or from other States to enter and clear thereat . . . . They moved the following proposition:
>
> "'The legislature of the United States shall not oblige vessels belonging to citizens thereof, or to foreigners, to enter or pay duties or imposts in any other State than in that to which they may be bound, or to clear out in any other than the State in which their cargoes may be laden on board; nor shall any privilege or immunity be granted to any vessel on entering or clearing out, or paying duties of imposts in one State in preference to another.'"
>
> On the same day Mr. [James] McHenry [of Maryland] and General [Charles Cotesworth] Pinckney [of South Carolina] submitted a proposition . . . relating to the establishment of new ports in the States for the collection of duties or imposts, which concluded as follows:
>
> "All duties, imposts and excises, prohibitions or restraints, laid or made by the legislature of the United States, shall be uniform and equal throughout the United States."[23]

The two provisions had related purposes, or so this history is deemed to show: to limit the powers granted to Congress in the Commerce and Taxing Clauses,[24] and, as Professor Nelson Lund has argued, to "remov[e] artificial and parochial obstacles to free trade."[25] The rules were intended, that is, to prevent restrictions on commerce that unfairly discriminate against goods associated with one part of the country.

The two clauses were then separated in the final document, although the assumption is that the clauses should still be interpreted in a consistent way. The *Knowlton* Court said the separation occurred in the Committee of Style, with the Committee's simultaneously deleting the requirement that duties, imposts, and excises be "equal throughout the United States," and moving the Uniformity Clause to its present place in the constitutional structure.[26]

The Committee of Style did delete the reference to equality, and that is important in understanding what the Clause means today: duties, imposts, and excises must be uniform but they need not be equal throughout the United States. But the *Knowlton* Court did not get the chronology quite right. It was not the Committee of Style that moved the Uniformity Clause to a new position in the constitutional structure. In fact, the draft that emerged from the Committee contained no reference to uniformity at all. The Uniformity Clause had simply disappeared in the redrafting process.[27]

The deletion of the Uniformity Clause probably did not reflect any major policy decision by Gouverneur Morris's Committee. The deletion was almost certainly an oversight, which was quickly rectified by the full Convention. On September 14, as the Convention was winding down and the constitutional text was being finalized, the Uniformity Clause was reinstated in the draft Constitution—placed in its present position in Article I, section 8, clause 1, by unanimous vote.[28]

DIRECT-TAX APPORTIONMENT RULE

> ***Representatives and direct Taxes shall be apportioned among the several States which may be included within this Union, according to their respective Numbers, which shall be determined by adding to the whole Number of free Persons, including those bound to Service for a Term of Years, and excluding Indians not taxed, three fifths of all other Persons.***—Article I, section 2

> ***No Capitation, or other direct, Tax shall be laid, unless in Proportion to the Census or Enumeration herein before directed to be taken.***—Article I, section 9, clause 4

The indirect taxes governed by the Uniformity Clause—the imposts, duties, and excises—were the relatively noncontroversial forms of taxation discussed at the Constitutional Convention. In addition, most founders accepted the idea that the national government had to have power to impose *direct* taxes—a category including, at a minimum, capitation and land taxes—at least in some circumstances. The Constitution clearly made it permissible for Congress to enact direct taxes, but the concern about governmental abuse of such taxes was pervasive at the Convention and in state ratifying conventions.

Because direct taxes were considered relatively dangerous, they required more stringent limitations than the uniformity rule that applied to indirect taxes. Even Alexander Hamilton, when he was writing as Publius, recognized that some limits had to be imposed on the taxing power. For duties, imposts, and excises—those levies subject to the uniformity rule—the dangers were minimal. Such levies come with built-in protections, as Hamilton explained in Federalist 21:

> It is a signal advantage of taxes on articles of consumption that they contain in their own nature a security against excess. They prescribe their own limit, which cannot be exceeded without defeating the end proposed—that is, an extension of the revenue. . . . If duties are too high, they lessen the consumption; the collection is eluded; and the product to the treasury is not so great as when they are confined within proper and moderate bounds. This forms a complete barrier against the material oppression of the citizens by taxes of this class, and is itself a natural limitation on the power of imposing them.[29]

Direct taxes were different, however: "In a branch of taxation where no limits to the discretion of the government are to be found in the nature of the thing, the establishment of a fixed rule, not incompatible with the end, may be attended with fewer inconveniences than to leave that discretion altogether at large."[30] Limits on the direct-taxing power ("fixed rules" short of prohibition) may be necessary and desirable to cabin governmental power.

The direct-tax apportionment rule is such a fixed rule. It requires that direct-tax liability be apportioned among the states on the basis of respective state populations (a computation that originally required special counting rules for slaves and "Indians not taxed"). The rule may have other purposes as well, but it is a limitation on governmental power to impose direct taxes. "An actual census or enumeration of the people must furnish the rule," Hamilton wrote in Federalist 36, "a circumstance which effectually shuts the door to partiality or oppression. The abuse of this power of taxation seems to have been provided against with guarded circumspection."[31] The apportionment rule makes direct taxes more difficult to implement than they otherwise would be.

The Convention backed into apportionment as the mechanism for limiting national power to enact direct taxes. Apportionment was initially discussed in connection with representation in Congress, and only later did representation and direct taxation become inextricably linked.

Determining the basis of representation in Congress was not easy for the delegates to the Constitutional Convention. Creation of a bicameral Congress was only part of the answer; a battle also raged about how representation in the House of Representatives should be determined. Should it be based on wealth, population, the states' respective contributions to national revenue, some combination thereof, or something else?

There was sentiment for wealth or the level of contributions as a measure;[32] it was only over time that sentiment shifted in favor of using population. The shift was in part because population could be seen as a surrogate for wealth, albeit a poor one.[33] According to Madison's notes, on June 12, Dr. William Samuel Johnson of Connecticut argued that "wealth and population were the true, equitable rule of representation; but he conceived that these two principles resolved themselves into one; population being the best measure of wealth."[34]

Population had another merit as well. It was possible to determine with reasonable accuracy, and some of the difficulties in apportioning tax liability under the Articles of Confederation could be avoided. On July 6, Charles Pinckney of South Carolina noted that

> [t]he value of land had been found on full investigation to be an impracticable rule. The contributions of revenue including imports & exports, must be too changeable in their amount; too difficult to be adjusted; and too injurious to the noncommercial states. The number of inhabitants appeared to him the only just & practicable rule.[35]

And while Pinckney was right that state-by-state contributions to the national government are nearly impossible to measure because of the indeterminate effects of duties, imposts, and excises, population can serve as a measure of other forms of governmental revenue if an apportionment rule is in place.[36]

If population was to be the measure for representation, how should slaves be counted? Here was a potentially convention-busting issue. The Southern states wanted the slaves to be counted fully. Charles Pinckney of South Carolina "thought the blacks ought to stand on an equality with whites."[37] In contrast, delegates from the Northern states wanted slaves to be counted as less-than-full persons; they argued, among other things, that full counting would give the

Southern states representation based on property rather than population. In the words of Elbridge Gerry of Massachusetts, who became an anti-federalist: "[P]roperty [is] not the rule of representation. Why then shd. the blacks, who were property in the South, be in the rule of representation more than the cattle & horses of the North."[38] The three fifths rule finally adopted came close to splitting the difference.

The three fifths rule was not new at the Convention. It was derived from a mechanism adopted in 1783, under the Articles of Confederation, to apportion requisitions among the states. That rule was intended to provide rough equality between the North and the South, and, when the idea first appeared at the Convention, no one suggested that another fraction would be more appropriate. Indeed, the rule was included in a June 11 motion made by James Wilson of Pennsylvania and seconded by Charles Pinckney of South Carolina,[39] two people with widely divergent views on almost any other conceivable topic, suggesting that a compromise had already occurred behind the scenes.[40]

The Convention nearly deadlocked on the issue of representation. In an attempt to avert such a disaster, Gouverneur Morris, representing Pennsylvania, introduced a motion on July 12 to add to a clause tying representation to wealth *and* population, a "proviso that taxation shall be in proportion to Representation."[41] Madison described the proposal's "object [as] lessen[ing] the eagerness on one side, & the opposition on the other, to the share of Representation claimed by the [Southern] States on account of the Negroes."[42]

The Morris proposal was new but, Professor Edwin Seligman wrote in 1911, "the proposition in its reverse form—that representation should be proportioned to taxation—had occasionally been advanced, both in the Continental Congress and in the convention."[43] For example, on July 9, three days before Morris introduced his motion, Rufus King of Massachusetts noted that "[e]leven out of 13 of the States had agreed to consider Slaves in the apportionment of taxation; and taxation and Representation ought to go together."[44]

After a number of objections had been raised to the Morris proposal, including concern that the proviso could lead to the revival of the discredited requisitions process, Morris answered that he

> supposed [the objections] would be removed by restraining the rule to *direct* taxation. With regard to indirect taxes on *exports* & imports & on consumption, the rule would be inapplicable. Notwithstanding what had been said to the contrary he was persuaded that the imports & consumption were pretty nearly equal throughout the Union.[45]

The Morris motion received immediate support from widely divergent parties—General Charles Cotesworth Pinckney of South Carolina and James Wilson of Pennsylvania. Pinckney "liked the idea. He thought it so just that it could not be objected to." Wilson "approved the principle, but could not see how it could be carried into execution; unless restrained to direct taxation."[46]

The Southern states were particularly worried about excessive taxation because it was feared taxation would fall hardest on the South. Linking taxation and representation would limit the risk that one part of the country could cripple another part through direct taxation, and it would prevent a future Congress from trying to destroy slavery through taxation. At the Virginia ratifying convention, Madison responded to this fear as it had been expressed by George Mason: "The taxation of this state being equal only to its representation, such a tax [i.e., one directed at slavery] cannot be laid as he supposes."[47] Slaves were to be counted as less than whites for purposes of representation, which was bad from a Southern perspective, but were also to be counted as less than whites for measuring a state's apportioned direct-tax liability, which was good for the South.

Coupling direct taxation and representation worked as a compromise because the increased representation attributable to slaves came at a cost to a state, an increased direct-tax liability for the state's inhabitants. Madison discussed this point in Federalist 54. After noting that population would be used to govern both representation and direct taxation, he stressed that the rules are "by no means founded on the same principle."[48] The tension between the two principles, despite the "common measure," is a good thing:

> As the accuracy of the census to be obtained by the Congress will necessarily depend . . . on the disposition, if not on the co-operation of the States, it is of great importance that the States should feel as little bias as possible to swell or to reduce the amount of their numbers. . . . By extending the rule to both objects, the States will have opposite interests which will control and balance each other and produce the requisite impartiality.[49]

At the Virginia ratifying convention, Edmund Randolph similarly explained the relationship between representation and direct taxation. After noting that "[r]epresentatives and taxes go hand in hand," he asked rhetorically whether Congress could assign 15/65 of the national taxes to Virginia, which had only 10/65 of the population: "Were they to assume such a power, it would be a usurpation so glaring, that rebellion would be the immediate consequence."[50]

Gouverneur Morris came to regret his motion at the Constitutional Convention. He later "hoped the Committee would strike out the whole of the clause . . . . He had only meant it as a bridge to assist us over a certain gulph; having passed the gulph the bridge may be removed."[51] But the compromise language developed a life of its own. It survived, with minor modification, in Article I, section 2 of the Constitution. The Supreme Court wrote, nearly a hundred years later in Springer v. United States (1881): "The builder [of the bridge] could not remove it, much as he desired to do so."[52]

The corresponding adjustment to the language of Article I, section 9, clause 4 to refer to "other direct . . . [t]ax" in addition to capitation taxes seems to have been a technical correction, with no substantive effect. Why should direct taxation be limited in one provision but not in the other? Some commentators over the years have suggested that the apportionment rule was intended to have special power because, as Arthur Graves wrote in 1910, "the qualification of direct taxes is the only provision in the entire Constitution which appears twice in that instrument. This fact ought to teach us to hold it in still higher regard and to respect the more the earnestness and intent of the framers who placed it there."[53] There is no evidence, however, that the duplication was intended to have this effect (although the fact that the apportionment rule appears in two places does suggest that the rule was not a mistake or an inadvertence).

In any event, the change to Article I, section 9 was not made simultaneously with consideration of the Morris motion. The new language was added on the motion of George Read of Delaware near the end of the convention, on September 14, with no objection. Read was apparently concerned that the government might use the direct-tax power to disproportionately impose levies on states that had been delinquent under the requisitions system. "He was afraid that some liberty might otherwise be taken to saddle the States with a readjustment by this rule, of past Requisitions of Congs—and that his amendment by giving another cast to the meaning would take away the pretext."[54]

Direct taxes could be abused, and the direct-taxing power was intended to be limited, but this is not to say that direct taxation was supposed to be impossible. In fact, the power to impose direct taxes was thought to be critical, at least in emergencies. For example, Virginia Governor Edmund Randolph, the mover and shaker behind the Virginia Plan and someone who favored a strong national government (although he eventually refused to sign the Constitution), exclaimed at the Virginia ratifying convention that "this power of imposing direct taxes has been proved to be essential to the very existence of the Union."[55] For Randolph, direct taxes were essential parts of a major revenue system needed to replace the ineffective requisitions process: "Money is the nerve—the life and soul of a government. . . . Ought [the general government] to depend for the means of its preservation on other bodies?"[56]

But because taxing individuals was fundamentally different from the requisitions process, resistance from American citizens could be expected. Taxes are generally disliked, and new forms of taxation inevitably are greeted with skepticism. Hamilton wrote in Federalist 12, "It is evident from the state of the country, from the habits of the people, from the experience we have had on the point itself that it is impracticable to raise any very considerable sums by direct taxation."[57] Although essential to meet the extraordinary revenue needs of wartime, when the impracticable can become the practicable, direct taxation could not be counted upon to meet the expenses of operating an ordinary government.

And direct taxation would not ordinarily be necessary. Ratification debates on the Constitution, including commentary in *The Federalist*, are full of reassurances that the bulk of governmental revenue would be raised through duties, imposts, and excises—none of which is a direct tax (and all of which, not surprisingly, are usually characterized as indirect taxes, although that is not a term used in the Constitution). In support of the proposition that "[d]irect taxation can go but little way towards raising a revenue," Oliver Ellsworth made the point vividly at the Connecticut ratifying convention in January 1788:

> To raise money [through direct taxation], people must be provident; they must constantly be laying up money to answer the demands of the collector. But you cannot make people thus provident. If you would do any thing to the purpose, you must come in when they are spending, and take a part with them. This does not take away the tools of a man's business, or the necessary utensils of his family: it only comes in when he is taking his pleasure . . . .[58]

Ellsworth argued that imposts were likely to be the most frequently used method of raising revenue by the national government, and imposts would not be fatal limitations on the states' ability to raise revenue.[59]

At the Virginia ratifying convention, James Madison emphasized that national defense requires the availability of extraordinary taxing powers, but those powers will not be necessary to meet the day-to-day expenses of government:

> When, therefore, direct taxes are not necessary, they will not be recurred to. It can be of little advantage to those in power to raise money in a manner oppressive to the people. . . . Direct taxes will only be recurred to for great purposes. . . . [I]t is necessary to establish funds for extraordinary exigencies, and to give this power to the general government; for the utter inutility of previous requisitions on the states is too well known.[60]

Duties, imposts, and excises were likely to be enough to cover ordinary governmental expenses, but they might not be able to meet emergency needs. Duties, imposts, and excises have natural limits; that is why they are generally safe. Raise indirect taxes too high and revenue will decrease, because consumption will decline and efforts devoted to evasion will increase. Furthermore, duties, imposts, and excises could not be counted on in the most extreme of emergencies. As Madison noted at the Virginia convention on June 11, 1788, if war came, when revenue needs would dramatically increase, imports, and therefore the revenue from imports, were almost certain to fall.[61] Additional sources of revenue were essential, and if the Constitution foreclosed other revenue possibilities, dangerous experimentation could follow, as Hamilton noted in Federalist 35: "[I]f the avenues to [resources] were closed, HOPE, stimulated by necessity, might beget experiments, fortified by rigorous precautions and additional penalties [against smuggling], which, for a time, might have the intended effect, till there had been leisure to contrive expedients to elude these new precautions."[62] The apportionment rule did not close the avenue to direct taxation, but it put speed bumps in the road.

THE EXPORT CLAUSE

No Tax or duty shall be laid on Articles exported from any State.
—Article I, section 9, clause 5

Whether to permit the national government to tax exports occupied a surprising amount of time and effort at the Constitutional Convention. It was generally agreed that the government should be able to tax imports (many founders thought that would be the nation's primary source of revenue in ordinary times), but the debates about other forms of taxation, including taxes on exports, were often contentious.

To many Federalists, exports were an appropriate subject of taxation. The nation needed revenue, and exports were one obvious, readily available source of funds. As reported in Madison's notes, Alexander Hamilton argued early at the Constitutional Convention, on June 18, "Whence then is the national revenue to be drawn? from Commerce, even from exports which notwithstanding the common opinion are fit objects of moderate taxation, from excise, &c &c. These tho' not equal, are less unequal than quotas."[63] And taxes on exports were thought to be relatively easy to administer, something stressed even by some anti-federalists worried about how intrusive other forms of taxation could be. Brutus, for example, thought a tax on exports and imports "could be raised by simple laws, with few officers, with certainty and expedition, and with the least interferences with the internal police of the states."[64]

Three of the most significant participants at the Constitutional Convention—Gouverneur Morris, representing Pennsylvania; James Wilson, also representing Pennsylvania; and James Madison, of Virginia—spoke in favor of a national power to tax exports, as did many others, and the largely silent but influential George Washington supported such a power. (The views of Madison and Washington were not enough, however, to carry the Virginia delegation, which ultimately voted against the power to tax exports.) Morris thought the power to tax exports was essential. As he argued on August 16, "Taxes on exports are a necessary source of revenue. For a long time the people of America will not have money to pay direct taxes. Seize and sell their effects and you push them into Revolts . . . ."[65] Although most founders focused on taxing *imports* as the easiest way to fund the new government, Morris emphasized "that it would not in some cases be equitable to tax imports without taxing exports; and that taxes on exports would be often the most easy and proper of the two."[66] Indeed, Morris suggested that a proviso restricting export taxation would be "so radically objectionable, that it might cost the whole system the support of some members."[67]

His state, Virginia, wound up opposing export taxation, as did all the Southern states, but Madison agreed with Morris, arguing both in favor of a national power to tax exports and against state power to do so:

> 1. the power of taxing exports is proper in itself, and as the States cannot with propriety exercise it separately, it ought to be vested in them collectively. 2. it might with particular

advantage be exercised with regard to articles in which America was not rivalled in foreign markets, as Tobo. &c. . . . [T]he price would be thereby raised in America, and consequently the taxes be paid by the European Consumer. 3. it would be unjust to the States whose produce was exported by their neighbours, to leave it subject to be taxed by the latter.[68]

And, emphasized Madison, the United States needed to have available the power to tax exports in the future, even if it did not do so now: "we are not providing for the present moment only . . . ."[69] This last argument, that the national government needed to have the power to tax exports even if it ordinarily would not exercise that power, was advanced by many others at the Convention, including John Dickenson of Delaware and Thomas Fitzsimons of Pennsylvania.[70]

Wilson, too, "was decidedly [against] prohibiting general taxes on exports."[71] Echoing Madison, he noted that granting the power did not mean it would always be used: "[T]he power had been attacked by reasoning which could only have held good in case the Genl Govt. had been *compelled*, instead of *authorized*, to lay duties on exports."[72] But the power needed to be available: "To deny [it] is to take from the Common Govt. half the regulation of trade."[73]

Taxing exports was nevertheless a touchy subject. The strongest support for prohibition came from Southern delegates, who feared that a tax on exports could be used to the South's detriment. In the late eighteenth century, the South was the primary exporter of goods, largely textiles, tobacco, and related products. The Southern states were, George Mason of Virginia proudly said, the "staple States."[74] A general tax on exports would therefore hit the South hardest, and, even if that were not so, many of the Southern delegates were afraid Northern states would gang up against the South to enact targeted duties. Mason put the concern this way:

"[A] majority when interested will oppress the minority". . . . If we compare the States in this point of view the 8 Northern States have an interest different from the five Southn. States,—and have in one branch of the legislature 36 votes agst 29. and in the other, in the proportion of 8 agst 5. The Southern States had therefore good ground for their suspicions. The case of Exports was not the same with that of imports. The latter were the same throughout the States: the former very different.[75]

And it was not only Southern delegates who worried about export taxation's potential for destroying the union through targeted duties. For example, Elbridge Gerry of Massachusetts, who became an anti-federalist, "thought the legislature could not be trusted with such a power. It might ruin the Country. It might be exercised partially, raising one and depressing another part of it."[76] In 1833, Justice Joseph Story explained the Export Clause and a couple of other provisions as follows:

The obvious object of these provisions is, to prevent any possibility of applying the power to lay taxes, or regulate commerce, injuriously to the interests of any one state, so as to favour or aid another. If congress were allowed to lay a duty on exports from any one state

> it might unreasonably injure, or even destroy, the staple productions, or common articles of that state. The inequality of such a tax would be extreme. In some of the states, the whole of their means result from agricultural exports. In others, a great portion is derived from other sources; from external fisheries; from freights; and from the profits of commerce in its largest extent. The burthen [*sic*] of such a tax would, of course, be very unequally distributed. The power is, therefore, wholly taken away to intermeddle with the subject of exports.[77]

Justice Story's reference to "these provisions" was to the Export Clause and the provisions following it in Article I, section 9, generally preventing Congress from favoring one port over another (the Port Preference Clause), or requiring vessels bound to or from one state from being subject to regulation or taxation in another state.

A related argument, with a more neutral ring, was that taxing exports would punish industrious behavior. The states producing the most for exportation, whether they were in the North or the South, would obviously be burdened most by export taxation, and it would be crazy for the nation to create a disincentive to productivity. For example, Oliver Ellsworth of Connecticut argued on August 21 that taxing exports "will discourage industry, as taxes on imports discourage luxury."[78] Founders sensitive to economic forces noted other unhappy effects as well. John Francis Mercer of Maryland worried that taxes on exports would "encourag[e] the raising of articles not meant for exportation."[79]

Finally, Southern opponents of export taxation argued, quite reasonably, that Northerners in 1787 might see Southern exportation as a source of immediate revenue, but the respective interests of the sections could shift over time. George Mason "hoped the Northn. States did not mean to deny the Southern this security [of prohibiting taxes on exports]. It would hereafter be as desirable to the former when the latter should become the most populous."[80] The argument that the North might suffer in the long run helped stiffen the resistance of a few northern delegates already worried that, as Oliver Ellsworth of Connecticut put it, "the taxing of exports would engender incurable jealousies."[81]

None of those concerns was frivolous, and something else was at stake as well. Although some of the arguments against export taxation were phrased in sectionally neutral terms, it was clearly the South that was most concerned about export taxation. A critical issue to the South was the effect of taxes on the "peculiar institution": duties directed at agricultural exports could be used to strike indirectly at slavery. If Southern agriculture were seriously harmed by excessive taxation, slavery itself could be in jeopardy. Taxing exports would have been an emotional subject in any event, but with the slavery connection it became a potentially convention-destroying issue.

When apportioning taxation among the states on the basis of population was first seriously addressed at the Convention, on July 12, Gouverneur Morris suggested that apportionment ought to be limited to direct taxation (as is now the case):[82] "Notwithstanding what had been said to the contrary he was persuaded that the imports & consumption were pretty nearly equal throughout the Union," and apportionment was therefore unnecessary to make sure taxes on items of consumption did not result in sectional abuse. Accordingly, he said, "[w]ith regard to indirect taxes on *exports* & imports & on consumption, the rule would be inapplicable."[83] General Charles Cotesworth Pinckney of South Carolina agreed that it made sense to limit apportionment to direct taxation, but part of what Morris had said scared him:

> He was alarmed at what was said yesterday, concerning the Negroes [how slaves should be counted in determining a state's representation in the House of Representatives]. He was now again alarmed at what had been thrown out concerning the taxing of exports. S. Carola. has in one year exported to the amount of £600,000 Sterling all which [*sic*] was the fruit of the labor of her blacks. Will she be represented in proportion to this amount? She will not. Neither ought she then to be subject to a tax on it. He hoped a clause would be inserted in the system restraining the Legislature from a [*sic*] taxing Exports.[84]

A couple of weeks later, General Pinckney emphasized how important the connection between slavery and exportation was. He "reminded the Convention that if the Committee [of Detail] should fail to insert some security to the Southern States agst. an emancipation of slaves, and taxes on exports, he shd. be bound by duty to his State to vote agst. their Report."[85] This was no idle threat. What was at stake in the debates on export taxation was whether the thirteen colonies would be able to agree on a Constitution at all: South Carolina and Georgia in particular were unwilling to compromise. As Madison put in an 1787 letter to Thomas Jefferson, "S. Carolina & Georgia were inflexible on the point of the slaves."[86] (Pinckney's fellow South Carolinian Pierce Butler had also stated at the Convention, on August 22, "that he never would agree to the power of taxing exports.")[87] That is why the draft prepared by the Committee of Detail provided the security Pinckney demanded: "No Tax or Duty shall be laid by the Legislature, on Articles exported from any State."[88]

Gouverneur Morris was not convinced that there was anything especially dangerous in the power to tax exports. Skeptics could find something to worry about with *any* power granted to the new national government, he said: "However the legislative power may be formed, it will if disposed be able to ruin the Country."[89] But, in Morris's view, such doomsday concerns should not shut down the process of creating a Constitution. Of course, the delegates should do what they could to minimize risks, but, unless the national government was to be powerless—unless, that is, there was going to be no *nation*—the risks could not be eliminated. Morris thought "local considerations ought not to impede the general interest,"[90] and he saw that happening with a short-sighted focus on exports.

To try to soften the resistance of his fellow Southerners, Madison played down the importance of sectional effects on export taxation, taking a number of not entirely consistent positions. At one point, he argued that the feared negative effects on the South were overblown:

> As to the fear of disproportionate burdens on the more exporting States, it might be remarked that it was agreed on all hands that the revenue [would] principally be drawn from trade, and as only a given revenue would be needed, it was not material whether all should be drawn wholly from imports—or half from those, and half from exports—The imports and exports must be pretty nearly equal in every State—and relatively the same among the different States.[91]

At another time he suggested that there might be a case for the South's initially bearing a disproportionate part of the burden: "The Southn. States being most in danger and most needing naval protection, could the less complain if the burden should be somewhat heaviest on them."[92] And he tried to turn George Mason's your-turn-will-come argument, used to scare Northern delegates about what export taxation could eventually bring to their part of the country, into something that might placate the South: "[T]ime will equalize the situation of the States in this matter."[93]

But, even if they had been internally consistent, assurances of this sort could go only so far. Whatever Morris and Madison thought, the parade of horribles was marching through the Convention. The fears were real, whether or not well founded, and piecemeal solutions were unlikely to work. Trying to craft a provision that would have protected against sectional taxation or that would have carved out specified categories of exported products from the taxing power could have tied up the Convention for weeks, with no guarantee of success: "To examine and compare the States in relation to imports and exports will be opening a boundless field," said Roger Sherman of Connecticut.[94] ("Mr Clymer [of Pennsylvania] remarked that every State might reason with regard to its particular productions, in the same manner as the Southern States.")[95] To end the bickering, Sherman argued, "It is best to prohibit the National legislature in all cases. The States will never give up all power over trade. An enumeration of particular articles would be difficult invidious and improper."[96] The alternative to prohibiting export taxation—particularly with the slavery subtext in the debates—was no constitution at all: "A power to tax exports would shipwreck the whole."[97]

Several unsuccessful attempts were made to amend the draft Clause, to preserve some role for national taxation of exports. For example, George Clymer of Pennsylvania thought export taxation should be permitted as long as it was being done for regulation of trade, but not otherwise. He therefore recommended "inserting after the word 'duty' [in the draft language of the Clause] the words 'for the purpose of revenue,'"[98] thus precluding export taxation that had as its only purpose raising revenue. Clymer's motion was rejected, suggesting that the founders considered a tax's purpose to be irrelevant under the Export Clause.

A more significant effort at amendment was an attempt, also in late August, to add a supermajority requirement, which, it was hoped, would protect sectional interests in the ordinary course, but would make it possible for the national government to tax exports in extraordinary circumstances. Madison moved, with a second by James Wilson, "to require 2/3 of each House to tax exports—as a lesser evil than a total prohibition."[99] But, as Madison put it, " it passed in the Negative."[100] Five states voted *yes* (New Hampshire, Massachusetts, New Jersey, Pennsylvania, and Delaware), and six voted *no* (Connecticut, Maryland, Virginia, North Carolina, South Carolina, and Georgia). Virginia's vote reflected a division in the delegation: George Washington joined Madison in the affirmative, but Mason, Edmund Randolph, and John Blair voted *no*. After that, the total prohibition passed 7–4 (with Massachusetts joining the six *no* votes on the Madison resolution),[101] and a later attempt by Gouverneur Morris and others to recommit the issue, with the hope that "the clauses relating to taxes on exports & to a navigation act . . . may form a bargain among the Northern & Southern States,"[102] also failed.

During the ratification period, there was relatively little public discussion of the merits of the Export Clause, and that should not be surprising. Anti-federalists concerned about the national taxing power had no reason to criticize a provision that was a limitation on that power. The Clause might not have gone far enough for most anti-federalists, but it was not a negative. For supporters of the Constitution, criticizing the Export Clause would have been counterproductive. Although prominent Federalists favored a national power to tax exports, a Constitution with an Export Clause was better than no Constitution at all. Besides, since it was necessary for political reasons to stress limits on the national taxing power—any serious, public suggestion that the power was boundless would have been fatal to ratification—the Export Clause was likely to be praised even by those who wished it were not there.

3

The Direct-Tax Clauses in the Courts from *Hylton* to the Sixteenth Amendment

What the Direct-Tax Clauses mean today depends on which of two very different conceptions is given primacy. In two cases decided a century apart, Hylton v. United States (1796), which considered the constitutionality of a tax on carriages, and Pollock v. Farmers' Loan & Trust Co. (1895), which considered the constitutionality of the 1894 income tax, the Supreme Court viewed the Clauses in nearly diametric ways. *Hylton* and *Pollock* were important historical events—as hard as it may be to believe, there was a time when some Supreme Court tax cases attracted public attention—and this chapter is therefore partly history, setting the stage for the Sixteenth Amendment. But because these cases both continue to be important in interpreting the Direct-Tax Clauses today, the chapter is also analysis, with critical commentary on the decisions.

The Supreme Court in *Hylton*, which concluded that the carriage tax was not a direct tax and therefore did not have to be apportioned among the states on the basis of population, gave the Direct-Tax Clauses very little scope indeed. In contrast, the Court in *Pollock* (although its narrow holding was overturned by the Sixteenth Amendment) read the Clause much more broadly, invalidating the 1894 income tax on the ground that the tax was a direct tax that had not properly been apportioned. At a technical level, it may be possible to reconcile the two holdings, but, as will become apparent, the jurisprudential foundations of the two cases come from different legal worlds.

This chapter is divided into four parts: *Hylton*, decided in 1796; the period between *Hylton* and the 1895 *Pollock* decision—a period during which the Court adhered to what it had said in *Hylton*; *Pollock* itself; and the period immediately after *Pollock*. The discussion is almost entirely of Supreme Court decisions. Although lower courts hear direct-tax cases—a claim that a levy is an unapportioned direct tax is a staple of frivolous tax-protester litigation—it is the Supreme Court cases, of course, that have set the agenda.

HYLTON

Hylton is worth special attention because it has affected so much of the jurisprudence and commentary on the meaning of "direct taxes." *Hylton* is understood to have limited the term to at most capitation and real-estate taxes, and proponents of a limited conception of the Direct-Tax Clauses continue to emphasize what they see as the continuing vitality of *Hylton*. To many commentators today, what the *Hylton* Court said about the Direct-Tax Clauses is definitive: no more need be said.

Hylton was decided in 1796, only seven years after the federal government began operating under the Constitution. At issue was a tax on carriages "kept by or for any person, for his or her own use, or to be let out to hire, or for the conveying of passengers." The carriage tax provided for annual levies ranging from ten dollars for each coach to one dollar for "every two wheel carriage."[103] It was enacted in 1794, at the urging of Secretary of the Treasury Alexander Hamilton, by a Congress filled with founders, when a war scare with Britain had made additional revenue essential.[104]

If the carriage tax was a direct tax, it was invalid, because it had not been apportioned among the states on the basis of population. If it was not direct, however, it was presumably constitutional. It was geographically uniform, and no other constitutional limitation apparently applied. The issue was thus straightforward, although decidedly not simple: Was the tax direct or was it not?

Hylton is fascinating for many reasons, including the fact that the Supreme Court had no jurisdiction to hear the matter. It was a test case crafted out of whole cloth by a number of Virginians unhappy with the tax—"everyone knew that the case . . . was feigned," writes historian William Casto[105]—and it was embraced by a Federalist bench that, one might infer, wanted to make a statement about national power. Hylton claimed to have 125 carriages for his own use (more, wrote Edward Whitney, "than then existed in Virginia")[106], presumably because the threshold jurisdictional amount for Supreme Court review was \$2000 (125 carriages with tax and penalties totaling \$16 per carriage). Even if believed, the patently phony claim should not have worked: for Supreme Court jurisdictional purposes, the dollar amount at issue was supposed to *exceed* \$2000,[107] and the parties had agreed that any liability of Hylton's could be discharged for only sixteen dollars, equaling the tax due on one carriage plus penalties.[108] Nevertheless, *Hylton* went ahead without any justices' questioning the Court's authority to hear the case or directly questioning the Court's power to nullify congressional acts on constitutional grounds. The Court thus implicitly accepted its power to nullify an act of Congress seven years before the better known decision in Marbury v. Madison (1803).

In early Supreme Court style, the *Hylton* opinions were written seriatim. Of the four participating justices, all of whom supported the tax, three (James Iredell, William Paterson, and Samuel Chase) wrote opinions. Although there was no single opinion for the Court, *Hylton* is usually interpreted as standing for a couple of propositions.

Proposition I is that the apportionment rule should apply only when it is easy to apply. In Justice Chase's words:

> The Constitution evidently contemplated *no taxes* as *direct* taxes, but only *such* as Congress could lay in *proportion to the census*. The rule of *apportionment* is only to be adopted in such cases, where it can *reasonably* apply; and the *subject* taxed, must ever determine the application of the rule.[109]

Justice Iredell agreed: "As all direct taxes must be *apportioned*, it is evident, that the constitution contemplated none as direct, but such *as could be apportioned*. If this cannot be *apportioned*, it is, therefore, not a *direct* tax in the sense of the constitution."[110] Because the justices said the carriage tax could not be reasonably apportioned, it was not a direct tax.

Two justices provided examples of the supposedly absurd results of apportioning a tax on property that was not uniformly distributed across the country. For example, Justice Chase wrote:

> Suppose two States, equal in census, to pay 80,000 dollars each, by a tax *on carriages*, of 8 dollars on every carriage; and in one State there are 100 carriages and in the other 1000. The owners of carriages in one State, would pay *ten times* the tax of owners in the other. A. in one State, would pay for his carriage 8 dollars, but B. in the other state, would pay for his carriage, 80 dollars.[111]

Although commentators have suggested that carriages may have been more common in the South than elsewhere, the justices simply took it for granted that carriages were not uniformly distributed across the country.[112]

Proposition II of *Hylton* is that, in Justice Chase's words, the direct taxes "contemplated by the Constitution, are only *two*, to wit, a *capitation*, or *poll* tax, *simply*, without regard to *property*, *profession*, or any *other circumstance;* and a tax on LAND." Justice Chase said he was not giving a "judicial opinion" on that point[113]—it was dictum—but he might as well have. Justice Iredell agreed with Chase, stating only that "[i]n regard to other articles, there may possibly be considerable doubt."[114] Although Justice Paterson was unwilling to concede that no other taxes could be direct taxes, he too concluded that capitation and real-estate taxes were the "principal" examples of direct taxes.[115]

Both Proposition I, that direct taxes are only those that can be practicably apportioned, and Proposition II, that the only direct taxes are capitation and real-estate taxes, make the direct-tax apportionment rule substantially less important than it might otherwise have been. And it is these propositions that, with the important exception of *Pollock*, have defined the Direct-Tax Clauses for over two centuries.

None of the *Hylton* justices, Federalists all, made a serious attempt to tie his analysis to the language or structure of the Constitution, perhaps because none liked the apportionment rule. Justice Paterson wished he could ignore it. He characterized the rule as "radically wrong; it cannot be supported by any solid reasoning. . . . The rule . . . ought not to be extended by construction."[116]

A fundamental problem in trying to make sense of *Hylton* is that Propositions I and II point in different directions. It is true that a capitation tax might have been easily apportionable. Indeed, had it not been for the special counting rules for slaves and for Indians not taxed, the apportionment rule would have been redundant for a lump-sum capitation tax.[117] But an apportioned land tax could not be simple, as Justice Paterson recognized.[118] A real-estate tax apportioned on the basis of population would have different tax structures in different states, unless the tax base, be it land value or acreage, is distributed across the country in a way that is proportionate to state populations. Such a uniform distribution is unlikely, to say the least.

To be sure, if Congress wants to impose a tax on the value of land and it puts aside valuation questions (questions that nearly destroyed the requisitions process under the Articles of Confederation), having different structures in different states is not an overwhelming conceptual problem. Congress can figure out what the appropriate rate in each state should be. And Congress did impose a number of direct taxes on real estate (land, improvements, dwelling houses, and slaves, who were considered to be inextricably linked to land value) between 1798 and 1861—all reflecting valiant attempts to meet the apportionment requirement.[119] If it is possible to come up with a comprehensible system for real estate, it ought to be possible to do it for anything else, including carriages. But it is not possible to do so in a way consistent with Proposition I.

Each proposition also has problems of its own. In discussing Proposition I, Professor David Currie complained that "[t]he opinions should have begun by investigating what the word 'direct' meant; on its face it does not begin to suggest taxes that may be apportioned fairly."[120] Even more important, the assumption that the apportionment rule should apply only to taxes with bases that are uniformly distributed across the country has the effect of nullifying any potential effect of the "rule." The apportionment rule is to be applied only in those cases in which it makes no difference, a peculiar way to interpret a constitutional limitation.

Proposition II, the idea that the term "direct taxes" means only poll taxes and land taxes, also has no obvious grounding in constitutional text and structure. It is fairly clear that poll and land taxes were understood at the time of the founding to be direct taxes. With respect to a capitation tax, which is mentioned in the Constitution itself, there is no doubt whatsoever, and with respect to a land tax, the contemporaneous commentators were in agreement. But the assumption that the term could encompass only those two kinds of taxes hardly jumps out from the constitutional text. Furthermore, it is not at all clear that the apportionment rule, which in form is a limitation on the taxing power, should be applied only to those forms of taxation known in 1787.

The source of the reasoning in *Hylton* is nonetheless fairly clear. The justices bought into some of the arguments of Alexander Hamilton, no friend of limitations on the national taxing power. Hamilton's arguments to the Court in *Hylton*, which have survived in fragmentary form, are therefore worth examining.

No longer Secretary of the Treasury in 1796, when *Hylton* was heard and decided, Hamilton nevertheless argued on behalf of the government in support of the carriage tax. In time-honored lawyerly style, Hamilton took a number of contradictory stances. He also advanced positions that contradicted arguments he had made in his preconstitutional writings.

Hamilton first emphasized the uncertainty of the constitutional terms—and thus the leeway available to the Court in interpreting those terms:

> What is the distinction between *direct* and *indirect* taxes? It is a matter of regret that terms so uncertain and vague in so important a point are to be found in the Constitution. We shall seek in vain for any antecedent settled legal meaning to the respective terms—there is none.[121]

However, as author of many numbers of *The Federalist*, when one of his goals was to reassure skeptics about the limited power of the future government, Hamilton generally used the term *direct taxes* as if his readers would understand the reference. When he was more precise in a few cases, he explicitly distinguished direct taxes from indirect taxes like imposts, excises, and duties on articles of consumption.[122]

In fact, Hamilton urged the Court to adopt something that is, except for one interesting addition, very much like the precise definition of direct taxes that it did adopt:

> The following are presumed to be the only direct taxes.
> Capitation or poll taxes.
> Taxes on lands and buildings.
> General assessments, whether on the whole property of individuals, or on their whole real or personal estate; all else must of necessity be considered as indirect taxes.[123]

In the same argument in which he had said no precise definition was possible, Hamilton came up with one.

Hamilton supplied some theory to justify the categorization of taxes on real estate. He argued that, in the writings of political theorists like John Locke, taxes upon land are called *direct* and all others *indirect*, because "all taxes fall ultimately upon land, and are paid out of its produce, whether laid immediately upon itself, or upon any other thing."[124] He had to admit that, because of the specific reference to capitation taxes, the Constitution includes more than real-estate taxes in the category of direct taxes. But, except for his allusion to "general assessments," he rejected the possibility that it might include still other levies.

Hamilton's argument that all taxes are ultimately taxes on land would convince no modern reader, and it is not clear that other founders were thinking the same way. Perhaps Hamilton's most potentially telling argument was that the carriage tax would have been characterized as an excise under English law. "[W]here so important a distinction in the Constitution is to be realized," argued Hamilton, "it is fair to seek the meaning of terms in the statutory language of that country from which our jurisprudence is derived."[125] That point was worth further attention, which it did not get from the Court in *Hylton.*

Hamilton's final argument ridiculed the proposition that looking to the economic incidence of a tax could be used to distinguish direct and indirect taxes: "Shall we call an indirect tax, a tax which is ultimately paid by a *person, different* from the one who pays it in the first instance?" If such a test had been applied in *Hylton*, the carriage tax would have been characterized as both direct and indirect and that, Hamilton argued, would have been "an absurdity."[126] The tax on carriages used by the owner was direct, in that the owner could not have shifted the liability to others. In contrast, the tax on carriages hired out might have been indirect if the owner could have shifted the burden to the lessees. To determine whether a shift in liability had occurred would have required a difficult, sometimes impossible, factual analysis. With such uncertainty about the incidence of a tax, Hamilton argued, the appropriate interpretational rule is deference. Judicial rulings should not "defeat the express and necessary authority of the government."[127]

But while writing in his *Federalist* capacity a few years earlier, Hamilton had endorsed the shiftability argument, and many founders drew just such a distinction between direct and indirect taxes. For administrative reasons, it is impractical to have the validity of every tax depend on whether *in fact* its burden is shifted. But the test was intended by the founders to look to the form of the imposition. If a tax is imposed on ownership, it is assumed not to be shiftable—a direct tax. If it is imposed on the sale or lease of property so that the burden might be shifted to the buyer or lessee, it is indirect. As Hamilton put it in Federalist 35, "The maxim that the consumer is the payer is so much oftener true than the reverse of the proposition."[128] And if a tax has both direct and indirect characteristics, as the carriage tax did—not shiftable as to ownership, but shiftable as to leasing—it can be partly valid and partly invalid. As we know today, it is not at all absurd to hold that a generally constitutional statute has unconstitutional aspects.

Hamilton's arguments, shaky though they were by modern standards, are important because Hamilton's ultimate position was adopted, more or less completely, by the Court that defined the Direct-Tax Clauses. And they matter because of who Hamilton was. *Hylton* has acquired special standing among commentators because of Hamilton's participation, how soon the case was decided after the Constitution's ratification, and who was on the Court. Of the four participating justices, Wilson, Paterson, and Chase had been members of the constitutional convention, and Iredell had been a member of the North Carolina ratifying convention.[129]

Those are relevant considerations in trying to make sense of late-eighteenth-century meaning, but they should not automatically be controlling. For one thing, the reservations of constitutional skeptics were not represented on the *Hylton* Court; the Court was made up of Federalists sympathetic to the power of a Federalist government. *Hylton* was part of a process of government building, *Federalist* government building—confirmed by the Court's rush to decide a case over which it should have had no jurisdiction—and the niceties of constitutional interpretation might have given way to meet the "exigencies of government."[130] The early Supreme Court, notes Professor Casto, "sought to support the political branches of the new government, not to oppose them";[131] the justices generally "bent to the wheels of government with enthusiasm and success."[132] A broad definition of "direct taxes" would have curtailed the "government's overriding need for a flexible and pragmatic authority to raise revenues."[133]

The reservations of some important constitutional supporters were also not represented on the *Hylton* Court. James Madison, for a notable example, voted against the carriage tax in Congress because he thought it was direct and not apportioned. He said on the floor of the House of Representatives that he was afraid it would "break down one of the safeguards of the Constitution."[134]

Perhaps the most interesting opinion in *Hylton* was that of Justice Paterson, a major participant at the Philadelphia convention, who made a more careful attempt than Chase and Iredell did to explain the validity of the carriage tax. Paterson and Chase had both concluded that "[a]ll taxes on expenses or consumption are indirect taxes,"[135] but Paterson made an effort to give intellectual content to the direct-indirect distinction: "Indirect taxes are circuitous modes of reaching the revenue of individuals, who generally live according to their income."[136] Paterson quoted Adam Smith's *The Wealth of Nations*:

> [T]he state not knowing how to tax directly and proportionably the revenue of its subjects, endeavours to tax it indirectly, by taxing their expence, which it is supposed in most cases will be nearly in proportion to their revenue. . . .
>
> Consumable commodities . . . may be taxed in two different ways; the consumer may either pay an annual sum on account of his using or consuming goods of a certain kind, or the goods may be taxed while they remain in the hands of the dealer . . . . [T]he coach tax and plate tax are examples of the former method of imposing; the greater part of the other duties of excise and customs of the latter.[137]

An income tax as we understand it today—when the state *does* know how to tax income—was the clearest example to Smith of a direct tax.

FROM *HYLTON* TO *POLLOCK*

The analysis in the various *Hylton* opinions, particularly those of Chase and Iredell, is striking in its failure to tie "constitutional" conclusions to the Constitution: From what sort of textual or structural analysis does one conclude that the apportionment rule should be interpreted so as to impose no complicating limitations on the taxing power (Proposition I), or that the only direct taxes can be capitation and real-estate taxes (Proposition II)? Nevertheless, *Hylton* did give some content to provisions that were not self-defining. It gave later generations of judges, who would otherwise have had to struggle with a difficult constitutional phrase, the comfort that precedent provides.

That limited view of the meaning of direct taxes prevailed for a century. Proposition II in particular was cited often. For example, in Veazie Bank v. Fenno (1869), the Court limited the definition of "direct taxes" to a *Hylton*-like understanding. *Veazie Bank* considered whether a Civil War tax on state bank notes—arising from "[t]he necessity of adequate provision for the financial exigencies created by the late rebellion"—was direct.[138] The Court looked to the direct-tax statutes enacted to that time (none has been enacted since) and noted that all had been on real estate: "[P]ersonal property, contracts, occupations, and the like, have never been regarded by Congress as proper subjects of direct tax."[139] Slaves had been taxed under most of the statutes, but that was because, after the first direct-tax statute in 1798, Congress "regarded slaves, for the purposes of taxation, as realty."[140]

In *Veazie Bank*, the Court nearly read the Direct-Tax Clauses out of the Constitution by looking to the overall taxing power conferred by Article I, Section 8:

> The comprehensiveness of the power, thus given to Congress, may serve to explain, at least, the absence of any attempt by members of the Convention to define, even in debate, the terms of the grant. The words used certainly describe the whole power, and it was the intention of the Convention that the whole power should be conferred. The definition of particular words, therefore, became unimportant.[141]

Similarly, in Springer v. United States (1881), the Court upheld a Civil War tax that apparently fell primarily on earned income (the tax is described in Chapter 4) against a challenge that it was an unapportioned direct tax: "*[D]irect taxes*, within the meaning of the Constitution, are only capitation taxes, as expressed in that instrument, and taxes on real estate . . . ."[142]

During the first post-*Hylton* century, the Court's reluctance to use the Direct-Tax Clauses to invalidate taxing statutes was furthered by a tendency to see challenged levies that might otherwise have presented conceptual difficulties as "duties, imposts, and excises"—not direct taxes. If taxes on real estate are direct taxes, what about an estate tax that could apply to real estate? Not a direct tax on property, said the Court in Scholey v. Rew (1875), but an excise on the passage of value, and excises need not be apportioned.[143] Moreover, in *Springer*, the Court characterized the Civil War income tax as "within the category of an excise or duty."[144] As the nineteenth century neared its end, "taxes" had come to mean only direct taxes, and "direct taxes" had come to mean only poll and real-estate taxes.

POLLOCK

By the time the *Pollock* controversy reached the Supreme Court in 1895, legal commentators had little reason to think that the Direct-Tax Clauses imposed any serious limits on the congressional taxing power. Indeed, facing the body of unfriendly precedent from *Hylton* to *Springer*, Pollock's lawyers invited the Court to reverse a "century of error" about the meaning of "direct taxes."[145] And, in so doing, the lawyers threw in frightening images of a "communistic march," characterizing the principles of the income tax as being as "communistic, socialistic—what shall I call them—populistic as ever have been addressed to any political assembly in the world."[146] It is hard to imagine today, but, as one commentator has stated, *Pollock* "would prove the most contentious and emotion-laden [case] of the era, far more so than *Plessy v. Ferguson.*"[147]

Pollock considered the constitutionality of an 1894 income tax that effectively applied—at a two percent rate—only to those with incomes over $4000, a very high figure for 1894 (the origins of the tax are described in Chapter 4). That high exemption amount gave the tax a class flavor, and, because individuals with the highest incomes were concentrated in a few industrialized states, it gave the controversy a sectional taste as well. (Because of a high exemption amount, citizens of Massachusetts, New Jersey, New York, and Pennsylvania had paid four-fifths of the total collected for the Civil War-era income tax.)[148]

Procedurally, *Pollock* and its companion, Hyde v. Continental Trust Co. (1895), were peculiar. Like *Hylton*, they were test cases, and as with *Hylton*, there should have been doubts about the Court's jurisdiction. Pollock and Hyde were not directly challenging the application of the income tax to them. Instead, each sued a corporation in which he held stock to prevent the corporation from complying first with the corporate income tax—the payment of which would have reduced the value of the shareholders' interests—and second with reporting obligations arising from the corporation's responsibilities as trustee for individual taxpayers.[149] As Edward Corwin later noted, "Such a suit is clearly moot, both parties having the same interest in having the law declared void."[150] The constitutionality of the tax was argued by the United States government—by Assistant Attorney General Edward Whitney, who appeared by "leave of court"—not by a named party.

In its initial consideration of the case, the Supreme Court, by a 6–2 vote—one justice did not participate because of illness—took a position that in many respects fit within the existing precedential framework. The Court accepted the *Hylton* dictum that a tax on real estate is direct and further concluded that there is no constitutionally significant difference between a tax on real estate and a tax on income from real estate. Because either tax diminishes the value of property, the apportionment rule that applies to one should apply to the other as well.[151]

Economic understanding supported the Court's conclusion, Chief Justice Melville Fuller wrote, looking to the shiftability of the tax:

Ordinarily all taxes paid primarily by persons who can shift the burden upon some one else, or who are under no legal compulsion to pay them, are considered indirect taxes; but a tax upon property holders in respect of their estates, whether real or personal, or of the income yielded by such estates, and the payment of which cannot be avoided, are direct taxes.[152]

The political economists' understanding did not necessarily control for purposes of constitutional law, the majority admitted, but a review of history led to the same result. The apportionment rule, wrote Fuller, was in part a response to the fundamental deficiency of the requisitions process: "[T]here were no means of compulsion, as Congress had no power whatever to lay any tax upon individuals."[153] With the power to tax individuals came a check—the apportionment requirement. And as Fuller emphasized, "The men who framed and adopted [the Constitution] had just emerged from the struggle for independence whose rallying cry had been that 'taxation and representation go together.'"[154]

Although Fuller referred to both personal and real property in his first *Pollock* opinion—as if the same principle should apply to both categories—the justices could agree only on the constitutional treatment of the tax as it applied to income from real estate. Split 4–4 on other issues, they were unable to rule on the validity of the tax as applied to income from personal property, nor were they able to confront the constitutionality of the income-tax statute as a whole.[155] Because of the uncertainty, and the pressure to deal with it, the Court heard the case a second time in 1895.

As a result of the second hearing, and also apparently because of a shift in one justice's vote, the Court held, over four vigorous dissents, that income from personal property should be treated the same as income from real property: "[W]e are unable to conclude that the enforced subtraction from the yield of all the owner's real or personal property . . . is so different from a tax upon the property itself, that it is not a direct, but an indirect tax, in the meaning of the Constitution."[156] As Professor Owen Fiss has noted, "[I]t would have seemed anomalous to draw a line between the income from real property and the income from personal property."[157] It would make no sense, that is, to require apportionment of a tax on rents, but not a tax on dividends and interest.

With the income from property constitutionally removed from the base of an unapportioned tax, and with an exemption amount of $4000, the statute was gutted. The Court therefore concluded that the entire statute had to fall, including the part—the tax on earned income—that the Court hinted might have survived constitutional scrutiny (the hint was that a tax on income from "professions, trades, employments, or vocations" was an excise tax not subject to apportionment).[158]

The whole problem could have been avoided if the Supreme Court had been willing to characterize the 1894 income-tax statute as a duty or an excise, which need not be apportioned, the sort of thing the Court had often done in the past, and had in fact done with the Civil War income tax in Springer v. United States

(1881). But the *Pollock* Court refused to do so, and recognized that many of its prior decisions had made the Direct-Tax Clauses paper tigers: "Direct taxation was not restricted in one breath, and the restriction blown to the winds in another."[159]

Pollock was a marked change in Direct-Tax Clause jurisprudence. One caustic, contemporaneous commentator criticized the Court for overruling "in effect three direct adjudications made by itself," "refin[ing] away to the vanishing point two other of its decisions," "crippl[ing] an important and necessary power and function of a coordinate branch of government," and "deliver[ing] an opinion in which is laid down a doctrine that is contrary to what has been accepted as law for nearly one hundred years."[160]

Because of the way the Court focused on income from real estate in the first *Pollock* decision, *Hylton* and *Pollock* may be consistent at a technical level. But in terms of judicial outlook, the opinions are irreconcilable. *Pollock* has come to be viewed by many as an unprincipled case, an aberration, a product of its time from a reactionary Court scared of class warfare.[161] As one commentator stated, "With the possible exceptions of the *Dred Scott* and *Legal Tender* cases, no other decision has heaped upon the Court such criticism and condemnation."[162] The use of the Direct-Tax Clauses, wrote Robert McCloskey, was only a superficially plausible effort to ground in constitutional text an effort that was aimed at quelling the revolution: "The direct tax clause, so long neglected as a constitutional restraint, provided the judges with an objective formulation of their prejudice in favor of wealth."[163] The reactions of some critics to the perceived "judicial usurpation" were extreme. Former Oregon Governor Sylvester Pennoyer, for example, called for the impeachment of the "nullifying judges."[164] If nothing else, the decision seemed lawless to many commentators. In a 5–4 decision, so much turns on one justice's vote.

The dissenting justices certainly thought something indefensible had happened in *Pollock*. In a scathing opinion, Justice John Marshall Harlan asserted that "it is not possible for this court to have rendered any judgment more to be regretted."[165] Justice Howell Jackson described *Pollock* as "the most disastrous blow ever struck at the constitutional power of Congress."[166] And Justice Henry Billings Brown called the decision "a surrender of the taxing power to the moneyed class."[167]

It is commentators' rejection of *Pollock*'s reasoning and outcome that provides the underpinning for the current understanding of Congress's plenary taxing power, as discussed in Chapter 1. If *Pollock* was wrong, and *Hylton* reigns, the apportionment rule has little scope, applying at most to capitation and real-estate taxes. Nevertheless, *Pollock* reached a defensible result. Some of the language in the arguments and in the opinions may have been more bombastic than was justified and, as with *Hylton*, the Court did an inadequate job of explaining what a direct tax is. But *Pollock's* reinvigoration of the Direct-Tax Clauses deserves more attention than the casual dismissal it so often receives from courts and commentators.

That the *Pollock* income tax affected only a small percentage of the American population, Owen Fiss argues, gave credibility to the proposition that this was not a taxing statute to which *Hylton* and its progeny should have been applied perfunctorily: "The income tax [was] an egalitarian measure intended to put the burden of taxation on the rich. It posed a fundamental question about the nature of the state and its capacity to intervene in the social sphere."[168] The tax was, in Louis Eisenstein's phrase, "class legislation of the most obvious kind."[169]

Moreover, the Court was not necessarily misguided in equating, for constitutional purposes, a tax on income from property with a tax on ownership of property. As Fiss argues, any distinction between the two "did not make a great deal of sense from an economic perspective, since the value of a property is the income it can generate."[170] Or, as Lord Coke had stated, in language quoted in *Pollock*, "[W]hat is the land, but the profits thereof?"[171]

Not all property is income producing—personal residences, for example, produce no taxable income—and a tax on real-estate income therefore does not necessarily have the same effect as a tax on all real-estate value. But a tax on income can diminish the value of an income-generating property just as much as a direct property tax does. If Congress had explicitly used income generated by property as a rough-and-ready surrogate for value (and the most common valuation methods today require capitalizing the future income stream that an asset will generate), there would have been no question that the tax was direct.

AFTER *POLLOCK*

Pollock was precedent-shattering, but it had little influence outside the income-tax area. After (and despite) *Pollock*, the Supreme Court continued to view the Direct-Tax Clauses narrowly. Some cases were easy. For example, in Thomas v. United States (1904), a stamp tax on a memorandum or contract of sale of stock certificates was determined not to be direct; it sounded more like a duty, impost, or excise: "The sale of stocks is a particular business transaction in the exercise of the privilege afforded by the laws in respect to corporations of disposing of property in the form of certificates."[172]

More important, in several cases the Court made it clear that it intended to give *Pollock* no expansive interpretation; the *Pollock* analysis was not to be extended to overturn other once-settled rules. In Knowlton v. Moore (1900), for example, the Court concluded that nothing in *Pollock* required overruling Scholey v. Rew (1875), which had held that an inheritance tax is not direct.[173] The Court rejected an interpretation of *Pollock* that depended on the shiftability of the tax; the taxpayer had argued that a death duty is a direct tax because the tax liability cannot be shifted to someone else.[174] The Court suggested that theory is not the governing principle, practice is: "[F]or the purpose of deciding upon its validity a tax should be regarded in its actual, practical results, rather than with reference to those theoretical or abstract ideas whose correctness is the subject of dispute and contradiction among those who are experts in the science of political economy."[175]

The incentive that existed prior to *Pollock* for courts sympathetic to a broad interpretation of the taxing power to characterize a levy as a duty, impost, or excise—and thus to avoid apportionment issues—was, if anything, increased by *Pollock*'s being on the books. What about a corporate-income tax enacted after *Pollock*, but before the income-tax amendment? In Flint v. Stone Tracy Co. (1911), it was held to be indirect because it was a tax on the privilege of "actual[ly] doing . . . business in a certain way"—that is, "in a corporate capacity"—rather than "upon property solely because of its ownership."[176]

Pollock was gasping for breath, but it was still alive. And whatever the merits of the reasoning in *Pollock*, the holding made enactment of an unapportioned income tax difficult, if not impossible. If there was ever to be an unapportioned income tax in the United States, amending the Constitution was probably going to be necessary.

4

The Income Tax and the Sixteenth Amendment

The Congress shall have power to lay and collect taxes on incomes, from whatever source derived, without apportionment among the several States, and without regard to any census or enumeration.—Sixteenth Amendment

From the time of the decision in Hylton v. United States (1796) until Pollock v. Farmers' Loan & Trust Co. (1895), the judicial assumption had been that the only taxes subject to the apportionment requirement were capitation taxes and real-estate taxes. It was only with the expansive interpretation of direct taxes in *Pollock*, striking down an 1894 income tax, that the rules of the game changed. At that point, supporters of an income tax had to think seriously about a constitutional amendment to permit an unapportioned income tax.

The income tax had first been used in the United States during the Civil War. Enacted in 1862, the Civil War tax was graduated, applying to incomes over $600 at a three percent rate and to incomes over $10,000 at a five percent rate[177] (in 1864, rates were increased to five, seven and a half, and ten percent for income ranges $600–$5000, $5000–$10,000, and over $10,000, respectively).[178] From the beginning, the tax was intended as an emergency measure—not until 1894 did many think such a tax might become a permanent part of the revenue system[179]—but it had some inherent appeal, especially among the vast majority of Americans who were not subject to the tax. It survived, in modified form, until 1872.

It could have lasted longer. There was sentiment among some congressmen to make the income tax a permanent part of the national system: it was thought to be fair, it reached the wealthy, and it did not have the unfortunate effects of the consumption taxes (tariffs and excises) that had been previously used to fund the national government. As Ohio Senator John Sherman explained:

> A few years of further experience will convince the body of our people that a system of national taxes which rests the whole burden of taxation on consumption, and not one cent on property or income, is intrinsically unjust. . . . [T]he consumption of the rich does not bear the same relation to the consumption of the poor as the income of the one does to the wages of the other.[180]

Whatever its intellectual justification, the Civil War tax expired because by the early 1870s there was no longer an urgent need for revenue; tariffs were bringing in enough to keep the country going. But good economic times did not last, and demands on government increased. The period between the 1872 expiration of the Civil War tax and the enactment of the 1894 income tax saw several panics and depressions, including one in 1893 (which gave a sense of immediacy to the 1894 debates). That period nevertheless also saw an astonishing accumulation of wealth by some very visible Americans. The contrast between wealth and suffering was one of the reasons several radical political parties, including the People's (Populist) party, were created in the late nineteenth century.[181]

THE 1894 INCOME TAX

Understanding what Congress was trying to do with the 1894 income tax, which was invalidated by the Supreme Court in *Pollock*, is important in understanding the purposes behind the Sixteenth Amendment.

Commentators generally see the late nineteenth-, early twentieth-century proponents of an income tax as trying to reorient the tax system. As historian Gerald Eggert put it in describing the background of the 1894 income tax:

> Congressional debates made it clear . . . that the tax was, in part, a response to the widespread demand to equalize the tax burdens borne by the various classes. The tariff, which was the federal government's chief source of revenue, lay most heavily on the poorer classes—ran the argument—while the proposed income tax would be paid by the wealthier classes.[182]

Edward Whitney (Assistant Attorney General at the time of *Pollock*) explained the 1894 tax in the same way: "The [Democratic] party controlling the House of Representatives, accepting the theory that the prevailing taxes on consumption bore especially hard on the smaller incomes, undertook to make up the deficit with a compensatory duty upon the larger ones."[183]

The 1894 income tax is often called a *populist* measure, and the People's party was in the forefront of the income tax movement. In 1892, the platform of the party proclaimed, "*We demand a graduated income tax.*"[184] The reason for the plank was obvious: Populists thought the wealthy were not paying their fair share under the tariff regime. Populist Senator William A. Peffer of Kansas said bluntly: "We propose to equalize taxation as far as it is possible to do so, and we propose to make the wealth of the country bear its just and fair proportion of the taxes of the country."[185]

The income tax had populist antecedents and populist support; no similar plank had appeared in the Democratic and Republican platforms. But the People's party did not have enough power to get its way without help, and the idea of an explicitly graduated tax fell by the wayside quickly. Nevertheless, the allure of an income tax was unmistakable to many members of the old-line parties, particularly Democrats, who had taken control of both Houses of Congress and who saw an opportunity for party realignment. Consumption taxes like tariffs were thought to be shifted to purchasers, and, if that was right, a poor man bore the same tax burden in buying a bag of sugar as did a rich man. The tax burdens, that is, had nothing to do with respective abilities to pay the taxes, and that was not fair.

The difference between an income tax and a consumption tax—one is consistent with ability to pay, one is not—was stressed throughout the congressional debates. The bill began in the House of Representatives, where Democratic Representatives Benton McMillin of Tennessee, chairman of the Ways and Means Subcommittee on Internal Revenue and a longtime proponent of income taxation, and the already legendary William Jennings Bryan of Nebraska recommended a two-percent tax on incomes of $4000 or more. That proposal, with changes in detail, in many ways mirrored the Civil War income tax, and it survived the subsequent legislative wrangling as an amendment to a major tariff revision bill.

McMillin explained the income tax legislation in this way:

> I ask of any reasonable person whether it is unjust to expect that a small per cent of this enormous revenue shall be placed upon the accumulated wealth of the country instead of placing all upon the consumption of the people. . . . And yet when it is proposed to shift this burden from those who can not bear it to those who can; to divide it between consumption and wealth; to shift it from the laborer who has nothing but his power to toil and sweat, to the man who has a fortune made or inherited, we hear a hue and cry raised by some individuals that it is unjust and inquisitorial in its nature . . . .[186]

The wealthy were not paying their share because of the form American taxation had taken. High and low income people who, McMillin posited, spend about the same on necessities "pay the same taxes to the Government, because taxes are to be paid upon what they consume!"[187]

Many other congressmen, like Senator Henry M. Teller of Colorado, made the same questionable point, that the rich were paying no more than the poor under the tariff system: "The man who holds millions of dollars' worth of property pays no more, perhaps, under the general taxes levied upon consumption than the man who has not any property."[188] Other income tax supporters went further, suggesting the rich might even have been paying *less* than the poor.[189] It is hard to imagine that, on the average, the rich were not paying far more in tariffs than the poor, something opponents of the income tax pointed out. But, silliness aside—opponents provided their absurd examples, too—the income tax supporters made an important point: A rich man with ten times the income or wealth of a poor man might pay more in consumption taxes, but he probably did not pay anything close to ten times as much. Assuming the burden of tariffs was shifted to consumers, the poor man almost certainly paid a higher percentage of his income and wealth in taxes than did the rich. And, said McMillin, the relative burdens on the poor had been growing: "The taxes having continually increased upon consumption, and no corresponding increase having been placed upon accumulation, we see such colossal fortunes amassed as were never concentrated in any other age or in any other country of the world."[190]

Having the wealthy pay more to support the government was thought to be fair in and of itself, but there were other reasons why tax obligations should be connected with ability to pay. For one thing, income tax supporters believed the rich had disproportionately benefitted from national policies. The rich were rich *because of* what government had done. Moreover, the wealthy received more from government—the value of protecting property, for example, goes up with the value of property protected, or so it was argued—and income tax proponents argued that the wealthy should have to pay for the extra services.

Finally, the case for an income tax had a civic-virtue component. Some thought participation in politics by the wealthy was skewed by their disproportionately low tax bills.[191] If the wealthy had to pay more in taxes, the argument went, they would pay more attention to government and help curb its excesses.

To conform to ability-to-pay standards, tax law had to relieve burdens on consumption. That was the constant theme advanced by income tax supporters. The House Ways and Means Committee report on the 1894 legislation made the point like this: "The wealth of this country amounts to more than $65,000,000,000, and the question arises whether it is not just and fair that a portion of this money should be raised by a tax on the earnings of wealth instead of imposing it all, or nearly all, on consumption."[192]

Because of the push for fairness, the disputes inevitably had a class-versus-class flavor. With a proposed rate of only two percent, the charges of socialism seem a bit much today: "vicious, socialistic and un-American"[193] and "the most socialistic measure which was ever enacted in this country,"[194] noted a couple of typical authors. But there *was* a class aspect to the legislation. The tax affected only about one percent of the population, the legislative attack on the wealthiest of the wealthy was no accident, and once the principle of an income tax had been accepted, there was no guarantee that rates would stay low. Lawyer James C. Carter, representing a bank nominally defending the tax before the Supreme Court, conceded it was "class legislation in th[e] sense [of distinguishing between rich and poor]. That was its very object and purpose."[195]

The revolution was not really coming, of course, but one can understand how some thought it might be. In any event, tax opponents were as capable of exaggeration as the most populistic of Populists. For example, Senator George F. Hoar of Massachusetts intoned: "We all want if we can to see a time when we can get rid of the internal-revenue system altogether. It is odious, it is a sore, it is an irritation, it is a sting in all parts of the country."[196] Indeed, characterizing the tax as populist would, it was hoped, bring the legislation down. Populist Senator William V. Allen of Nebraska complained, "Every Senator that has spoken against the income tax has taken the occasion to say that it was Populistic,"[197] and he was pretty much correct.

Income tax opponents did not limit themselves to questioning the populist origins of the tax; they also marshaled an arsenal of substantive arguments against the tax, and in favor of a consumption tax system. The income tax had historically belonged to the states,[198] they argued, and it ought to be used by the national government only in emergencies, if at all.[199] It was socialistic,[200] nothing but class legislation,[201] and it was sectional in purpose—aimed at the East, where the wealthy were concentrated.[202] Moreover, it was a pernicious tax that would encourage Americans to lie about their economic situations and, if the tax was going to be enforced, require that government agents pry into the private affairs of citizens. "Inquisitorial" was an often used adjective.[203]

Yet another argument was made against the income tax and, implicitly, in favor of the existing consumption taxes. Although *Pollock* is often described as having been a shock to Court-watchers in 1895, potential constitutional problems were raised in the 1894 debates. New York Senator David Bennett Hill stated (with a touch of hyperbole, one imagines), "I have never talked with a lawyer or the bench of a court who has not stated that he believes this is a direct tax, and therefore unconstitutional."[204] Others agreed that enacting an income tax would bring serious constitutional challenges.[205]

President Cleveland stayed on the sidelines during the debates. He had called for "a small tax upon incomes derived from land and certain corporate investments,"[206] but he considered it politically inexpedient for the Democratic party to push for a broader tax on personal incomes.[207] He therefore allowed the 1894 income tax legislation to become law without his signature.[208]

ON TO THE SIXTEENTH AMENDMENT

When the Supreme Court struck down the 1894 income tax in Pollock v. Farmers' Loan & Trust Co. (1895), as described in Chapter 3, the reaction in many quarters was outrage. The possibility of a constitutional amendment that would clearly permit an unapportioned income tax was raised immediately after the Court handed down its decisions in 1895, but little of significance happened until 1909. Because the Court soon began to nibble away at the scope of *Pollock*, some held out hope no amendment would be necessary.

Hope that the Court might unequivocally repudiate *Pollock* was dashed, however. There was an obvious chicken-and-egg problem. If the Court were going to reconsider the constitutionality of an unapportioned income tax, Congress would have to enact such a tax, and, with *Pollock* on the books, that would be a bold step indeed. But if Congress did not act, the Court would have no opportunity to reexamine its decisions—even though many observers thought the Court was ready to do just that.

Pressures for Congress to act were also reduced because Congress had found alternative means of raising revenue. To help fund the Spanish-American War, for example, Congress enacted an "excise" tax on the gross receipts of companies refining petroleum or sugar, lessening any sense of urgency about an income tax. (In Spreckels Sugar Refining Co. v. McClain (1904), the Supreme Court upheld the tax as an indirect one not requiring apportionment.) And throughout this period, the attention of progressives was focused on other matters, like antitrust. Although they were the primary mainline party supporting income taxation, the Democrats had no income tax plank in their 1904 platform.[209]

The movement for an income tax began to hit its stride near the end of the first decade of the twentieth century. Democratic Representative Cordell Hull of Tennessee introduced income tax legislation in 1907, and the Democratic party called for an income tax amendment in its 1908 platform:[210]

> [W]e favor an income tax as part of our revenue system, and we urge the submission of a constitutional amendment specifically authorizing congress to levy and collect a tax upon individual and corporate incomes, to the end that wealth may bear its proportionate share of the burdens of the federal government.[211]

Support for an income tax had been building among Republicans as well. In 1906 President Theodore Roosevelt stated that a "graduated income tax of the proper type would be a desirable feature of federal taxation, and it is to be hoped that one may be devised which the supreme court will declare constitutional."[212] How to do that was not clear, however, and Roosevelt showed only sporadic interest in the project. But the seed had been planted, and Roosevelt's successor, William Howard Taft, also appeared to accept the constitutionality and the desirability, at least in emergencies, of an income tax. In accepting the Republican nomination in 1908, Taft stated, "I believe that an income tax, when the protective system of customs and the internal revenue tax shall not furnish enough for governmental needs, can and should be devised which, under the decisions of the Supreme Court, will conform to the Constitution."[213] Furthermore, "insurgent Republicans" had come to Congress willing to join with Democrats and any remaining Populists to push for an income tax.[214]

Support was there, but income tax proponents had to resolve the difficult threshold question: whether to seek a new statute or to go first for a constitutional amendment. That issue was the subject of much of the discussion leading to the Sixteenth Amendment.

To Amend or Not to Amend

The merits of income taxes came close to being an afterthought in congressional deliberations in 1909 because there was little more to say. The positions on both sides had been exhaustively developed in 1894, and the substantive arguments were a reprise of 1894—with discussion about how income taxes are different from consumption taxes.

The focus of much of the debates in 1909, in form at least, was on whether a constitutional amendment was the way to proceed. Many income tax supporters thought no amendment was necessary. Moreover, some advocates, like Cordell Hull, resisted an amendment because, they worried, a few people in a few states could prevent ratification and thereby delay, if not altogether destroy, the movement. Without the support of House Speaker Joseph Cannon, Hull could not get his own proposal for reenactment of the 1894 legislation onto the fast track,[215] but in the Senate there were income tax supporters ready and willing to move ahead.

In 1909 Senators Joseph W. Bailey of Texas, a Democrat, and Albert B. Cummins of Iowa, a Republican, both introduced legislation to add an income tax provision, modeled on the 1894 statute, to a tariff bill. Their thinking was straightforward. The Court in *Hylton* and other cases had read the Direct-Tax Clauses narrowly. The Court in 1895 had rescued the Clauses, but the Court had been intensely divided (5–4), and it later seemed to have retreated. Furthermore, the composition of the Court had changed. Why bother with a constitutional amendment if the Court was likely to uphold an income tax anyway? In introducing his version of an amendment to the tariff bill, Senator Bailey said he did not believe

> that opinion [in *Pollock*] is a correct interpretation of the Constitution, and I feel confident that an overwhelming majority of the best legal opinion in this Republic believes that it was erroneous. With this thought in my mind, and remembering that the decision was by a bare majority, and that the decision itself overruled the decisions of a hundred years, I do not think it improper for the American Congress to submit the question to the reconsideration of that great tribunal.[216]

Bailey and Cummins favored the statutory route although they recognized the Court might adhere to *Pollock* and strike down a new statute. The status quo was unacceptable. As Cummins said, "If that opinion is to stand in its full scope and with its full vigor, then the United States must abandon for all time, or until the Constitution is amended, the exercise of a power and authority which had been recognized for a hundred years before the opinion was announced." Congress can interpret the Constitution as well as the Court, Cummins said, and pushing for a statutory change was an obligation: "I believe it to be the bounden duty of Congress at this time to again invoke the deliberate reexamination of this question by the Supreme Court." The Cummins legislation, like that introduced by Senator Bailey, "challenges the opinion of the Supreme Court."[217]

The risk of a negative decision from the Court was not a reason to stand pat, argued income tax supporters. Quite the contrary. If the Court rejected a new income tax statute, the case for a constitutional amendment would be clear. But without a new judicial decision on the books, an amendment could get bogged down precisely because it would not be clear the amendment was needed.

Not surprisingly, those resisting the Bailey-Cummins legislation stressed the Court's honor. Some amendment supporters, like Nebraska Senator Norris Brown, had urged deference to *Pollock* all along. Others, like Rhode Island Senator and Republican majority leader Nelson Aldrich, whose motives were not necessarily high-minded, agreed: "The imposition of an income tax now is not only an attempt to adopt an unconstitutional provision, but it is an assault, a rebuke in any way, of the Supreme Court of the United States."[218] (It is now generally accepted that Aldrich "supported" a constitutional amendment rather than a statutory fix because he thought an amendment would die in the ratification process. If that had happened, the income tax would have been dead for decades, or so he apparently hoped.)

Since commentators today almost universally reject *Pollock*, it has become easy to question the motives of everyone who pushed for a constitutional amendment rather than a new income tax statute. Perhaps everyone was not acting with the best of intentions, but it was hardly frivolous to worry about offending the Supreme Court. The potential for real conflict was there, and public confidence in the Court may have been at stake, too. *Pollock* had been decided only fourteen years earlier; it was no old-and-cold decision of a bygone era.

In any event, in 1909, President Taft weighed in with support for a constitutional amendment, stressing, among other things, the desirability of "stability of judicial construction of the Constitution."[219] (Taft coupled his recommendation with a proposal for a corporate income tax.) The Senate Finance Committee, which reported out the language that became the Sixteenth Amendment, recommended the conservative route as well:

> The committee decided that it would be unwise to pass an income-tax amendment [to a tariff] in form and substance like those introduced by the Senator from Texas [Bailey] and the Senator from Iowa [Cummins]. We felt that, in view of the decision . . . in the Pollock case, it would be indelicate, at least, for the Congress of the United States to pass another measure and ask the Supreme Court to pass upon it, when they had already passed upon the proposition . . . .[220]

Other reasons, some legitimate and some perhaps not so legitimate, also pointed toward amending the Constitution before again enacting an income tax. For one thing, while the Supreme Court might uphold a new statute, a later Court could reverse course as, it was said, had happened in 1895. Only an amendment would protect against future judicial usurpation of congressional power. Senator Thomas H. Carter of Montana, a Republican, argued that, "in the midst of that bewildering condition, it is infinitely better for us to refer the constitutional amendment to the several States, so that the question involving the power of Congress to levy an income tax may be forever and effectually put at rest."[221]

And, as noted above, it was probably the case that some "supporters," like Nelson Aldrich, viewed the proposals as a way to resist the 1909 move for an income tax and to send the issue to the states, where the possibility of rejection was high (only twelve states needed to say *no*). That rejection could then be used to resist future income tax pressures.[222] An income tax might have been inevitable—today it looks that way—but not all congressmen wanted it to happen on their watch.

Income tax proponents certainly thought there was something fishy about "support" for an amendment. Idaho Senator William Borah pulled no punches: "[T]he great, controlling, overwhelming proposition, supported by the unquestionable facts surrounding us, is the fact that it is here as a measure to defeat the income tax . . . ."[223] Senator Cummins said the amendment was "brought forward here, not by its original author, the Senator from Nebraska [Norris Brown], but by its more recent sponsors, simply as one of the instruments to defeat the income-tax provision . . . , and I shall vote for it without the slightest hope that it will ever become a part of the Constitution."[224]

Mississippi Senator Anselm J. McLaurin, who wanted an income tax and who thought an amendment unnecessary, was also pessimistic about what the amendment process would bring:

> Whatever may be the intention in bringing forward the proposed amendment, I think the effect will be to defer the enactment of any law providing for an income tax. I think the effect of it will be that there will be probably more than a fourth of the States of the Union which will refuse to ratify the action of Congress.

Worse, predicted McLaurin, that failure "would be urged as a very plausible argument before the Supreme Court of the United States that the people are not in favor of an income tax."[225]

Regardless of the motives of amendment "supporters," however, real income tax proponents had to accept reality. There would be no income tax until the Constitution was amended. As Representative William C. Adamson of Georgia put it, "I do not believe it necessary to amend the Constitution in order to levy an income tax, but the majority will not let us have it any other way. It were more proper, easier, and quicker to amend the Supreme Court than to amend the Constitution." But, Adamson argued, if we have to do it, let us do it fast: "Let all lovers of their country press the matter at once and continuously before all state legislatures."[226] And history was on the side of the tax. It was going to happen—if not now, later: "Representatives here admit that they do not expect to pass an income-tax law after this amendment is adopted. If they do not, men sent here in their places will."[227]

The Language of the Amendment: Taxes on Incomes

There was a lot going on in 1909—the Bailey-Cummins proposals to enact an income tax without waiting for a constitutional amendment, tariff revision, and a presidential proposal for a corporate income tax to operate at least until the

Constitution could be amended to permit a personal income tax. Despite the confusing mass of material, it is possible to get a good sense of what the Sixteenth Amendment was supposed to do, and that was to remove only *taxes on incomes* from the apportionment requirement.

A key player was Republican Senator Norris Brown of Nebraska. Senator Thomas P. Gore of Oklahoma introduced a resolution providing for a constitutional amendment on March 25,[228] but the important chronology began in late April, when Brown proposed the following language: "The Congress shall have power to lay and collect taxes on incomes and inheritances."[229] Brown, like many others, was leery of enacting another statute that might be rejected by the Supreme Court: "It is for that reason, Senators, that I present to you to-day the imperative and commanding necessity for an amendment to the Constitution which will give the court a Constitution that can not be interpreted two ways."[230]

However meritorious a constitutional amendment might have been in the abstract, Senator Isidor Rayner of Maryland quickly pointed out that Brown's language was useless. Congress already had the *power* to tax incomes and inheritances, he noted. The problem, at least with an income tax, was that the Court had said such a tax must be apportioned: "[I]f this amendment . . . were to go through, it would not affect the [Direct-Tax Clauses] and there would still have to be an apportionment."[231] Rayner was obviously right, and this Brown proposal went nowhere.

A month and a half later, on June 16, President Taft gave his support to a constitutional amendment, stressing the danger of enacting a tax based on the hope the Court might reverse itself.[232] Although Taft may have favored a personal income tax, he proposed enactment of a corporate tax (something thought to be permissible already) until the Constitution could be amended. We do not know for sure why Taft took this position—it has been suggested Senator Aldrich manipulated Taft to kill any possibility of a personal income tax in 1909—but the Taft proposals took the wind out of the sails of those who favored enacting an individual tax without first amending the Constitution.

The next day, June 17, with the President now officially on the side of a constitutional amendment, Senator Brown tried again, proposing the following language: "The Congress shall have power to lay and collect direct taxes on incomes without apportionment among the several States according to population."[233]

If the goal was to permit an unapportioned income tax, Brown's language seemed to work: it removed any "direct taxes on incomes" from the apportionment requirement. But Senator McLaurin was not satisfied. The impediment they were facing was the Direct-Tax Clauses, he argued, so why not strike out the references to direct taxes in the Constitution, leaving apportionment to apply only to capitation taxes? That would "accomplish all that [Brown's] amendment proposes to accomplish and not make a constitutional amendment for the enacting of a single act of legislation."[234]

Brown said *no:* "That may be true, Mr. President; *but my purpose is to confine it to income taxes alone*, and to forever settle the dispute by referring the subject to the several States."[235] Had the McLaurin proposal been accepted, it would have made analysis of the taxing power far simpler today, but Brown's intention was unmistakable, to limit the Amendment to "taxes on incomes." Nothing that happened later in the amendment process changed that critical language or that basic intention.

Senator Brown did not explain why he resisted the apparently friendly McLaurin suggestion, but one can imagine legitimate reasons for drafting the amendment the way Brown did. His proposal kept the changes narrow, limiting the effect to income taxes—which was, after all, what tax proponents were pushing for—and a narrow proposal made ratification easier. Maybe Brown was leery of eliminating the apportionment rule, making an unapportioned real-estate tax possible. Or perhaps he was concerned about the unknown. If Brown was not sure what might be included in the category of "direct taxes," or what sorts of taxes might be devised in the future, he might well have resisted giving future Congresses the power to enact any tax without significant limitation.

Whatever Brown's reasons, he was not willing to broaden the language, and his proposal was sent to the Finance Committee. The form of the Amendment that emerged in June, with an explanation of why a constitutional amendment should be sought, read somewhat differently, but it was still limited to "taxes on incomes": "The Congress shall have power to lay and collect taxes on incomes, from whatever source derived, without apportionment among the several States and without regard to any census or enumeration."[236] With a comma added, that is the way the Amendment now reads.

The committee had deleted Brown's reference to "direct taxes" and added the phrase "from whatever source derived." How these changes occurred is not clear—the committee sessions were closed, with no record of the deliberations—but theories abound. For example, according to Professor Sidney Ratner, writing in mid-twentieth century, "These crucially important and liberal changes were introduced by Senator Aldrich at the suggestion and the insistence of Senator Knute Nelson of Minnesota .... Nelson, although a conservative and Standpat Republican ..., seems to have become responsive to the progressive upsurge in Minnesota ...."[237] Roy and Gladys Blakey, relying on a letter published in 1920, also named Nelson: "[I]t was there amended at the insistence of Nelson ... to include the phrase 'from whatever source derived' and omit the word 'direct' ...."[238] John Buenker suggested Nelson's "object was to foreclose the possibility of any class of income being held exempt from taxation by the Court."[239]

Writing at the time, in 1911, Professor Edwin Seligman noted simply, and correctly: "No explanation was made of the change, and when Senator Aldrich reported the amendment, he asked to have it disposed of without debate. It was indeed debated, but the discussion was exceedingly slight."[240] Seligman added:

In the House the discussion was a little longer, but still occupied only four hours, and one of the members protested . . . : "I imagine that nothing which I may be able to say will defeat the prearranged programme[;] but for the House to perform its part in such a solemn transaction as amending the Constitution . . . without having the form of the amendment seriously considered by one of its committees, strikes me as a proceeding of extraordinary levity."[241]

That is nevertheless exactly what happened.

The Income Tax as a Reaction to the Inadequacies of Consumption Taxes

The Sixteenth Amendment was intended to remove only "taxes on incomes" from the apportionment requirement, not to abolish the Direct-Tax Clauses. But even if that is all the Amendment did, it was a lot: the category of "taxes on incomes" was hardly trivial. It was what members of Congress had been talking about since 1894 (and, in some cases, since 1862).

"Taxes on incomes" was a far-reaching concept, but congressional discussions leading to the resolution that became the Sixteenth Amendment do not reflect an open-ended understanding of that concept. From the beginning, supporters of the modern income tax stressed that it was necessary to tie taxation to ability to pay—to ensure that the wealthy who had benefitted from the American system would pay their fair share of the nation's tax liability. Ability to pay was also offered as a justification for graduating an income tax, of course—for taxing higher levels of income at higher rates. But even a proportional income tax—a tax imposed at a flat rate—was seen as consistent with ability to pay, particularly when contrasted with the consumption taxes that had dominated the national revenue system through most of the nation's history. (All income taxes seriously proposed in the late nineteenth century were progressive in that each had a substantial exemption amount, with the nominally flat rate coming into play only for high incomes.)

In short, by taxing more than what was spent on consumption and, as a result, reaching the wealthy in a way that tariffs did not, the income tax was considered fundamentally different from taxes on consumption. In Professor Michael Graetz's words, "[W]hen this nation adopted the Sixteenth Amendment, achieving fairness in the distribution of the tax burden was the essential reason for taxing income and for taxing it at progressive rates."[242]

On the merits—in discussing both the proposed statutory changes introduced by Senators Bailey and Cummins and the possibility of a constitutional amendment—income tax debates in 1909 mirrored those of 1894. Indeed, Representative Champ Clark of Missouri suggested there was nothing more to say: "My own opinion is that there is not very much necessity for speech making on this occasion or on this proposition. The income tax is a Democratic proposition. We put it in the tariff bill of 1894. A very large majority of us have been in favor of it ever since."[243]

As discussed earlier, the significant debate in 1909 was about whether to seek a constitutional amendment. But, on the question of what an income tax is, the debates on the proposed statutory changes and on the proposed constitutional amendment were really one big debate.

As was true in 1894, much of the discussion in 1909 was about how an income tax would further the ability-to-pay principle in a way that consumption taxes did not. Senator Bailey explained his amendment to the tariff bill: "I believe [the income tax] is the only tax ever yet devised by the statesmen of the world that rises and falls with a man's ability to pay it."[244]

When Cummins introduced his bill, Senator Augustus Octavius Bacon of Georgia pressed him to justify it. Would Cummins favor the income tax if enough revenue could be raised by tariffs? Bacon wanted to know "whether it was rested upon the importance of shifting the burden of taxation from the great masses of consumers, so far as we may be able to do it, to rest it in part, at least, upon the shoulders of those who have the wealth of the country." Cummins finally answered: "[I]f I could change the situation I would so rearrange and readjust these schedules as to decrease the revenue derived from the custom-houses and place it where it should belong—upon those fortunate people who enjoy large incomes." Said Bacon: "Now the Senator has stated exactly the thing I wanted him to state."[245]

Ability to pay dominated discussions of income tax proponents in 1909: Income taxes are consistent with that principle, consumption taxes are not. What follows is a representative sample of statements made on the floors of Congress; there are many more examples.

Senator Bailey (Texas): "Under any circumstances an income tax is more equitable than a tax on consumption. It is more just as between the different classes, and it better conforms to that sound canon of taxation which enjoins upon us to lay all taxes on those who can bear them . . . ."[246]

Senator William Borah (Idaho): An income tax was needed to supplement the tariffs "in order that we may arrive as nearly as we can, as human ingenuity can make it, at a tax which is levied upon a man's ability to pay and in accordance with what he derives as a measure of benefit from his Government."[247] He added, "We believe that every tax system based upon consumption should be supplemented by a system which taxes property and the wealth of the country . . . ."[248]

Senator Cummins (Iowa): "[A]n income tax, levied upon those who ought to bear the burdens of government, . . . will meet even that principle more perfectly than to levy duties upon things that the people must use, and impose the weight of government only by the rule of consumption."[249]

Representative Ollie M. James (Kentucky): "[N]o tax was ever more unjust . . . than a tax upon consumption . . . . A tax upon what some people eat and what they wear would deny them the necessities of life, while others, rolling in opulence . . . , would not feel such a tax."[250]

Representative Robert Lee Henry (Texas): "Equality in taxation should be the north star to light our pathway and direct our feet in the enactment of such statutes. No tax more equitably and wisely distributes the burdens of government than an income tax."[251]

Representative Adam M. Byrd (Mississippi): A tariff falls "upon consumption and not upon wealth, upon what one eats and wears and not upon his property; it means that the citizen who can scarcely provide food and raiment for his wife and children contributes as much or more to the support of the Government as does the multimillionaire."[252]

Representative William Sulzer, a Democrat (New York): "At the present time nearly all the taxes . . . are levied on consumption—on what the people need to eat and to wear and to live; on the necessaries of life; and the consequence is that the poor man . . . pays practically as much to support the Government as the rich man . . . ."[253]

Representative David A. De Armond (Missouri), a veteran of the 1894 battles: "There is no good reason why taxation should not be according to ability to pay—according to wealth, according to income. Your tariff tax is a tax upon necessity, a tax in proportion to the amount you buy, a tax in proportion to what you must have, not a tax in proportion to what you possess."[254]

Representative Courtney W. Hamlin (Missouri): "The tariff tax is levied entirely upon consumption. The laboring man must expend his income for food, fuel, clothing, and tools of industry, and these taxes are heavier upon the necessities." He added that Democrats had always argued for shifting the burden of government "at least partially . . . from the backs of the poor to those who can bear it; to divide these burdens between wealth and consumption; to divide them between the man who has nothing but his labor and the man who has incomes many times greater."[255]

Representative William R. Smith (Texas): "No one can contend that our system of indirect taxation [has no] objectionable features, because . . . its burdens are measured by what the citizen's needs require him to purchase for consumption and not by the amount of his wealth, nor by his ability to pay."[256]

Overall, the tone of the debates was more civil than in 1894. There were fewer Populists around, and, given the reduced opposition to an income tax, less reason to debate with "agrarian ferocity."[257] But except for differences in tone, passages could be moved from 1894 to 1909 and back again without changing the nature of the debate in either year.

Opponents also made the same points that had been made in 1894. An income tax, it was said, was socialistic and inquisitorial.[258] It ought to be available, if at all, only in emergencies.[259] And, as in 1894, there were references about the extent to which an income tax helps, or hinders, civic virtue.[260]

But the opposition went nowhere. The joint resolution containing the Amendment passed unanimously in the Senate (77–0)[261] and in the House a week later, after about four hours' debate, by a vote of 318 to 14.[262] The level of opposition was greater than the votes suggest, because of absences and abstentions, but the votes were nevertheless overwhelmingly favorable.

RATIFICATION AND ITS AFTERMATH

The ratification fight was often intense, but the Amendment was ratified in less than four years. As Randolph Paul wrote, "[T]he fears [that the] amendment would be blocked proved to be unfounded and the struggle for the amendment had the quality of anti-climax."[263] There were bumps along the way, most significantly opposition from New York Governor Charles Evans Hughes. Hughes worried that the language "from whatever source derived" would permit taxing "not only incomes from ordinary real or personal property, but also incomes derived from State and municipal securities,"[264] something *Pollock* had precluded under the doctrine of intergovernmental immunity (a subject discussed in Chapter 10).[265] If the Amendment was intended to overturn *Pollock*, Hughes's fears about New York finances were not trivial.[266]

Opponents of the Amendment latched onto the Hughes argument, which delayed ratification in a few states, but Hughes received assurances that the Amendment was intended to remove apportionment only for income taxes already within congressional power, not to extend taxing power to new categories of income.[267] Thereafter, ratification went surprisingly fast. By early 1913, forty-two states, including New York, had ratified the Amendment.[268]

A new income tax followed almost immediately in 1913.[269] That first statute seems quaint to modern readers, with rates on income above $3000 ranging from one to seven percent, and we have certainly moved far beyond what anyone could have imagined in 1909 or 1913. In 1909, Senator William Borah responded to the charge that an income tax is necessarily socialistic, by sarcastically criticizing positions taken by opponents:

> When the State or the Government sees fit to lay a [tariff] which may take 30 per cent of the income, the fruits of the labor, of the man of ordinary means, that is the exercise of constitutional power. But when you lay a tax of 2 per cent upon incomes, so slight a burden that it would scarcely be felt, that is socialism. Man's intelligence should not be so universally discredited. But he says if you can levy a tax of 2 per cent you may lay a tax of 50 or 100 per cent. Who will lay the tax of 50 or 100 per cent? Whose equity, sense of fairness, of justice, of patriotism does he question? Why, the representatives of the American people . . . .[270]

How could the "representatives of the American people" do such a thing? The marginal rates never reached 100 percent, of course, but they got close—and they got there fast, rising to a top wartime rate of 77 percent in 1918.[271]

New York Governor Hughes's fear about the demise of the doctrine of intergovernmental tax immunity as it applied to interest on state and municipal bonds turned out to be well founded, as will be discussed in Chapter 10, but that did not happen officially until South Carolina v. Baker (1988). And it did not happen because of the Sixteenth Amendment. The Court in 1988 determined that exempting state and municipal bond interest from federal income taxation had never been mandated by the Constitution properly understood.

Post–Sixteenth Amendment Litigation and the Vitality of *Pollock*

Before ratification of the Sixteenth Amendment, the Supreme Court had cut back sharply on the scope of *Pollock*. And after ratification (until 1920), the Court continued to express skepticism about the wisdom of its 1895 decision. The merits of *Pollock* were of course irrelevant to the enactment of an unapportioned "tax on incomes"; the Amendment took care of *Pollock*'s narrow holding. But the merits of *Pollock*'s broader reasoning is important in gauging the extent to which taxes other than levies on incomes might be characterized as direct taxes—a subject to be discussed in Chapter 8.

In Brushaber v. Union Pacific Railroad Co. (1916), a stockholder sued to enjoin a corporation from complying with corporate income tax provisions enacted after the effective date of the Sixteenth Amendment—a procedural posture similar to that in *Pollock.* The *Brushaber* Court interpreted the Amendment as merely having eliminated the need to consider the source of income (that is, whether it was attributable to property or services) in determining whether an income tax must be apportioned.[272] But, the Court also seemed to have been saying, source of income should ordinarily not have been an issue; an income tax is generally an excise tax, not subject to apportionment. Only in unusual cases, suggested the Court, could a tax on income be so closely tied to property that it would become a direct tax. *Brushaber* effectively characterized *Pollock* as a substance-over-form decision dependent on its peculiar facts.

In another case decided the same year, Stanton v. Baltic Mining Co. (1916), the Court said *Brushaber* "simply prohibited the previous complete and plenary power of income taxation possessed by Congress from the beginning from being taken out of the category of indirect taxation to which it inherently belonged"[273]—again, an income tax is an excise—and being tested "by a mistaken theory deduced from the origin or source of the income taxed."[274] *Pollock*, the Court appears to have been saying in 1916, was based on a mistaken theory.

Did the Court in 1916 mean to be repudiating its 1895 decision in *Pollock*? Had the understanding of the Direct-Tax Clauses returned to that of Hylton v. United States (1796)? Was the Sixteenth Amendment therefore completely unnecessary as a technical, legal matter (although it may have been required as a practical, political matter)? These questions will be considered in Chapters 7 and 8.

Notes to Part I

1. "Essays of Brutus I," *New York Journal* (Oct. 18, 1787), *reprinted in* 2 *The Complete Anti-Federalist* (Herbert J. Storing ed., Chicago: University of Chicago Press, 1981): pp. 363, 366.

2. *See* Charles J. Bullock, "The Origin, Purpose and Effect of the Direct-Tax Clause of the Federal Constitution. I," *Political Science Quarterly* 15 (1900): pp. 217, 218–19.

3. *The Federalist No. 21,* at 143 (Alexander Hamilton) (Clinton Rossiter ed., New York: Mentor Books, 1961).

4. *See* Roger H. Brown, *Redeeming the Republic: Federalists, Taxation, and the Origins of the Constitution* (Baltimore: Johns Hopkins University Press, 1993): p. 318 n.38.

5. Brown, *Redeeming:* p. 12.

6. *The Federalist No. 30,* at 189 (Alexander Hamilton) (Clinton Rossiter ed., New York: Mentor Books, 1961).

7. 2 Jonathan Elliot, *The Debates in the Several State Conventions on the Adoption of the Federal Constitution* (Philadelphia: J. B. Lippincott Co., 1836) 233 (June 20, 1788), quoted in *New York v. United States,* 505 U.S. 144, 165–66 (1992).

8. 2 Elliot, *Debates:* p. 56 (Jan. 21, 1788), quoted in *New York v. United States,* 50 U.S. at 165.

9. *New York v. United States,* 505 U.S. at 165.

10. Herbert J. Storing, *What the Anti-Federalists Were For* (Chicago: University of Chicago Press, 1981): pp. 35–36.

11. *See* 2 Max Farrand ed., *The Records of the Federal Convention of 1787* (New Haven: Yale University Press, 1937): p. 359 (Aug. 21, 1787).

12. Luther Martin, "Mr. Martin's Information to the General Assembly of the State of Maryland" (1788), reprinted in 2 Storing, *Complete:* pp. 27, 55.

13. Martin, *Mr. Martin's Information:* p. 56.

14. *See* "Address of a Minority of the Maryland Ratifying Convention," *Md. Gazette* (May 6, 1788), reprinted in 5 Storing, *Complete:* pp. 92, 97.

15. "Speech of George Mason in the Virginia State Ratifying Convention" (June 4, 1788), reprinted in 5 Storing, *Complete:* pp. 255, 259.

16. "Speech of Patrick Henry in the Virginia State Ratifying Convention" (June 5, 1788), reprinted in 5 Storing, *Complete:* pp. 211, 223.

17. 1 *Annals of Congress* 773 (Joseph Gales ed., 1834) (Aug. 22, 1789).

18. 2 Elliot, *Debates:* p. 233 (June 20, 1788), quoted in *New York v. United States,* 505 U.S. at 165–66.

19. 3 Elliot, *Debates:* p. 122 (June 7, 1788).

20. 3 Elliot, *Debates:* pp. 251–52 (June 11, 1788).

21. *See The Federalist No. 36,* at 219 (Alexander Hamilton) (Clinton Rossiter ed., New York: Mentor Books, 1961).

22. *See* Robert Middlekauff, *The Glorious Cause: The American Revolution, 1763–1789* (New York: Oxford University Press, 1982): pp. 597–99.

23. *Knowlton,* 178 U.S. at 103 (quoting 5 Elliot, *Debates:* pp. 478–79) (citations omitted).

24. *Knowlton,* 178 U.S. at 103–04.

25. Nelson Lund, "The Uniformity Clause," *University of Chicago Law Review* 51 (1984): 1193, 1212.

26. *Knowlton,* 178 U.S. at 105.

27. See 2 Farrand, *Records:* p. 594 (noting that Madison's copy of the draft prepared by the Committee includes the Uniformity Clause only as an interlineation by Madison).

28. 2 Farrand, *Records:* p. 614 (Sept. 14, 1787).

29. *See The Federalist No. 21,* at 142–43.

30. *The Federalist No. 21,* at 143.

31. *The Federalist No. 36,* at 220.

32. *See* 1 Farrand, *Records:* pp. 196–97 (June 11, 1787).

33. *The Federalist No. 54,* at 336 (James Madison) (Clinton Rossiter ed., New York: Mentor Books, 1961).

34. *See* 1 Farrand, *Records:* p. 593 (July 12, 1787).

35. 1 Farrand, *Records:* p. 542 (July 6, 1787).

36. *See The Federalist No. 54,* at 336 (arguing in favor of apportionment of taxation "notwithstanding the imperfection of the rule as applied to the relative wealth and contributions of the States").

37. 1 Farrand, *Records:* p. 542 (July 6, 1787).

38. 1 Farrand, *Records:* p. 201 (June 11, 1787).

39. 1 Farrand, *Records:* p. 201 (June 11, 1787).

40. Brown, *Redeeming:* p. 318 n.38.

41. 1 Farrand, *Records:* p. 592 (July 12, 1787).

42. 2 Farrand, *Records:* p. 106 n.* (July 24, 1787).

43. Edwin R. A. Seligman, *The Income Tax* (New York: Macmillan, 1914): p. 550 (citing Bullock, *Origin:* p. 233 n.3).

44. 1 Farrand, *Records:* p. 562 (July 9, 1787).

45. 1 Farrand, *Records:* p. 592 (July 12, 1787).

46. 1 Farrand, *Records:* p. 592 (July 12, 1787).

47. 3 Elliot, *Debates:* p. 453 (June 15, 1788).

48. *The Federalist No. 54,* at 336.

49. *The Federalist No. 54,* at 340–41.

50. 3 Elliot, *Debates:* p. 121 (June 7, 1788).

51. 2 Farrand, *Records:* p. 106 (July 24, 1787) (footnote omitted).

52. *Springer,* 102 U.S. at 596.

53. Arthur C. Graves, "Inherent Improprieties in the Income Tax Amendment to the Federal Constitution," *Yale Law Journal* 19 (1910): 505, 515.

54. 2 Farrand, *Records:* p. 618 (Sept. 14, 1787).

55. 3 Elliot, *Debates:* p. 122 (June 7, 1788).

56. 3 Elliot, *Debates:* p. 115 (June 7, 1788).
57. *The Federalist No. 12,* at 92 (James Madison) (Clinton Rossiter ed., New York: Mentor Books, 1961).
58. 2 Elliot, *Debates:* p. 191 (Jan. 7, 1788).
59. *See* 2 Elliot, *Debates:* pp. 191–92 (Jan. 7, 1788).
60. 3 Elliot, *Debates:* pp. 95–96 (June 16, 1788).
61. 3 Elliot, *Debates:* p. 253 (June 11, 1788).
62. *The Federalist No. 35,* at 213 (Alexander Hamilton) (Clinton Rossiter ed., New York: Mentor Books, 1961).
63. 1 Farrand, *Records:* p. 286 (June 18, 1787).
64. "Essays of Brutus VII," *New York Journal* (Jan. 3, 1788), reprinted in 2 Storing, *Complete:* pp. 400, 404.
65. 2 Farrand, *Records:* p. 307 (Aug. 16, 1787).
66. 2 Farrand, *Records:* p. 305 (Aug. 16, 1787).
67. 2 Farrand, *Records:* p. 306 (Aug. 16, 1787).
68. 2 Farrand, *Records:* p. 306 (Aug. 16, 1787).
69. 2 Farrand, *Records:* p. 307 (Aug. 16, 1787).
70. *See* 2 Farrand, *Records:* p. 361 (Aug. 21, 1787); 2 Farrand, *Records:* p. 362 (Aug. 21, 1787).
71. 2 Farrand, *Records:* p. 307 (Aug. 16, 1787).
72. 2 Farrand, *Records:* p. 362 (Aug. 21, 1787).
73. 2 Farrand, *Records:* p. 362 (Aug. 21, 1787).
74. 2 Farrand, *Records:* p. 306 (Aug. 16, 1787).
75. 2 Farrand, *Records:* pp. 362–63 (Aug. 21, 1787).
76. 2 Farrand, *Records:* p. 307 (Aug. 16, 1787).
77. 2 Joseph Story, *Commentaries on the Constitution of the United States* (Boston: Hilliard, Gray & Co., 1833) § 1011, at 469–70 (footnote omitted).
78. 2 Farrand, *Records:* pp. 359–60 (Aug. 21, 1787).
79. 2 Farrand, *Records:* p. 307 (Aug. 16, 1787).
80. 2 Farrand, *Records:* p. 305 (Aug. 16, 1787).
81. 2 Farrand, *Records:* pp. 359–60 (Aug. 21, 1787).
82. *See* U.S. Const. Art. I, § 2, cl. 3; U.S. Const. Art. I, § 9, cl. 4.
83. 1 Farrand, *Records:* p. 592 (July 12, 1787).
84. 1 Farrand, *Records:* p. 592 (July 12, 1787).
85. 2 Farrand, *Records:* p. 95 (July 23, 1787).
86. Letter from James Madison to Thomas Jefferson (Oct. 24, 1787), reprinted in 10 *The Papers of James Madison* (Robert A. Rutland and Charles Hobson eds., Chicago: University of Chicago Press, 1977): pp. 206, 214.
87. *See also* 2 Farrand, *Records:* p. 374 (Aug. 22, 1787).
88. 2 Farrand, *Records:* pp. 142, 168.
89. 2 Farrand, *Records:* p. 307 (Aug. 16, 1787).
90. 2 Farrand, *Records:* p. 360 (Aug. 21, 1787).
91. 2 Farrand, *Records:* p. 361 (Aug. 21, 1787).
92. 2 Farrand, *Records:* pp. 306–07 (Aug. 17, 1787).
93. 2 Farrand, *Records:* p. 307 (Aug. 17, 1787).
94. 2 Farrand, *Records:* p. 308 (Aug, 16, 1787).
95. 2 Farrand, *Records:* p. 363 (Aug. 21, 1787).

96. 2 Farrand, *Records:* p. 361 (Aug. 21, 1787).

97. 2 Farrand, *Records:* p. 308 (Aug. 16, 1787).

98. 2 Farrand, *Records:* p. 363 (Aug. 21, 1787).

99. 2 Farrand, *Records:* p. 363 (Aug. 21, 1787).

100. 2 Farrand, *Records:* p. 363 (Aug. 21, 1787).

101. 2 Farrand, *Records:* pp. 363–64 (Aug. 21, 1787).

102. 2 Farrand, *Records:* p. 374 (Aug. 22, 1787).

103. Act of June 5, 1794, Ch. 45, § 1, 1 Stat. 373, 374 (repealed 1802).

104. *See* William R. Casto, *The Supreme Court in the Early Republic: The Chief Justiceships of John Jay and Oliver Ellsworth* (Columbia: University of South Carolina Press, 1995): p. 101.

105. Casto, *Supreme:* p. 102.

106. Edward B. Whitney, "The Income Tax and the Constitution," 20 *Harvard Law Review* (1907): 280, 283 n.1.

107. *See* Judiciary Act of 1789, Ch. 20, § 22, 1 Stat. 73, 84.

108. *Hylton,* 3 U.S. (3 Dall.) at 172.

109. *Hylton,* 3 U.S. (3 Dall.) at 174 (Chase, J.).

110. *Hylton,* 3 U.S. (3 Dall.) at 181 (Iredell, J.).

111. *Hylton,* 3 U.S. (3 Dall.) at 174; *see also Hylton*, 3 U.S. (3 Dall.) at 181–82 (Iredell, J.).

112. *Compare* David P. Currie, *The Constitution in the Supreme Court: The First One Hundred Years, 1789–1888* (Chicago: University of Chicago Press, 1885): p. 34 (questioning validity of assuming without inquiry that carriages were distributed unevenly), *with* Casto, *Supreme:* p. 101 (stating that carriages were in fact more widespread in the South).

113. *Hylton,* 3 U.S. (3 Dall.) at 175 (Chase, J.).

114. *Hylton,* 3 U.S. (3 Dall.) at 183 (Iredell, J.).

115. *Hylton,* 3 U.S. (3 Dall.) at 177 (Paterson, J.).

116. *Hylton,* 3 U.S. (3 Dall.) at 178 (Paterson, J.).

117. *See* Owen M. Fiss, *History of the Supreme Court of the United States: Troubled Beginnings of the Modern State, 1888–1910* (New York: Macmillan, 1993): p. 92.

118. *See Hylton,* 3 U.S. (3 Dall.) at 180 (Paterson, J.) (stating that "a tax upon land, where the object is simple and uniform throughout the states, is scarcely practicable").

119. *See* Act of Aug. 5, 1861, Ch. 45, 12 Stat. 292; Act of Mar. 5, 1816, Ch. 24, 3 Stat. 255; Act of Feb. 27, 1815, Ch. 60, 3 Stat. 216; Act of Jan. 9, 1815, Ch. 21, 3 Stat. 164; Act of Aug. 2, 1813, Ch. 37, 3 Stat. 53; Act of July 14, 1798, Ch. 75, 1 Stat. 597.

120. Currie, *Constitution in the Supreme Court:* p. 34.

121. Brief for the United States, *Hylton v. United States*, 3 U.S. (3 Dall.) 171 (1796) [hereinafter *Hamilton's Brief*], reprinted in 8 *The Works of Alexander Hamilton* (Henry Cabot Lodge ed., Fed. ed., New York: G. P. Putnam's Sons, 1904): pp. 378, 378–79.

122. *See, e.g., The Federalist No. 12,* at 93; *The Federalist No. 21,* at 143; *The Federalist No. 36,* at 219.

123. *Hamilton's Brief:* p. 382.

124. *Hamilton's Brief:* p. 381.

125. *Hamilton's Brief:* p. 383.

126. *Hamilton's Brief:* p. 379.

127. *Hamilton's Brief:* p. 380.

128. *See The Federalist No. 35,* at 212.

129. *See* Marjorie E. Kornhauser, "The Constitutional Meaning of Income and the Income Taxation of Gifts," *Connecticut Law Review* 25 (1992): 1, 22, n.92.

130. *Hylton*, 3 U.S. (3 Dall.) at 173 (Chase, J.).

131. Casto, *Supreme:* p. 247.

132. Casto, *Supreme:* p. 250.

133. Casto, *Supreme:* p. 104.

134. 4 *Annals of Congress* 730 (1794).

135. *Hylton,* 3 U.S. (3 Dall.) at 180 (Paterson, J.); *see Hylton*, 3 U.S. (3 Dall.) at 175 (Chase, J.).

136. *Hylton,* 3 U.S. (3 Dall.) at 180 (Paterson, J.).

137. *Hylton,* 3 U.S. (3 Dall.) at 180–81 (Paterson, J.) (quoting Adam Smith, *The Wealth of Nations* (Edward Cannan ed., New York: Random House, 1937) (1776): pp. 821, 827.

138. *Veazie Bank,* 75 U.S. (8 Wall.) at 536.

139. *Veazie Bank,* 75 U.S. (8 Wall.) at 543.

140. *Veazie Bank,* 75 U.S. (8 Wall.) at 544.

141. *Veazie Bank,* 75 U.S. (8 Wall.) at 541.

142. *Springer,* 102 U.S. at 602.

143. *Scholey,* 90 U.S. (23 Wall.) at 348.

144. *Springer,* 102 U.S. at 602; *see also Scholey*, 90 U.S. (23 Wall.) at 34 ("it is expressly decided that the term ['direct taxes'] does not include the tax on income").

145. Robert G. McCloskey, *The American Supreme Court* (Chicago: University of Chicago Press, 1960): p. 94.

146. *Pollock*, 157 U.S. at 532.

147. John Steele Gordon, *Hamilton's Blessing: The Extraordinary Life and Times of Our National Debt* (New York: Walker, 1997): p. 87.

148. *See* Willard L. King, *Melville Weston Fuller* (New York: Macmillan, 1950): p. 195.

149. *See Pollock,* 157 U.S. at 430–32.

150. Edward S. Corwin, *Court over Constitution* (Princeton: Princeton University Press, 1938): p. 178.

151. *See Pollock,* 157 U.S. at 581.

152. *Pollock,* 157 U.S. at 558.

153. *Pollock,* 157 U.S. at 559–60.

154. *Pollock,* 157 U.S. at 556.

155. *See Pollock,* 157 U.S. at 586.

156. *Pollock,* 158 U.S. at 618.

157. Fiss, *History:* p. 89.

158. *Pollock,* 158 U.S. at 637. The distinction between earned income and income from real estate provided a way for the *Pollock* Court to avoid repudiating its 1881 decision in *Springer*. The *Springer* decision had not relied on the earned-income point, however, and this distinction seems to have been one of convenience rather than principle.

159. *Pollock,* 158 U.S. at 622.

160. Francis R. Jones, "Pollock v. Farmers' Loan and Trust Company," *Harvard Law Review* 9 (1895): 198, 198.

161. *See, e.g.,* Kornhauser, *Constitutional:* pp. 23–24.

162. David G. Farrelly, "Justice Harlan's Dissent in the Pollock Case," *Southern California Law Review* 24 (1951): 175, 182.

163. McCloskey, *American:* p. 94.

164. Sylvester Pennoyer, "The Income Tax Decision, and the Power of the Supreme Court to Nullify Acts of Congress," *American Law Review* 29 (1895): 550, 558.

165. *Pollock,* 158 U.S. at 664–65 (Harlan, J., dissenting).

166. *Pollock,* 158 U.S. at 706 (Jackson, J., dissenting).

167. *Pollock,* 158 U.S. at 695 (Brown, J., dissenting).

168. Fiss, *History:* p. 77.

169. Louis Eisenstein, *The Ideologies of Taxation* (New York: Ronald Press, 1961): p. 21.

170. Fiss, *History:* p. 88.

171. 1 Edward Coke, *The First Part of the Institutes of the Lawes of England* (London: Societie of Stationers, 1628) Ch. 1, § 1, at 4v, quoted in *Pollock,* 157 U.S. at 580.

172. *Thomas,* 192 U.S. at 371.

173. *Knowlton,* 178 U.S. at 78–83.

174. *Knowlton,* 178 U.S. at 81–82.

175. *Knowlton,* 178 U.S. at 83 (quoting Nicol v. Ames, 173 U.S. 509, 516 (1899)).

176. *Flint,* 220 U.S. at 150.

177. *See* Act of July 1, 1862, Ch. 119, §§ 89–93, 12 Stat. 432, 473–75.

178. Act of June 30, 1864, Ch. 173, § 116, 13 Stat. 223, 281.

179. *See* Roy G. Blakey and Gladys C. Blakey, *The Federal Income Tax* (New York: Longmans, Green & Co., 1940): p. 7.

180. "Internal Taxes and Tariff" (statement of Mar. 15, 1872), *reprinted in* John Sherman, *Selected Speeches and Reports on Finance and Taxation, from 1859 to 1878* (New York: D. Appleton, 1879): pp. 336, 348–49.

181. *See* Sidney Ratner, *Taxation and Democracy in America* (New York: John Wiley & Sons, 1967): pp. 145–67.

182. Gerald G. Eggert, "Richard Olney and the Income Tax Cases," *Mississippi Valley Historical Review* 48 (1961): 24–25.

183. Whitney, *Income Tax:* p. 284.

184. *Quoted in* 26 Cong. Rec. app. 601 (Jan. 30, 1894) (statement of Populist Colorado Rep. Lafe Pence) (emphasis added).

185. 26 Cong. Rec. 6634 (June 21, 1894).

186. 26 Cong. Rec. app. 413 (Jan. 29, 1894).

187. 26 Cong. Rec. app. 415 (Jan. 29, 1894).

188. 26 Cong. Rec. 6692 (June 22, 1894).

189. *See, e.g.*, 26 Cong. Rec. app. 293 (Jan. 31, 1894) (statement of Populist Senator Omer Ken of Nebraska).

190. 26 Cong. Rec. app. 415 (Jan. 29, 1894).

191. *See, e.g.*, 26 Cong. Rec. app. 76 (Jan. 23, 1894).

192. H.R. Rep. No. 53–276, at 3 (1894).

193. Amasa J. Parker, Jr., "Income Tax of 1894—Its Provisions and Constitutionality," *Albany Law Journal* 50 (1894): 416, 421.

194. "Current Topics," *Albany Law Journal* 51 (1895): 17, 22.

195. *Pollock,* 157 U.S. at 518 (oral argument for appellee).

196. 26 Cong. Rec. 6630 (June 21, 1894).

197. 26 Cong. Rec. 6707 (June 21, 1894).

198. *See, e.g.*, 26 Cong. Rec. 6694 (June 22, 1894) (statement of Ohio Sen. Sherman).

199. *See, e.g.*, 26 Cong. Rec. app. 207 (Jan. 26, 1894) (statement of Pa. Rep. Robert J. Adams, Jr.).

200. *See, e.g.*, 26 Cong. Rec. 6695 (June 22, 1894) (statement of Sen. Sherman).

201. *See, e.g.*, 26 Cong. Rec. app. 303 (Jan. 30, 1894) (statement of Me. Rep. Seth L. Milliken).

202. *See, e.g.*, 26 Cong. Rec. 6627 (June 21, 1894) (statement of Del. Sen. Anthony Higgins).

203. *See, e.g.*, 26 Cong. Rec. app. 395 (Jan. 30, 1894) (statement of N.Y. Rep. Joseph C. Hendrix).

204. 26 Cong. Rec. 6637 (June 21, 1894).

205. *See, e.g.*, 26 Cong. Rec. 6629 (June 21, 1894) (statement of Sen. Hoar).

206. Quoted in Seligman, *Income Tax:* p. 496.

207. Ratner, *Taxation:* pp. 173–74.

208. Ratner, *Taxation:* p. 189.

209. *See* Blakey & Blakey, *Federal:* p. 21.

210. *See* Blakey & Blakey, *Federal:* p. 22.

211. Quoted in Seligman, *Income Tax:* pp. 591–92.

212. Quoted in Seligman, *Income Tax:* p. 591.

213. Quoted in Blakey & Blakey, *Federal:* p. 23.

214. *See* W. Elliot Brownlee, "Historical Perspective on U.S. Tax Policy Toward the Rich," in *Does Atlas Shrug? The Economic Consequences of Taxing the Rich* (Joel B. Slemrod ed., New York: Russell Sage Foundation, 2000): pp. 28, 39.

215. *See* Kyvig, *Explicit:* p. 201.

216. 44 Cong. Rec. 1351 (Apr. 15, 1909).

217. 44 Cong. Rec. 1422 (Apr. 21, 1909).

218. 44 Cong. Rec. 3931 (June 29, 1909).

219. Presidential Message, "Tax on Net Income of Corporations," S. Doc. No. 61–98, at 2 (1909); *see* Ratner, *Taxation:* p. 286.

220. 44 Cong. Rec. 3936 (June 29, 1909) (statement of Cal. Sen. Frank P. Flint).

221. 44 Cong. Rec. 3995 (July 1, 1909).

222. *See* Kyvig, *Explicit:* pp. 202–03; Ratner, *Taxation:* p. 307.

223. 44 Cong. Rec. 3992 (July 1, 1909).

224. 44 Cong. Rec. 3974 (June 30, 1909).

225. 44 Cong. Rec. 4067 (July 3, 1909).

226. 44 Cong. Rec. app. 119 (July 12, 1909).

227. 44 Cong. Rec. app. 121 (July 12, 1909).

228. S.J. Res. 8, 61st Cong., 44 Cong. Rec. 263 (Mar. 25, 1909).

229. S.J. Res. 25, 61st Cong., 44 Cong. Rec. 1568 (Apr. 28, 1909).

230. 44 Cong. Rec. 1568 (Apr. 28, 1909).

231. 44 Cong. Rec. 1569 (Apr. 28, 1909).

232. *Presidential Message:* p. 2; Ratner, *Taxation:* p. 286.

233. S.J. Res. 39, 61st Cong., 44 Cong. Rec. 3377 (June 17, 1909).

234. 44 Cong. Rec. 3377 (June 17, 1909).

235. 44 Cong. Rec. 3377 (June 17, 1909) (emphasis added).

236. S.J. Res. 40, 61st Cong., 44 Cong. Rec. 3900 (June 28, 1909).

237. Ratner, *Taxation:* p. 299.

238. Blakey & Blakey, *Federal:* p. 61.

239. John D. Buenker, *The Income Tax and the Progressive Era* (New York: Garland, 1985): p. 127.

240. Seligman, *Income Tax:* p. 595.

241. Seligman, *Income Tax:* pp. 595–96 (quoting 44 Cong. Rec. 4391 (July 12, 1909) (statement of Mass. Rep. Samuel W. McCall)).

242. Michael J. Graetz, *The Decline (and Fall?) of the Income Tax* (New York: W. W. Norton & Co., 1997): p. 222.

243. 44 Cong. Rec. 4392 (July 12, 1909).

244. 44 Cong. Rec. 1351 (Apr. 15, 1909).

245. 44 Cong. Rec. 1429 (Apr. 21, 1909).

246. 44 Cong. Rec. 1538 (Apr. 26, 1909).

247. 44 Cong. Rec. 1680 (May 3, 1909).

248. 44 Cong. Rec. 1682 (May 3, 1909).

249. 44 Cong. Rec. 3968 (June 30, 1909).

250. 44 Cong. Rec. 4398 (July 12, 1909).

251. 44 Cong. Rec. 4412 (July 12, 1909).

252. 44 Cong. Rec. 4416 (July 12, 1909).

253. 44 Cong. Rec. 4417 (July 12, 1909).

254. 44 Cong. Rec. 4420 (July 12, 1909).

255. 44 Cong. Rec. 4433 (July 12, 1909).

256. 44 Cong. Rec. app. 127 (July 12, 1909).

257. W. Elliot Brownlee, *Federal Taxation in America: A Short History* (Cambridge: Cambridge University Press, 1996): p. 38 (describing 1894 debates).

258. *See, e.g.,* 44 Cong. Rec. 4390 (July 12, 1909) (statement of N.Y. Republican Rep. Sereno E. Payne, chair of Ways and Means Committee).

259. *See, e.g.,* 44 Cong. Rec. 4391 (July 12, 1909) (statement of Mass. Rep. Samuel W. McCall) ("[W]hy not . . . limit it expressly to time of war?").

260. *See, e.g.,* 44 Cong. Rec. 4109 (May 27, 1909).

261. 44 Cong. Rec. 4121 (July 5, 1909).

262. 44 Cong. Rec. 4440 (July 12, 1909).

263. Randolph E. Paul, *Taxation in the United States* (Boston: Little Brown, 1954): p. 97.

264. Ratner, *Taxation:* 304 (quoting Special Message from the Governor, New York Senate, No. 3, at 5 (1910)).

265. *Pollock,* 157 U.S. at 584–86.

266. *See* Paul, *Taxation:* p. 97.

267. *See* Evans v. Gore, 253 U.S. 245, 260–61 (1920); *see also* Buenker, *Income Tax:* pp. 255–61.

268. *See* Buenker, *Income Tax:* p. 158.

269. Income Tax Law of 1913, Ch. 16, 38 Stat. 114.

270. 44 Cong. Rec. 3999 (July 1, 1909).

271. *See* Revenue Act of 1918, Ch. 18, §§ 210–211, 40 Stat. 1057 (1919); Brownlee, *Federal:* p. 45.

272. *Brushaber,* 240 U.S. at 18.

273. *Stanton,* 240 U.S. at 112.

274. *Stanton,* 240 U.S. at 113.

PART II

Analysis

5

The Uniformity Clause

> ***[A]ll Duties, Imposts and Excises shall be uniform throughout the United States.***
> —Article I, section 8, clause 1

The taxing power provided in Article I, section 8, clause 1 (the taxing power begins the list of enumerated powers) is very broad indeed: "The Congress shall have power to lay and collect Taxes, Duties, Imposts and Excises, to pay the Debts and provide for the common Defense and general Welfare of the United States." Included in the same clause, however, is an express limitation on the taxing power: "[B]ut all Duties, Imposts and Excises shall be uniform throughout the United States." This is the so-called Uniformity Clause.

A couple of points jump out at the careful reader. For one thing, the levies that are subject to the uniformity rule ("Duties, Imposts and Excises") seem to be only a subset of the levies that Congress can impose ("Taxes, Duties, Imposts and Excises"). The difference in the language used in the these two parts of the clause suggests that there are some levies ("Taxes") that need not be "uniform." (In fact, as will be discussed in more detail in Chapter 6, direct taxes, which are subject to a special apportionment rule, cannot be uniform as that term has come to be understood.)

A second point is that the list of permissible levies contains a number of terms that are bewildering to a modern reader and that are not defined at any point in the Constitution. What, if anything, distinguishes a "Duty" from an "Impost," for example? ("Imposts" have always been understood to apply to imports, but the founders used the term *duty* in that context as well.) What is an "Excise"? Is "Tax" a distinct category or is it an umbrella term that also encompasses the other levies (which is, presumably, the way we would talk about taxes today)?

The meaning of "Duties, Imposts and Excises" will be discussed at the end of this chapter, and the definition, like all definitions, is subject to some uncertainty at the edges. Despite the fuzziness, however, the Uniformity Clause is one constitutional limitation that lends itself to black-letter treatment: Duties, excises, and imposts (levies that are generally called "indirect taxes," to distinguish them from the "direct taxes" subject to the apportionment rule) must be geographically uniform to satisfy the Clause. This means that, as the Supreme Court wrote in Knowlton v. Moore (1900), "[W]herever a subject is taxed anywhere, the same must be taxed everywhere throughout the United States, and at the same rate."[1]

Professor Nelson Lund has pointed out that the Uniformity Clause began its life tied to what became the Port Preference Clause of Article I, section 9, clause 6, and, while the Port Preference Clause forbids discrimination along state lines, the Uniformity Clause makes no similar reference to the states as states.[2] Nevertheless, no court has ever attached any significance to this difference in language. The Uniformity Clause is understood to require uniformity state-by-state—nothing more, nothing less. Professor David Currie has noted the congressional assumption, in deliberations on an early whiskey tax, that the Uniformity Clause required only geographic uniformity of this sort.[3]

In a passage quoted by the Supreme Court in Ptasynski v. United States (1982), Justice Joseph Story, in his 1833 *Commentaries on the Constitution,* described the purpose of the Uniformity Clause as follows:

> [The purpose of the clause] was to cut off all undue preferences of one State over another in the regulation of subjects affecting their common interests. Unless duties, imposts, and excises were uniform, the grossest and most oppressive inequalities, vitally affecting the pursuits and employments of the people of different States, might exist. The agriculture, commerce, or manufactures of the State might be built up on the ruins of those of another; and a combination of a few States in Congress might secure a monopoly of certain branches of trade and business to themselves, to the injury, if not to the destruction, of their less favored neighbors.[4]

For example, Congress may not tax a particular type of property transfer in New York at a one percent rate (measured by the value of the property, say) and an otherwise identical type of property transfer in Delaware at a two percent rate. Nevertheless, the uniformity requirement does not preclude Congress from providing exemptions to the application of any particular tax—like not taxing the first $1 million of estate value—as long as the rules are applied uniformly, on a state-by-state basis, throughout the United States.

It is not hard to see why geographic uniformity was considered important at the Constitutional Convention. The Southern states in particular were concerned about oppressive levies targeted at their section of the country, and a number of constitutional provisions were intended to ensure that representatives of one set of states could not gang up to overtax citizens of another set of states. Requiring that the same base be taxed at the same rates is consistent with that general purpose.

But if the uniformity rule means only that "wherever a subject is taxed anywhere, the same must be taxed everywhere throughout the United States, and at the same rate," it does not come close to making sectional taxation impossible. For example, suppose Congress is considering the imposition of a national tax on a particular category of property. If the property is concentrated in a few states, a tax on that property can be sectional in its effects while satisfying the uniformity rule. A tax on sleighs that meets the uniformity rule (the same rate applicable in all states) would obviously have dramatically different effects on different states.

Indeed, almost any item that could conceivably be subject to national taxation is likely to be distributed unevenly across the country. Because of this, as Professor Lund has written, "virtually all . . . taxes [on goods and activities] have nonuniform *effects*. A tax on tobacco, for example, will affect the tobacco-growing regions more severely than others."[5] But if the tax is not a direct tax subject to the apportionment rule and is not on "Articles exported" (which would be prohibited by the Export Clause), the uniformity rule is the only constitutional constraint on Congress's power to impose such a tax. As long as the tax on tobacco applies at the same rate in all states, the uniformity rule is satisfied.

In the minds of many commentators, the uniformity rule, so understood, has "shriveled away to a mere flyspeck," or so Professor Bittker wrote about the rule's effect on the income tax.[6] "Uniformity" could have been interpreted in a broader way—to preclude progressive rates, for example, or taxes that have sectional effects. Indeed, uniformity challenges of that sort were made in Pollock v. Farmers' Loan & Trust Co. (1895) (the *Income Tax Cases*), based on a $4,000 exemption (which made the 1894 income tax applicable only to very high-income people) and on the fact that, because of the concentration of high incomes in the industrialized Northeast, the burden of the tax fell overwhelmingly on that region. Those issues were not resolved in 1895—the income tax was struck down on other grounds—but the Court soon explicitly limited the rule to geographic uniformity in Knowlton v. Moore (1900).[7]

Still, although the Uniformity Clause has not been as powerful as it might have been, it has more potential effect than the "flyspeck" comment suggests. Even if, narrowly defined, the Clause precludes only geographic discrimination of a very specific sort—taxing items in Utah at rates different from those that apply in Ohio, for example—that is not a meaningless principle.

We have come to take geographic uniformity so much for granted—the idea that a duty, impost, or excise must operate "with the same force and effect in every place where the subject of [the tax] is found," as the Supreme Court put it in the Head Money Cases (1884)[8]—that we forget it was not a given in 1787. It might not have been politically possible to do so, but, in theory, the Constitution could have permitted national duties, imposts, and excises to vary from state to state, taking into account differences in local conditions.

Suppose today's Congress wanted excise taxes to affect gasoline consumption in a geographically variable way. A policy maker might consider having the rate depend on usage in each state, hitting gas-guzzling populations harder than others. The main reason that such a geographically variable tax would not be suggested in Congress is probably that, even without constitutional constraints, it would be politically difficult to get the tax enacted. But another reason is that the Uniformity Clause looms in the background. Even if it wished to, Congress could not constitutionally enact such a tax.

SUPREME COURT CASE LAW INTERPRETING THE UNIFORMITY CLAUSE

A discussion of the Supreme Court's consideration of uniformity rule issues requires little space. The serious history did not begin until 1884, and the understanding outlined in the Head Money Cases (1884), in dictum, is pretty much the controlling understanding today, at least for facially neutral statutes. That understanding was followed, with some embellishment, in Knowlton v. Moore (1900). And in Ptasynski v. United States (1982), the Court expanded on the analysis required if Congress uses geographic terms in the process of defining subjects to be taxed.

Facially Neutral Statutes

The *Head Money Cases* considered the constitutionality of a charge (called a *duty* in the statute) imposed on carriers of immigrants coming by sea to American ports. The statute did not single out any particular states for taxability (or exemption from taxability). In effect, however, because the charge applied only to immigrants coming by sea, and not those crossing land borders, it affected only seafaring parts of the country. That geographically variable effect, said the challengers to the charge, violated the Uniformity Clause.[9]

The *Head Money* Court could have avoided discussing the meaning of uniformity altogether, because it wound up concluding that the charge was not a tax at all and therefore was outside the scope of the Uniformity Clause. (While the Court said the charge was not a "tax," what it should have said, to be precise, was that the charge was not a duty, impost, or excise. By its terms, the uniformity rule does not apply to "taxes" that are not duties, imposts, or excises.) The charge was to raise revenue for administrative purposes and to help immigrants on arrival in the United States, and the Court concluded that Congress had exercised its power over commerce, not its taxing power, in enacting the statute.[10]

Although the Court did not have to define uniformity, it threw judicial restraint to the winds and did so anyway, concluding that a tax is uniform if it "operates with the same force and effect in every place where the subject of it is found."[11] That language has come to define the Uniformity Clause. Thus, even if the charge at issue in the *Head Money Cases* had been characterized as a duty, impost, or excise, it would have met constitutional requirements: "Here [said the Court] there is substantial uniformity within the meaning and purpose of the Constitution."[12]

Requiring more than substantial uniformity would have been unrealistic, the Court concluded: "Perfect uniformity and perfect equality of taxation, in all the aspects in which the human mind can view it, is a baseless dream."[13] The Court assumed, without explanation, that the Constitution requires only a form of geographic uniformity that does not look to the actual effects of a facially neutral statute:

The uniformity here prescribed has reference to the various localities in which the tax is intended to operate. . . . Is the tax on tobacco void, because in many of the States no tobacco is raised or manufactured? Is the tax on distilled spirits void, because a few States pay three-fourths of the revenue arising from it?[14]

If it had been characterized as a duty for Uniformity Clause purposes—remember, all of this was dictum—the charge on immigrants would have been valid because it applied to immigrants at a port in Tennessee (if you could find one) just as it applied to immigrants at ports in New York.

Dictum though it was, the conception of the Uniformity Clause explicated in the *Head Money Cases* was followed in Knowlton v. Moore (1900) with a few embellishments and a bit more explanation. In *Knowlton*, the Court considered the constitutionality of an inheritance tax that exempted small legacies and provided for a graduated rate structure applicable to larger legacies.[15] The inheritance tax was challenged on the ground that, because it did not operate in the same way on all individuals and all property, it violated the Uniformity Clause.

This time the Court had to face the Uniformity Clause issues directly. The *Knowlton* Court characterized the challengers' conception of the uniformity rule as one of "intrinsic uniformity," something like the "perfect uniformity" argument raised sixteen years earlier, and once again it rejected that idea in favor of geographic uniformity.[16]

Several factors pointed to geographic uniformity as the goal of the Uniformity Clause, including the language of the Clause itself. The phrase "throughout the United States" would be surplusage if the word "uniform" meant that a tax must affect all persons or property identically, and constitutional phrases ought not to be treated as surplusage.[17] Furthermore, based on its examination of history, the Court concluded that the Clause was intended to prevent Congress from explicitly favoring one part of the country at the expense of another, not to preclude taxes that have incidental, nonuniform effects on individuals.[18] Indeed, as was discussed in Chapter 2, an early version of the Clause presented to the Constitutional Convention would have required that duties, imposts, and excises not only be "uniform," but also that they be "equal throughout the United States." But the reference to equality disappeared along the way in the Convention's deliberations.

Perhaps most important, if "intrinsic uniformity" were the goal, hardly any duty, impost, or excise on articles of consumption would satisfy the requirements of the Uniformity Clause because consumption of any particular type of good can vary substantially from state to state. That would have been a nonsensical result. No one could seriously have suggested that the founders intended to make such indirect taxes all but impossible.[19] Indeed, the evidence is overwhelming that the founders thought indirect taxes would fund the national government in the ordinary course of its business. For example, James Wilson, a staunch Federalist, emphasized that "the great revenue of the United States must, and always will, be raised by impost; for, being at once less obnoxious, and more productive, the interest of the government will be best promoted by the accommodation of the people."[20] In any event, if the founders really intended for the Uniformity Clause to prohibit, or nearly prohibit, duties, imposts, and excises, they picked peculiar language to evidence that intention.

Interpreting the Uniformity Clause in a geographic way also had the happy effect of tying the Clause to the apportionment rule that applies to direct taxes (a category that, at a minimum, includes capitation taxes and land taxes). The apportionment rule determines a state's percentage of the total direct-tax liability to be collected by computing the state's share of the national population (for example, a state with one tenth of the national population would be required to collect one tenth of any direct tax liability), clearly with the goal of preventing discrimination among states and regions. As the *Knowlton* Court clumsily put it, "Now, that the requirement that direct taxes should be apportioned among the several States, contemplated the protection of the States, to prevent their being called upon to contribute more than was deemed their due share of the burden, is clear."[21] Giving the Uniformity Clause an interpretation grounded in the same general purpose, said the Court, harmonized two related constitutional provisions.[22]

Geographic References in Taxing Statutes

The final chapter in the Supreme Court's involvement with the Uniformity Clause was United States v. Ptasynski (1982), where the Court accepted the general principles of the *Head Money Cases* and *Knowlton*, but addressed some issues unresolved in those cases. In particular, *Ptasynski* considered how to analyze a taxing statute where Congress *does* include an arguably discriminatory geographical reference. And it made explicit what had been implicit in the two prior cases—that a facially neutral taxing statute, one that does not use geographic references, does not implicate the Uniformity Clause.

Ptasynski considered a provision in the Crude Oil Windfall Profit Tax Act of 1980 that excluded "exempt Alaskan oil" from the application of an excise on the production of domestic crude oil.[23] "Exempt Alaskan oil" was one of several defined categories of oil from north of the Arctic Circle, where production was so expensive that Congress determined special treatment was justified. Taxpayers from the lower forty-eight states challenged the tax, arguing that the exemption for "Alaskan oil" violated the Uniformity Clause.

The *Ptasynski* Court accepted the proposition that the Uniformity Clause is primarily concerned with sectional discrimination. But, if that is so, how could an exemption for a particular category of Alaskan oil be reconciled with the *Head Money* rule, requiring that a levy governed by the Uniformity Clause "operate[ ] with the same force and effect in every place where the subject of it is found"?[24]

The Court dealt with part of the problem by defining it away. In one striking passage, the Court concluded that Congress can generally define the "subjects" of taxation as it wishes: "Where Congress defines the subject of a tax in nongeographic terms, the Uniformity Clause is satisfied"[25] (the Court cited *Knowlton* for this proposition, but the *Knowlton* Court had not made such a point—at least not explicitly).[26]

With this understanding, Congress can generally draft around a potential Uniformity Clause problem. As Professor Lund has bluntly said, "Congress may enact blatantly discriminatory indirect taxes without risking constitutional scrutiny: it need only take care to frame the 'subjects' of taxation in nongeographic terms."[27] With respect to the windfall profit tax itself, Lund noted, "Had the tax challenged in *Ptasynski* provided an exemption for all oil produced from wells that cost more than $1,000,000 to drill, there would presumably not have been even a colorable objection based on the [U]niformity [C]lause. . . ." That was so, even though "the effects of this definition might have been virtually identical to those of the geographic definition that Congress in fact used."[28]

Artful congressional drafting should generally avoid Uniformity Clause problems, but Congress had not been so artful in drafting the Windfall Profit Tax Act. It had, in fact, used a geographical reference—and an obvious one. Ultimately, however, congressional clumsiness (if that is what was involved) turned out not to be fatal.

The *Ptasynski* Court held that geographic references are not necessarily forbidden: "where Congress does choose to frame a tax in geographic terms, we will examine the classification closely to see if there is actual geographic discrimination."[29] Under this analysis, "actual geographic discrimination" is relevant only if the statute at issue uses geographic terms to define the subject being taxed. If a taxing statute is facially neutral—that is, if Congress uses no geographic references—one need not even ask whether there is geographic discrimination in fact.

If geographical references are used, as in the special treatment for "Alaskan oil," a court is obligated to look for actual geographic discrimination. Nevertheless, except in extraordinary cases (the sorts of factual situations found in law school hypotheticals), a court is unlikely to find it. The judicial search is conducted in a way that gives considerable deference to Congress's judgment. In *Ptasynski* itself, the Court concluded that, "[w]here . . . Congress has exercised its considered judgment with respect to an enormously complex problem, we are reluctant to disturb its determination."[30]

Thus, if Congress is dealing with an "enormously complex" problem—and what legislative problems are not?—a court is likely to defer to the congressional determination. The windfall profit tax unquestionably dealt with a complex problem: Congress had found that oil production is more difficult and expensive in northern Alaska than elsewhere, which justified preferential treatment for "exempt Alaskan oil."[31]

The *Ptasynski* Court also stressed that the problem Congress was dealing with in exempting certain Alaskan oil from the tax was "geographically isolated," a nondiscriminatory justification for framing an exemption in geographic terms.[32] In coming to that conclusion, the Court relied on a set of cases decided under the Bankruptcy Clause, the Regional Rail Reorganization Act Cases (1974). Those cases had held that Congress's power to establish "uniform Laws on the subject of Bankruptcies throughout the United States"[33]—the relevance of the Bankruptcy Clause to Uniformity Clause analysis was the common use of the term "uniform"—permitted Congress to enact special bankruptcy provisions for financially troubled railroads in one region of the country.[34] In the *Rail Act Cases*, the Court cited *Head Money* for the proposition that where Congress is addressing a geographically isolated problem, a law can be uniform even though it treats different regions differently.[35] (Although the Court had not made that point explicitly in *Head Money*, there is some plausibility to the proposition.)

At bottom, the special treatment for "exempt Alaskan oil" was not a Uniformity Clause problem because use of the term *Alaskan* was not really a geographical reference, at least not of the sort prohibited by the Clause. The term was a shorthand way of referring to a particular category of oil, one that Congress could have used nongeographic terms to describe. As the Court put it, "Had Congress defined this class of oil in nongeographic terms, there would be no question as to the Act's constitutionality. We cannot say that identifying the class in terms of its geographic boundaries renders the exemption invalid."[36]

"DUTIES, IMPOSTS AND EXCISES": INDIRECT TAXES VERSUS DIRECT TAXES

As interpreted, the Uniformity Clause thus prohibits only certain governmental charges that vary geographically in an explicit, and otherwise unjustified, way. But to what levies does the Clause potentially apply?

The uniformity rule by its terms applies only to "Duties, Imposts and Excises," not to all levies that fall within the omnibus taxing power of Article I, section 8, clause 1. None of those terms is defined in the Constitution, and one searches the case law (and the literature more generally) in vain for a concise set of definitions that will distinguish among duties, imposts, and excises.[37]

Be that as it may, the critical distinction is not between "duties," say, and "imposts," but between "Duties, Imposts and Excises," on the one hand, and other levies that are not subject to the Uniformity Clause. The basic distinction in the constitutional structure is between the sorts of indirect taxes for which uniformity (a relatively limited restriction) is appropriate, and those direct taxes subject to the much more restrictive apportionment rule discussed in Chapter 6.

The founders considered indirect taxes (generally taxes on the transfer of articles of consumption) to be relatively safe. Although an indirect tax may nominally be imposed on a shipper or a merchant, the founders assumed that the economic burden would be shifted to the ultimate consumer. As a result, the tax was avoidable in this important way: consumers could decide whether to buy the taxed good, and thus whether to pay the tax.

Indirect taxes may wind up affecting the price, and therefore the consumption, of the products to which they relate. In Federalist 21, Hamilton noted that "[i]mposts, excises, and, in general, all duties upon articles of consumption, may be compared to a fluid, which will in time find its level with the means of paying them."[38] Consumers will adjust their behavior to the cost of the products, a cost that may reflect the consumption taxes that have to be paid—the "imperceptible agency of taxes on consumption."[39]

Of course, it is not necessarily true that the burden of such an indirect tax can be passed on to the ultimate consumer, as Hamilton recognized: "It is not always possible to raise the price of a commodity in exact proportion to every additional imposition laid upon it. The merchant . . . is often under a necessity of keeping prices down in order to make a more expeditious sale."[40] Imagine widgets that sold for $1 before the imposition of a five percent tax. If those widgets compete with wudgets that are equally attractive, which also sell for $1 but which will not be taxed, the widget seller is going to have to eat the tax (charging only about ninety-five cents so that the total cost to the purchaser is $1) or he is not going to sell anything. Who will pay more than $1 to get a widget if he can buy a wudget for $1?

Nevertheless, the assumption of most founders was that an indirect tax is one which the ultimate consumer can generally decide whether to pay by deciding whether to acquire the taxed product. For the Hamilton of *The Federalist,* before he became an advocate trying to validate the *Hylton* carriage tax, it was enough to characterize consumption taxes as indirect in that they were usually passed on: "The maxim that the consumer is the payer is so much oftener true than the reverse of the proposition. . . ."[41]

That made indirect taxes safe from governmental overreaching, or so it was thought. At the Pennsylvania ratifying convention, James Wilson said an indirect tax is safe "because it is voluntary. No man is obliged to consume more than he pleases, and each buys only in proportion to his consumption. The price of the commodity is blended with the tax, and the person is often not sensible of the payment."[42] And, wrote Alexander Hamilton in Federalist 21, "The amount to be contributed by each citizen will in a degree be at his own option, and can be regulated by an attention to his own resources." Accordingly, "[i]t is a signal advantage of taxes on articles of consumption, that they contain in their own nature a security against excess."[43]

If the national government raises indirect tax rates too high, consumers will instead purchase untaxed goods or will otherwise engage in avoidance (and maybe even evasion) of the tax, thus actually reducing government revenues. As antifederalist Brutus explained, "[I]f [imposts] are laid higher than trade will bear, the merchants will cease importing, or smuggle their goods. We have therefore sufficient security, arising from the nature of the thing, against burdensome and intolerable impositions from this kind of tax."[44] In short, there is no incentive for government to abuse such taxes. Indeed, with the protections against governmental abuse characteristic of indirect taxes, it is impossible for the national government to gouge the taxpaying public.

In contrast, direct taxes have no similar built-in protections. They were thought to be dangerous precisely because they are not so easily avoided. A tax on the ownership of real estate, for example, cannot be shifted to anyone else, or so it was assumed. A confiscatory land tax was therefore seen as a greater danger than an indirect tax—dangerous to the individuals involved and dangerous to the affected states, whose tax bases could be decimated by overreaching federal taxation. If the national government soaked up too much revenue, little would be left to fund the needs of the states,[45] and the very existence of the states could be endangered.[46] The apportionment rule accordingly made such direct taxes more difficult to impose.

To be sure, not everyone thought that the direct-tax power would be exercised in an irresponsible way, even without specific constitutional protections. For example, James Madison believed the awesome responsibility of taxing individuals directly, rather than relying on a system of requisitions, would temper any tendency to congressional excess:

> [T]hose who fix the public burdens will feel a greater degree of responsibility, when they are to impose them on the citizens immediately than if they were to say what sum should be paid by the states. . . . Were they to exceed, in their demands, what were reasonable burdens, the people would impute it to the right source, and look on the imposers as odious.[47]

But the likely good faith of future Congresses, even when checked by informed public opinion, went only so far as a comforter, and many founders wanted an explicit restraint on congressional power.

The distinction between the relatively safe indirect taxes and the relatively dangerous direct taxes makes the constitutional structure coherent. Under this scheme, a levy is an indirect tax subject to the uniformity rule or a direct tax governed by apportionment, and the rules are necessarily mutually exclusive. A tax cannot be both indirect and direct (see Chapter 6). Historically there was a sense that there might also be a third category of levies that fell through the cracks at the Constitutional Convention and that would, as a result, be subject to neither the uniformity nor the apportionment rule. By its terms, the Uniformity Clause applies to "Duties, Imposts and Excises," not to "taxes," and the apportionment rule applies only to *direct* taxes. The possible category of levies governed by neither rule would consist of "taxes" (as distinguished from "Duties, Imposts and Excises") that are not "direct taxes."

No one at the Convention discussed such a possibility, but two of the justices in Hylton v. United States (1796) did so.[48] And Justice Story, in his 1833 *Commentaries*, discussed it at some length:

> Here, then, two rules are prescribed, the rule of apportionment . . . for *direct* taxes, and the rule of uniformity for *duties, imposts,* and *excises.* If there are any other kinds of taxes, not

embraced in one or the other of these two classes, (and it is certainly difficult to give full effect to the words of the constitution without supposing them to exist,) it would seem, that congress is left at full liberty to levy the same by either rule, or by a mixture of both rules, or perhaps by any other rule, not inconsistent with the general purposes of the constitution.[49]

Close linguistic analysis points in the direction suggested by the *Hylton* justices and Justice Story, but this is probably a case where we should resist reading too much into every word in the Constitution. It is doubtful that any founder could have distinguished with precision among the bewildering variety of terms used to refer to governmental levies: "Taxes, Duties, Imposts and Excises" in Article I, section 8;[50] "Duties, Imposts, and Excises" in the Uniformity Clause;[51] "Tax or Duty" in the Export Clause[52] and in the clause limiting a levy on the "Migration or Importation" of slaves to "ten dollars for each Person";[53] "Imposts or Duties" in the Import-Export Clause;[54] and "Tax" or "Taxes" in the Direct-Tax Clauses.[55] For purposes of the Uniformity Clause and the direct-tax apportionment rule, the constitutional structure makes the most sense if the term *taxes* in Article I, section 8, clause 1 is understood as an umbrella term that encompasses not only direct taxes, but also the indirect taxes—the duties, imposts, and excises that are imposed on articles of consumption. Indirect taxes must be uniform; other taxes must be apportioned.

In any event, no example of a tax that is governed by neither the uniformity rule nor the apportionment rule has ever been found, and the quest has been abandoned by all but the most determined. As Chief Justice Melville Fuller noted in Pollock v. Farmers' Loan & Trust Co. (1895): "although there have been from time to time intimations that there might be some tax which was not a direct tax nor included under the words 'duties, imposts and excises,' such a tax for more than one hundred years of national existence has as yet remained undiscovered. . . ."[56] And none has been discovered in the century since *Pollock*.

In a 1910 article anticipating ratification of the Sixteenth Amendment, Dwight Morrow thought he had found such a levy. The Supreme Court had concluded in *Pollock* that an income tax is direct. The Amendment removed "taxes on incomes" from the scope of the apportionment rule, but it did not change the characterization of an income tax. If *Pollock* was rightly decided, the modern income tax remains a direct tax (and is therefore arguably not subject to the uniformity rule), but the income tax is also explicitly exempted from apportionment by the Sixteenth Amendment.[57] *Voila!* As a direct tax, an income tax does not have to be uniform and, because of the Amendment, it does not have to be apportioned . . . or so it seemed.

Not requiring that income tax rates be geographically uniform could give Congress enormous flexibility in putting an income tax together (although the flexibility would still be constrained, of course, by the demands of the political marketplace). But that was not to be. The Supreme Court concluded in Brushaber v. Union Pacific Railroad Co. (1916) that the income tax, no longer required to be apportioned after the Sixteenth Amendment, is subject to the uniformity rule.[58] Like all other taxes that have been analyzed under the taxing provisions of the Constitution, the income tax must be governed by one of the two basic rules.

The result in *Brushaber* means that, even if the income tax is technically a direct tax (and on that point not all would agree), Congress cannot tax the income of New Yorkers at rates different from those that apply to Mississippians or define the income tax base differently in the two jurisdictions. The constitutional language may not mandate that result, but after *Brushaber,* it is hard to imagine that any national levy will ever be held exempt from both the uniformity and apportionment rules.

6

The Direct-Tax Apportionment Rule

Representatives and direct Taxes shall be apportioned among the several States which may be included within this Union, according to their respective Numbers, which shall be determined by adding to the whole Number of free Persons, including those bound to Service for a Term of Years, and excluding Indians not taxed, three fifths of all other Persons.—Article I, section 2

No Capitation, or other direct, Tax shall be laid, unless in Proportion to the Census or Enumeration herein before directed to be taken.—Article I, section 9, clause 4

Under the two Direct-Tax Clauses, direct taxes must be apportioned among the states on the basis of respective state populations. This requirement makes direct taxes cumbersome to use—except for "taxes on incomes," which were excepted from the apportionment rule by the Sixteenth Amendment. (As will be discussed in Chapter 8, the category of "direct taxes" includes, at a minimum, capitation and land taxes, and, especially if Pollock v. Farmers' Loan & Trust Co. (1895) was rightly decided, it may include much more.) Unless the base of a direct tax is spread across the country in a way that is proportionate to state populations—and except for the simplest form of head tax, it is hard to imagine a tax base so evenly distributed—an apportioned direct tax will have to have different rates in different states, or some other rickety mechanism will have to be used to satisfy the apportionment rule. The mechanics of apportionment can be worked out without a doctorate in mathematics, but the practical effect of the rule is to make enactment of a geographically variable direct tax politically difficult.

The rule, in short, is a hobble on congressional power to enact most direct taxes. Although several national taxes on real estate (generally including slaves as well) were enacted between 1798 and 1861,[59] no national tax has been apportioned since 1861. From Congress's perspective, avoiding the apportionment process is always desirable, and courts in the nineteenth century made it easy for Congress not to have to worry about apportionment. Until the decisions in *Pollock*, which invalidated an unapportioned income tax, courts were generally willing to classify challenged levies as something other than direct taxes and therefore not subject to apportionment.

Pollock changed the Supreme Court's conception of an income tax (and of direct taxes more generally), but after ratification of the Sixteenth Amendment in 1913, taxes on incomes were specifically excepted from apportionment. As a result, it no longer mattered whether *Pollock*'s characterization of an income tax as direct was correct. Whatever the proper status of a "tax on incomes," it does not have to be apportioned.

This history suggests why the Direct-Tax Clauses have disappeared from public consciousness. Indeed, if many taxes (including the monumental revenue-raiser that is the personal income tax) do not have to be apportioned, why should anyone care about apportionment? Commentators have come to ignore the Direct-Tax Clauses altogether or to characterize the apportionment rule, in Professor Calvin Johnson's words, as "a rule too silly to enforce"[60]—to argue that, on the merits, the rule *deserves* to be ignored. The rule seems to have become at best a historical curiosity, and in 2004, it is doubtful that many congressmen have any idea that there might still be taxes which, if enacted, would be subject to this peculiar requirement.

Nevertheless, it is not clear that apportionment is of only historical interest. For one thing, the Constitution contains *two* Direct-Tax Clauses. An interpreter need not go so far as to argue that the Clauses have extra effect for that reason (although such an argument has in fact been made)[61] to see the Clauses as creating a serious limitation on the taxing power. At a minimum, however, the two references to apportionment show that the rule was not an afterthought or an obvious mistake.

And for any tax that is a direct tax but is not a tax on incomes, apportionment remains a technical requirement. It may seem that no one cares anymore, but one cannot be sure that twenty-first century courts will see a constitutional rule as "too silly to enforce." It is therefore worth considering how apportionment would work, how it relates to the uniformity rule discussed in Chapter 5, and whether apportionment has legitimate (or at least arguably legitimate) purposes.

MECHANICS OF THE APPORTIONMENT RULE

When the apportionment rule applies, a state with one tenth of the national population must bear one tenth of the aggregate direct-tax liability, regardless of the state's proportion of the national tax base. (If Congress were simultaneously to enact more than one direct tax requiring apportionment—something that has not happened—the apportionment would presumably be done tax by tax, or so the language of Article I, section 9, clause 4 suggests.)

Under the original version of the apportionment rule, the population figures used to apportion direct taxes reflected the special counting rules for slaves and "Indians not taxed." The Fourteenth Amendment effectively ended the three fifths rule for slaves, and in 1924, American Indians were by statute made citizens of the United States (and were therefore generally made subject to U.S. taxation).[62]

The special counting provisions are thus gone, but the rule tying direct-tax liability to population remains in the Constitution.

If the apportionment rule were invoked today, it would almost necessarily lead to the sort of geographical variation that the uniformity rule precludes for duties, excises, and imposts. Of course, if state X with one tenth of the national population also has one tenth of the relevant national tax base, apportionment presents no particular problem: X's one tenth of the population will have to pay one tenth of the total direct-tax liability. The citizens of X might dislike the particular tax, and they might dislike the way the tax burden is distributed among the state's citizens and residents. But they should not feel that their state is being gouged by other states.

But suppose state X's share of the direct-tax base is only one twentieth of the national total. Each taxed item in state X will be subject to tax at a rate *double* the otherwise applicable average, or Congress will have to come up with some other, equally klutzy mechanism to make the apportionment numbers come out right. Whatever the mechanism adopted, the citizens of state X (particularly the citizens who might feel the pinch of a higher tax rate) are unlikely to see the tax as fair.

Because of the Sixteenth Amendment, a national income tax is no longer subject to apportionment, but as the federal tax most readers are familiar with, it still provides a nice example of the arguable perversity of apportionment. Assume as before that state X has one tenth of the national population but one twentieth of the national income. (With a *per capita* income one half the national average, X is a very poor state indeed.) If an income tax did have to be apportioned, the average X resident would still have to pay as much in income tax as is paid by the average person nationally. To get to that result, the federal tax rates applicable in state X would probably have to double the national average. Thus, because of apportionment, citizens and residents of poorer states would be subject to income taxation at rates *higher* than the national average, a regressive structure that would appall many—if a tax with such geographically variable terms were really to be enacted.

On the other hand, if state X's share of the direct tax base is one fifth of the national total, the taxed items (or the taxed income in the above example) would be subject to rates *one half* the national average. That would obviously be good for state X but bad for others. And these hypothetical results are so obviously absurd, say critics of apportionment, that they show the intellectual bankruptcy of the apportionment rule.

If Congress went ahead with direct taxation when there is significant geographical variation of this sort in the tax base, most of us would find the result peculiar and maybe even outrageous. The resulting statute would certainly look very different from the taxing provisions we are used to. Nevertheless, as the third part of this chapter will discuss, the apportionment rule is not nearly as nonsensical as it may at first seem, if it is understood as a deterrent to the enactment of such patently objectionable taxes.

THE RELATIONSHIP BETWEEN APPORTIONMENT AND UNIFORMITY

The above description of the mechanics makes the apportionment process sound more off-putting than it really is because not all levies are required to be apportioned. The Constitution effectively divides the tax universe into direct taxes, which do have to be apportioned (unless exempted by the Sixteenth Amendment), and other levies, which are usually called *indirect taxes.*

Indirect taxes is not a constitutional term, but it is a shorthand way to refer to the "Duties, Imposts and Excises"—a subset of the "Taxes, Duties, Imposts and Excises" that Congress has the "Power To lay and Collect"—that, under Article I, section 8, clause 1, must "be uniform throughout the United States." As was discussed in Chapter 5, the uniformity rule has been interpreted to require only geographic uniformity for indirect taxes, meaning that, "if a particular item is subject to tax, it must be taxed at the same rate throughout the United States, wherever it may be found."[63]

Under the constitutional scheme, no national levy is subject to both the apportionment rule and the uniformity rule. (That is presumably why the uniformity rule, by its terms, does not seem to apply to "taxes.") The uniformity requirement cannot apply to apportioned direct taxes because dividing up the burden of a direct tax on the basis of population, as the apportionment rule demands, would almost always lead to tax rates or other tax attributes that vary from state to state. Except in very unusual situations, an apportioned tax could not be geographically uniform.

For example, if a national tax on real estate is a direct tax (and ancient authority holds that it is), the tax rate can be uniform only if state real-estate values—or acreages, or whatever other measure might be used for the tax—and state populations happen to be proportionate. For a real-estate tax to have a uniform rate structure, a state with one tenth of the national population would have to have one tenth of the national real-estate value (or acreage), a state with one twentieth of the population would have to have one twentieth of the value (or acreage), and so on across the country. That is not the case, and it is hard to imagine that it could ever be the case.

An 1895 commentator stated that "the framers [undoubtedly] thought that, in a rough way at least, the land in any States would be valuable in proportion to their populations, or that the populations of the States would ultimately be roughly proportional to their areas."[64] The founders may have been thinking in that way, but at best the contemporaneous evidence would have pointed to rough proportionality. It should therefore have been apparent that taxes on real estate would have to have geographically variable terms to satisfy the apportionment rule. (In fact, the first direct tax on real estate, in 1798, contained a complex scheme to satisfy the apportionment requirement.)[65] The variation among states may not have been enormous with a tax on real estate in the late eighteenth century, but it would have been enough to violate the rule of geographic uniformity.

If a direct-tax base were absolutely uniform geographically (that is, the distribution of the tax base among the states correlated perfectly with population), the tax would seem to satisfy both the uniformity and apportionment rules simultaneously. While such a situation is theoretically possible, it is extremely unlikely in the real world. And even if it were to occur, only the apportionment rule would be technically applicable in that case.[66]

In short, the logic of the constitutional structure requires that apportionment and uniformity be mutually exclusive requirements. And the pervasive assumption is that any levy is covered by one rule or the other: a tax is either direct and therefore subject to apportionment, or indirect and therefore subject to the uniformity requirement.

The mutual exclusivity of the two rules is not a matter of debate—everyone agrees that no tax is governed by both the uniformity and apportionment rules—but, closely read, the constitutional language suggests that there could be a category of levies covered by *neither* rule. As was discussed in Chapter 5, however, no such levy has ever been identified, and it is unlikely that one will ever be found.

SHOULD THE APPORTIONMENT RULE BE IGNORED?

The direct-tax apportionment rule may be contained in two constitutional clauses, but it long ago disappeared from public discussion. No tax has been apportioned since 1861, nor has Congress seriously discussed apportioning a tax since that time. Furthermore, a number of commentators who have looked at the rule have concluded that it deserves to be ignored, except perhaps for capitation taxes, and who today advocates a capitation tax? (Besides, a lump-sum capitation tax would generally satisfy the apportionment rule anyway, now that the special counting rules for slaves and "Indians not taxed" are no longer relevant.)

This part critically considers some of the arguments that have been advanced for discarding apportionment as a serious requirement: that the founders intended no significant limitations on the taxing power to begin with; that the Direct-Tax Clauses are nonsensical in their operation; that the Clauses were inextricably linked to the odious system of slavery; and (as first discussed in Chapter 3) that we should defer to the founding-era Supreme Court's interpretation of the Clauses in Hylton v. United States (1796), which seemed to limit "direct taxes" to at most capitation and real-estate taxes.

The Founders' Intentions

Professor Calvin Johnson has argued that creating a workable national revenue system after the debacle of the Articles of Confederation was a critical reason for having a new constitution, and, at the Constitutional Convention, Johnson says, "Tax won."[67] The Constitution was a "pro-tax" document,[68] and, he argues, the founders therefore intended no significant limitations on the taxing power (other than the Uniformity and Export Clauses).

In some very important respects, tax did indeed "win" in Philadelphia. But properly understanding the Constitution does not require choosing between a nearly unlimited taxing power and no taxing power at all. The Constitution was intended to strengthen the national taxing power, but that fact needs to be put into perspective. The "national" government had had *no* power to tax individuals under the Articles of Confederation; all it could do was requisition funds from the states. Tax "won" when the delegates agreed to something as simple as permitting the national government to levy duties on imports.

Professor Johnson states that "[n]o proponent of this Constitution could have tolerated a hobble on federal revenue,"[69] but a lot of founders, including Federalists, insisted on restraints. The Constitution includes the Uniformity Clause and the Export Clause as well as the two Direct-Tax Clauses—hobbles all. The constitutional context, Professor Owen Fiss has properly noted, was "defined by the desire to prevent abuses of the power of taxation,"[70] and, without constraints on the national taxing power, the Constitution would not have been ratified.

Many commentators have also drawn support for an expansive conception of the taxing power by noting that the Federalists generally "won" in Philadelphia and in the ratifying conventions and that the anti-federalists generally lost.[71] And it is incontrovertible that nearly all Federalists wanted the national government to have a direct-taxing power. Nevertheless, it is a significant leap from that premise to the conclusion that the power was to be unconstrained. Constitution-writing is not an either-or process; the "winners" did not get everything they wanted in undiluted form.

For example, the Federalists generally opposed the Export Clause, discussed in Chapter 9, which prevents Congress from taxing "Articles exported."[72] Among the formidable opponents of limiting Congress's power to tax exports were Alexander Hamilton, James Madison, Gouverneur Morris, George Washington, and James Wilson, but the Clause survived—despite the overall Federalist victory. And most Federalists did not think that the taxing power should be unlimited: Madison thought the direct-tax apportionment rule was "one of the safeguards of the Constitution."[73]

Even the strongest proponents of a powerful national government did not say in public that the government was to be unconstrained in raising revenue. For example, Alexander Hamilton probably preferred an unlimited taxing power, and, in some passages in *The Federalist*, he suggested that only necessity, not constitutional language, should limit that power. But Hamilton was a realistic politician, who wanted the Constitution ratified, and he also stressed protections against abuse. In Federalist 36, for example, he praised the effect of the apportionment rule: "An actual census or enumeration of the people must furnish the rule, a circumstance which effectually shuts the door to partiality or oppression. The abuse of this power of [real-estate] taxation seems to have been provided against with guarded circumspection."[74] To say that the Federalists "won" is not to say that the Direct-Tax Clauses can be ignored.

Is the Apportionment Rule "Too Silly to Enforce"?

Professor Calvin Johnson has a more serious claim as well: with the Direct-Tax Clauses the founders unknowingly created a monster that, if given free rein, would have made a serious national government impossible. As Johnson has put it, "Apportionment of direct tax turned out to be a rule too silly to enforce, in those cases in which the tax base is not equal per capita among the states."[75] Presented with two badly broken constitutional clauses that would inevitably have produced bizarre results, Johnson argues, the *Hylton* Court acted in a statesmanlike way by slaying the monster. The Court did what it had to do.

If there were no way to make sense of the Direct-Tax Clauses, then perhaps the Clauses should be discarded. If a provision has no discernable reason for existence or if it just cannot work to effectuate any legitimate purpose, then perhaps it has to go—or, at a minimum, be interpreted in the most restrictive way possible. But the Clauses had their purposes, and the Clauses work in a defensible (albeit clunky) way.

It is true that the founders did not understand all of the consequences of the provisions they created. The founders thought in general that the direct-tax apportionment rule would prevent abuse—it would make direct taxes geographically "fair," among other things—but they did not prepare spreadsheets to study how the rule would work in a lot of hypothetical situations. Furthermore, there probably was no consensus (there certainly could not have been unanimity) about all of the taxes to which the Direct-Tax Clauses might apply in the future.

The most often quoted passage from Madison's notes in support of the idea that the founders were clueless is Rufus King's unanswered question on August 20: "Mr King asked what was the precise meaning of *direct* taxation? No one answ[ere]d."[76] The conventional wisdom is that, as Dwight Morrow explained in 1910, "Rufus King's question was not answered because no man in the Convention was able to answer it. He asked for a 'precise' definition of 'direct taxation.' As a matter of fact no man has yet satisfactorily answered that question."[77]

But criticisms of that sort cannot be a justification for ignoring the Clauses. Who knows for sure why people do *not* speak? Morrow's interpretation, which is based on no evidence, is not the only way to understand the silence that followed Rufus King's question. Professor Keith Dougherty has hypothesized, just as plausibly, that "[l]ack of discussion reflected the virtual consensus on the issue and perhaps the limited thought put into the details."[78] In any event, whatever the delegates were thinking about King's question, the silence cannot have been as powerful as Morrow suggested: it did not lead to a move to excise or restrict the Direct-Tax Clauses.

The founders did punt on the details—this was a *Constitution* they were writing—but we do have an idea of what they wanted. In fact, in other contexts, Rufus King himself acted as if he understood the meaning of "direct taxes." For example, at the Massachusetts ratifying convention, he stated, "It is a principle of this Constitution, that representation and taxation should go hand in hand."[79] When King later spoke out against requisitions, he again seemed to know what he was talking about:

> The first revenue will be raised from the impost, to which there is no objection, the next from the excise; and if these are not sufficient, direct taxes must be laid. . . . [I]f we mean to support an efficient federal government, which, under the old Confederation, can never be the case, the proposed Constitution is . . . the only one that can be substituted.[80]

The apportionment rule is clumsy, and it does not lend itself to adaptation to changing circumstances—the "infinite variety of causes" of the "wealth of nations" described by Hamilton in Federalist 21.[81] But the clumsiness makes the apportionment rule no less real, and it is a rule that was thought to have application to real taxes. In trying to reassure his fellow Virginians about the Constitution, Edmund Pendleton emphasized the practical, equalizing effect of the apportionment rule: "We have hitherto paid more than our share of taxes for the support of the government. . . . But by this system we are to pay our equal, ratable share only. Where is the danger of confiding in our federal representatives?"[82] Similarly, in correspondence, James Madison argued that the Southern states should support direct taxation because those states heavily consumed imports (and therefore were more affected than the North by import duties): "[D]irect taxes when necessary should come in aid of that fund; since being laid on all the States by an equal rule provided in the Constitution, they tend to equalize the general burden on every part of the Continent."[83]

Because the founders had not thought about the details, however, Professor Johnson argues that they did not understand the absurdity of the apportionment rule. The founders may have had geographical uniformity in mind in some general sense. But if the tax base is not distributed equally across the nation, rates will probably have to differ among the states, and who could have intended that? In Hylton v. United States (1796), Justice Chase had written (in language quoted in Chapter 3): "The rule of *apportionment* is only to be adopted in such cases, where it can *reasonably* apply; and the *subject* taxed, must ever determine the application of the rule."[84] And Justice Iredell agreed with that proposition: "As all direct taxes must be *apportioned,* it is evident, that the constitution contemplated none as direct, but such *as could be apportioned.*"[85]

Like the justices in *Hylton*, Professor Johnson can conjure examples to make apportioned taxes look ridiculous. In *Hylton*, Justice Chase hypothesized a distribution of carriages under which (if the carriage tax were treated as direct) owners in one state might have to pay ten times the amount of tax paid by owners in another equally populous state—a result that Chase considered ridiculous.[86] Extending the arguable absurdity with an even more implausible set of hypothetical facts, Johnson argues that, if apportionment were required with a carriage tax like the one in *Hylton*, "the poor fool to drive the first carriage into Kentucky would have to bear Kentucky's entire state quota."[87]

The *Hylton* justices thus concluded, as does Professor Johnson, that apportionment should be required only when there is a geographically uniform direct-tax base. But interpreting apportionment in that way—as applying only where the tax base is "equal per capita among the states"—renders two clauses meaningless that, in form at least, are limitations on congressional power. If apportionment is to apply only when it makes no difference, the rule is "enforced" only when there is nothing to enforce. Even with the Supreme Court's blessing, that is a peculiar way to interpret a constitutional provision.

In fact, the apportionment rule, while unwieldy, has a core of good (or at least defensible) sense, as a limitation on the congressional power to enact sectionally burdensome taxes. For the founders, the possibility of taxes targeted at particular sections of the country was not a trivial concern, and, by itself, the uniformity rule does nothing to prevent a tax directed at geographically concentrated items.

Part of the concern was slavery. The South was afraid that Congress might attack the peculiar institution by levying a tax on slaves, and the apportionment rule substantially lessened, if it did not eliminate, that possibility. Slaves were in fact taxed as part of several apportioned direct taxes on real estate, on the understanding that slaves were inextricably linked to the associated land, but no direct tax was ever levied on slaves alone, and with reason. Apportioning a tax on slaves would have required that a proportionate part of the tax come from states with no slave populations whatsoever—a result that no northern representative could have supported.

The apportionment rule nevertheless has application to *any* sectionally concentrated direct-tax base, not just to slaves. Suppose a tax is imposed on the ownership of sleighs. Although rates may be the same throughout the country, so that the uniformity rule is satisfied, only the North will bear the burden of the tax—*unless* the tax is direct. If the tax is direct, however, the burden must also fall on states with a sleigh deficit—with the liability of any state dependent on its fraction of the national population, not the concentration of sleighs in that state. Georgia representatives would have been as enthusiastic about an apportioned tax on sleighs as Massachusetts representatives would have been about an apportioned tax on slaves.

Although Professor Johnson and the *Hylton* justices emphasized that the apportionment rule, *if applied*, could lead to bizarrely different tax rates in different states—indeed, depending on how the taxed items are distributed, it could lead to *higher* rates in poorer states—this argument misses the point of the Direct-Tax Clauses. It is *because* the rule might lead to facially suspect results that the rule has effect as a deterrent.

The Clauses should mean that, in ordinary circumstances, a direct tax aimed at a sectionally concentrated tax base (that is, a base that is not at least approximately proportionate to population) will not be enacted. Who in Congress is going to vote for such a tax, except in an emergency like wartime, when revenue needs overwhelm other concerns?

While Representative Jones might initially be inclined to support a tax that seems to hit states other than his own, it is not as though he will be able to do that secretly (and it is not as though the congressmen from the adversely affected states are likely to vote for the tax). And, if the proposed tax is direct, it would wind up hitting Jones's constituents as well. The apportionment rule ensures that, regardless of the distribution of the tax base across the country (and even if Jones's state has few sleighs), Jones's constituents would have to pay their apportioned share of the total liability. How is Representative Jones going to defend a vote for such a statute on the floor of Congress, or to his constituents back home, or to anyone else?

If Congress is inclined to use direct taxes at all (and even supporters of direct taxation thought the United States would rely on *indirect* taxation in the ordinary course of its business), the apportionment rule pushes Congress in the direction of implementing only those direct taxes that have uniformly distributed bases. If the base of a proposed direct tax is "equal per capita among the states," to use Professor Johnson's phrase, the tax by definition will satisfy the apportionment rule, and it will be relatively easy to sell politically.

For a sectionally concentrated tax base, however, the apportionment rule should help prevent enactment of the tax, except in emergencies. Emergency revenue needs will occasionally trump fairness concerns—the founders did intend that direct taxation be possible—but ordinarily fairness (particularly when fortified by the apportionment rule) should win out. One hopes that a tax directed at a geographically concentrated tax base would not be enacted even without the apportionment rule, but if fairness is not enough to lead Congress to the right result, the rule should ordinarily clinch the case.

Perhaps some constitutional provisions are so nonsensical that they should be discarded for that reason, but the Direct-Tax Clauses do not approach that standard of absurdity. Commentators can reasonably disagree with the goal of cabining congressional power, or be indifferent to the purported dangers of sectional taxation, or find fault with the way the apportionment rule implements its goals in a particular case. But the rule is not "too silly to enforce."

The Connection with Slavery

Some have suggested that the apportionment rule was merely an accidental by-product of the fight about how slaves should be counted for purposes of representation—that it has little content because it was not the focus of the real controversy swirling through the constitutional convention—and that it should be disregarded for that reason. Writing at the turn of the twentieth century, for example, Charles Bullock said, "[T]he constitutional requirement concerning direct taxes originated in the struggle to effect a compromise on the question of representation for the slaves. It had no basis in any rational scheme for regulating taxation, and could have had none."[88] Professor Edwin Seligman, one of the intellectual fathers of the modern income tax, wrote at about the same time, "[T]he introduction of the words 'direct taxes' had no reference to any dispute over tax matters, but was designed solely to solve the difficulty connected with representation. . . ."[89] Seligman added, "The direct-tax clause was inserted into the constitution simply and solely as a concession to slavery, and with the disappearance of slavery and the adoption of the fourteenth amendment the very reason for its existence passed away."[90]

Professor Bruce Ackerman, Professor Calvin Johnson, and other modern commentators have also pointed to the Direct-Tax Clauses' unfortunate connection with slavery as a reason for jettisoning the Clauses. As Professor Ackerman puts it, "There is no longer a constitutional point in enforcing a lapsed bargain with the slave power."[91]

This is a widely held position, but it is not obviously correct. As a preliminary matter, it is questionable to conclude that, because the apportionment rule was part of a compromise, it was a meaningless requirement. Compromises work only if the components of the compromise have value to the disputing parties. And it is even more questionable to conclude that, because the apportionment rule was part of a compromise with slavery and slavery has ended, any reason to enforce the apportionment rule has disappeared. Obviously the Clauses took the form they did, with the three fifths counting rule for slaves, because of slavery. But the apportionment rule, which applies to both representation and direct taxation, was not pro-slavery.

In his notes on the Constitutional Convention, James Madison described Gouverneur Morris's proposal of "proportioning direct taxation to representation," ultimately reflected in Article I, section 2, as having the "object [of] lessen[ing] the eagerness on one side, & the opposition on the other, to the share of Representation claimed by the S. <Sothern> [*sic*] States on account of the Negroes."[92] By tying apportionment to both representation and direct taxation, the rule had the effect of increasing the South's representation (by counting slaves as three fifths of a person) but simultaneously increasing the South's share of any direct-tax liability (also by counting slaves as three fifths of a person).[93] Any incentive the Southern states might have had to overstate slave populations, so as to increase representation, would have come with a substantial cost: increased direct-tax liability. This was a compromise that worked because it fully satisfied neither side, and, viewed in its entirety, the compromise was not pro-slavery.

Madison discussed this point in Federalist 54. After noting that population would be used to govern both representation and direct taxation, he stressed that the rules are "by no means founded on the same principle."[94] The tension is a good thing:

> As the accuracy of the census to be obtained by the Congress will necessarily depend . . . on the disposition, if not on the co-operation of the States, it is of great importance that the States should feel as little bias as possible to swell or to reduce the amount of their numbers. . . . By extending the rule to both objects, the States will have opposite interests which will control and balance each other and produce the requisite impartiality.[95]

The compromise reflected in the Direct-Tax Clauses worked precisely because it was neither pro-slavery nor anti-slavery.

The compromise was not universally popular, of course; compromises never are. It dealt with a distasteful subject, slavery, and it elicited opposition because it was intended to have real effects. For example, Massachusetts anti-federalists objected to the fact that Massachusetts blacks would increase that state's share of the national tax burden more than would Southern blacks.[96] Such an objection was silly; the three fifths rule potentially imposed a much greater tax burden on Southern states than on Northern states, much more than not counting slaves at all would have done. But however misguided the concern of the Massachusetts anti-federalists, it is significant that they were concerned enough to object. The direct-tax capability of the national government was feared, and that is why the apportionment rule is in the Constitution.

As a result of the Civil War Amendments, the Constitution was stripped of its most egregious connections with slavery, including the three fifths rule. Discarding still other provisions because of a perceived slavery taint would expose the Constitution to a seemingly endless series of challenges. Where do we stop if we start unraveling the compromises that had some arguable connection with slavery? Was provision *A* too closely tied to tainted provision *B*? How do we tell? And what about *C*, which at one point was discussed in connection with *B*? If all constitutional provisions are up for grabs, one despairs of being able to invoke closure.

With the apportionment rule, Professors Johnson and Ackerman might respond, we have no difficulty figuring out what the compromise was. It is right there in Article I, section 2, with the three fifths rule used both for direct taxation and for representation. But note how counting slaves worked in the two situations. It was the apportionment rule for *representation* that was the real "bargain with the slave power"; counting slaves, even in part, for purposes of representation was a benefit to the South. In contrast, counting slaves for purposes of the apportionment rule for direct taxation potentially imposed a financial burden on the South. Finding taints only in provisions one disapproves of is not a helpful canon of constitutional interpretation in any event, and in this case the commentators get it backwards: They see the taint of slavery only on the side of the compromise that was intended to impose a *cost* on slave states.

Despite its tangential connection with slavery, the direct-tax apportionment rule had independent reasons for existence, such as deterring sectionally directed taxation. Given the founders' fears of the national taxing power, it is hard to imagine that the Constitution would have included no limitations on direct taxation had slavery not existed. The dangers of sectional taxation did not begin with slavery and did not disappear with the end of slavery. Yes, the limitation actually selected took a peculiar form, but that is not an indisputable reason for disregarding it.

Hylton as an Indication of Original Understanding

Chapter 3 discussed the merits of the opinions in Hylton v. United States (1796). Despite the good sense at the core of the apportionment rule, many commentators, with some reason, think that the opinions in *Hylton* are the best indication of what the original understanding of the Direct-Tax Clauses was. If Justice Iredell wrote that, "[a]s all direct taxes must be *apportioned,* it is evident, that the constitution contemplated none as direct, but such *as could be apportioned,*"[97] his statement is accepted as gospel, even though that conception had the effect of gutting the Clauses. Iredell and colleagues were "giants [who] walked upon the earth," in Professor Calvin Johnson's phrase, and "[t]hey knew the Constitution far better than we do."[98]

Obviously, *Hylton* is important evidence in interpreting the original understanding of the Direct-Tax Clauses. No one could seriously suggest otherwise. But there are reasons to read the *Hylton* opinions critically. The conceptions exhibited there were not tied to constitutional text, and they reflected a one-sided conception of original meaning. As Justice Souter explained in another context, in rejecting use of the founding generation's behavior as a necessarily determinative method of discerning original understanding, "[P]ublic officials, no matter when they serve, can turn a blind eye to constitutional principle."[99] The *Hylton* Court was a Federalist Court, which viewed its function as propping up, rather than checking, the Federalist government, and it generally is not a good idea to rely on those in power to define the limits of their power. We ought to be skeptical of founders' statements that, if given controlling weight, would have the effect of gutting constitutional provisions.

The dictum in *Hylton* limiting apportionment to capitation and real-estate taxes is especially suspect because it seems to preclude application of the apportionment rule, a limitation on congressional power, to any form of taxation that was unknown in 1787. It is true that, in their discussions of direct taxation, the founders expressed concern only about capitation taxes and real-estate taxes; those were the forms of direct taxation with which they were familiar. And obviously they could not have talked about forms of taxation that had not yet been devised. But what should we infer from those facts? It would be a peculiar Constitution indeed that governed only the specific sorts of behavior that could have been contemplated in 1787. That interpretive principle would render the Fourth Amendment irrelevant to electronic surveillance, for example, a position that no serious Fourth Amendment scholar advances.

WERE DIRECT TAXES INTENDED TO BE USED?

The apportionment rule was intended to hobble the direct-taxing power. It was intended, that is, to make it difficult to enact a direct tax with a base that is not spread evenly, or approximately evenly, across the country. But that is not to say that the apportionment rule, if taken seriously, was intended to be a "tax killer," in Professor Calvin Johnson's phrase,[100] or that it works to make direct taxation impossible. In fact, Congress enacted a number of apportioned direct taxes on real estate between 1798 and 1861.[101] These statutes, which included complex mechanisms to ensure compliance with the apportionment rule, show that apportioning direct taxes, while difficult, can be done.

After the fiscal disasters of the Articles of Confederation, most founders believed the government needed the power to levy direct taxes. Direct taxation "should be within reach in all cases of emergency," said James Wilson, but it should be used only if indirect taxation failed to raise sufficient revenue. It was indirect taxes—primarily imposts, Wilson suggested—that would fund the national government in the ordinary course: "[T]he great revenue of the United States must, and always will, be raised by impost; for, being at once less obnoxious, and more productive, the interest of the government will be best promoted by the accommodation of the people."[102]

But emergencies like war change the calculus; at such times the burden of apportionment can become temporarily tolerable. As Socius wrote in the *Carlisle Gazette* in November 1787, "As the grand revenue will arise from another source, [direct taxation] may never be applied to, but on such occasions, as may require great exertions. . . ."[103] That followed the English understanding of direct taxation. As Roy Douglas has explained, "Unlike customs duties, [direct taxes] had traditionally been levied as emergency measures only, to meet some special need, usually a war. . . ."[104] Indeed, all of the explicitly direct taxes on real estate enacted in the United States between 1798 and 1861—all of which were structured to satisfy the apportionment rule, something the English did not have to worry about—came into being during wartime or with the country's facing a likelihood of war.

TO WHAT DOES APPORTIONMENT APPLY?

However broad the category of direct taxes, the Sixteenth Amendment removed "taxes on incomes" from the apportionment requirement. What is left of the apportionment requirement today therefore depends not only on how the term *direct taxes* is understood, but also on the meaning of "taxes on incomes." Discussion of the current scope of the apportionment rule will therefore be deferred until Chapter 8, after consideration of the Sixteenth Amendment in Chapter 7.

7

The Sixteenth Amendment Today

The Congress shall have power to lay and collect taxes on incomes, from whatever source derived, without apportionment among the several States, and without regard to any census or enumeration.—Sixteenth Amendment

The Sixteenth Amendment was ratified in 1913, and since that time, the national government has relied heavily on the personal income tax as a source of revenue. Surprising though it may be, however, one cannot find clear, modern authority about the legal effect of the Amendment. The case law construing the Amendment is quite old; the Supreme Court has not tried to understand the meaning of "taxes on incomes" for more than half a century.

The practical effect of the Sixteenth Amendment was swift and certain, of course. With the Amendment on the books, Congress could enact an income tax without worrying about whether, under the Direct-Tax Clauses, the tax must be apportioned. Regardless of whether Pollock v. Farmers' Loan & Trust Co. (1895) was rightly decided, an unapportioned tax on incomes is constitutional (assuming the uniformity rule is satisfied). If *Pollock* was wrong and an income tax was not a direct tax to begin with, the Amendment was surplusage. If *Pollock* was right and an income tax is a direct tax, the Amendment removes taxes on incomes from the apportionment requirement. Either way, apportionment is not required for an income tax.

That general principle is clear, but its application in the real world is not necessarily obvious. By its terms, the Sixteenth Amendment exempts only *taxes on incomes* from apportionment, and that term is not self-defining. What *taxes on incomes* means depends on the validity of *Pollock* and what the Amendment was intended to do to *Pollock*—and those are issues about which there is not agreement. Was the Amendment intended to reinstate the pre-*Pollock* understanding of the Direct-Tax Clauses? Or was it intended to broaden congressional power even further, by eliminating the Clauses altogether? Or was it intended to accept the result and reasoning of *Pollock* as givens and then to carve out a limited exception to the *Pollock* Court's understanding of what taxes must be apportioned?

These are serious questions. At bottom, the practical issue is whether there are any taxes still subject to the apportionment requirement or whether the Amendment eliminated any significant effect that the Direct-Tax Clauses otherwise might have had.

CONCEPTIONS OF THE AMENDMENT

Students of the Sixteenth Amendment fall into at least two camps, with quite different conceptions of the legal situation in a post-Amendment world. At one extreme are those who think that the taxing power was always unencumbered, or generally unencumbered, by the Direct-Tax Clauses and that as a result the Amendment was surplusage. For proponents of this first conception, the Amendment simply cleaned up a mess left by the Supreme Court's wrongheaded decision in *Pollock*.

At the other extreme are those who, generally accepting the result in *Pollock* (that the term *direct taxes* has much broader scope than the Supreme Court's decision in United States v. Hylton (1796) suggested) and following the guidance of early Supreme Court cases interpreting the Sixteenth Amendment, understand the term *taxes on incomes* to have a limited (although important) meaning. The Amendment carved *taxes on incomes* out of the direct-tax apportionment rule, but it left the rule intact for a potentially significant body of other direct taxes.

There are of course variations—and variations on variations—of these two general conceptions of the Sixteenth Amendment. But it is not unfair to characterize the universe of legal commentators as being divided into those who think the meaning of the Amendment matters not at all (the many who accept Conception I) and those (the few adherents of Conception II) who think the meaning of the Amendment is critical in determining how broad the application of the Direct-Tax Clauses continues to be.

Conception I: The Amendment as Surplusage

Professor Daniel Shaviro has stated that "it is generally agreed that the amendment does not significantly constrain how taxable income can be defined by Congress and the courts,"[105] and he is clearly right about the extent of the scholarly agreement. By far most commentators today assume that the Amendment is irrelevant for purposes of determining the extent of the congressional taxing power.

Conception I actually takes two related, but slightly different forms. For some, the Amendment is surplusage because the taxing power, properly understood, was broad enough to permit an unapportioned income tax even without the Amendment. Under this view, the Amendment, if it did anything at all, merely clarified the already existing scope of the taxing power. The Supreme Court had gotten the meaning of "direct taxes" horribly wrong in *Pollock*, and the Amendment was intended not to validate (and then overturn) that case, but rather to show congressional disdain for *Pollock* and return the legal understanding of the Direct-Tax Clauses to its pre-*Pollock* state. The Sixteenth Amendment in 1913 was intended to do nothing more, the argument goes, than remove a temporary, illegitimate impediment to the plenary taxing power.

Proponents of Conception I can point to South Carolina v. Baker (1988), where the Supreme Court confirmed that case law had overruled the part of *Pollock* holding interest on a state bond immune from federal taxation under the doctrine of intergovernmental tax immunity (a subject discussed in Chapter 10).[106] That particular, narrow holding of *Baker* was not surprising; the Court had noted in Graves v. New York (1939), in language quoted in *Baker*, that "[t]he theory . . . that a tax on income is legally or economically a tax on its source, is no longer tenable."[107] A tax on municipal bond interest therefore does not breach principles of federalism because it is not a tax on the municipalities themselves. But *Baker* can also be interpreted as having repudiated *Pollock* in its entirety. If *Pollock*'s result depended on the notion that taxing income from property taxes the property itself—a tax on income from real estate is the equivalent of a direct tax on the real estate—and *Baker* repudiated that notion, then little or nothing of *Pollock* remains.[108] Because of the Sixteenth Amendment, the Court has had no occasion to reconsider the rest of *Pollock*; *Pollock* survives—adherents of Conception I might argue—only because there has been no occasion to bury it formally.

In Union Electric Co. v. United States (2004), for example, the United States Court of Appeals for the Federal Circuit stated that it had to accept *Pollock* as "the law" because the case had not been explicitly overruled, but the court noted that *Pollock*'s "reasoning appears to have been discredited."[109] The court then sidestepped the question of *Pollock*'s continuing significance by concluding that a special assessment on purchasers of enriched uranium was an excise—thus not a direct tax required to be apportioned regardless of whether *Pollock* still has some vitality.

One prominent proponent of Conception I is Professor Bruce Ackerman, who bluntly downplays the significance of the term "taxes on incomes." The Amendment was a response to *Pollock*, and "[w]hen the People mobilize to overrule the [Supreme] Court"—as "the People" did with the Sixteenth Amendment—"it seems particularly inappropriate for the Justices to respond in a niggling fashion."[110] If the scope of the Amendment were to be litigated today, Ackerman argues, the Court should not hesitate; it should proclaim (or actually re-proclaim) the plenary nature of the taxing power. Ackerman concludes that, "[u]nder the constitutional regime inaugurated by the New Deal, there are no significant limits on the national government's taxing, spending, and regulatory powers where the economy is concerned—other than the requirement that government compensate owners if their property is taken for public purposes."[111]

Like Ackerman, Professor Calvin Johnson argues that Congress carefully crafted the resolution that became the Sixteenth Amendment so as to indicate no acceptance of *Pollock*'s expansive conception of direct taxes.[112] Congress did this, the argument goes, so that after ratification of the Amendment, the law would revert to its pre-*Pollock* form—with the Supreme Court's decision in Hylton v. United States (1796) as the controlling understanding of the Direct-Tax Clauses. With *Hylton* resurrected as the unquestioned law of the land, the only direct taxes would presumably be capitation taxes and real-estate taxes. (Indeed, both Ackerman and Johnson actually go even further than that, arguing for a variety of reasons that real-estate taxes should no longer be treated as "direct taxes" subject to apportionment—a question that will be addressed in Chapter 8.)

At bottom, argue Ackerman and Johnson, the Sixteenth Amendment was nothing but a tactical maneuver. Most Amendment supporters thought *Pollock* was so clearly wrong that the Amendment, as a technical matter, should have been unnecessary. The problem was that the votes were not there to go ahead with a new income tax unless the Constitution was first amended.[113] The Amendment made it politically possible to get a new income tax on the books; it should not be interpreted, say Ackerman and Johnson, as a validation of the result in *Pollock*.

Under another variation of Conception I, which leads to the same substantive result—that the Direct-Tax Clauses and the Sixteenth Amendment do not constrain Congress in any significant way—commentators have argued that it is necessarily up to Congress to define what a "tax on incomes" is, just as Congress must give content to the terms *general welfare* or *public use*.[114] If Congress says a particular provision is part of a tax on incomes, that ends the Sixteenth Amendment analysis, or so it is argued: Apportionment is not required.

Victor Thuronyi has put the argument this way: "Because people have different views of tax equity, there is no 'true' concept of income."[115] Instead, the concept "is by its nature highly practical, flexible and ad hoc,"[116] and that flexibility has constitutional implications:

> [T]he Constitution allows Congress to provide for the common defense. Can a congressional funding of a missile be challenged on the basis that, in fact, the missile . . . decreases our security? Apart from standing concerns, such a challenge surely would be summarily rejected by the courts on the basis that the common defense is an inherently malleable term the meaning of which must be left to the judgment of Congress. The same should apply to the meaning of income in the sixteenth amendment.[117]

Professor Marjorie Kornhauser agrees that "incomes" is an "inherently malleable term":

> [T]he Sixteenth Amendment must give Congress a fully vested power to tax *all* income, however Congress defines it, without worrying about fine distinctions. Such an interpretation yields a meaning of income that is broad and evolutionary. Income's meaning is to be determined by Congress, not the Court, and that meaning changes over time as congressional conceptions of income change and become more sophisticated.[118]

A constitutional provision obviously cannot constrain Congress if it is up to Congress to define what the provision means. The ultimate effect of Conception I therefore is that, in the words of Professor Lawrence Zelenak, "[w]hen Congress is the final arbiter of constitutionality, if enough legislators believe the provision is *probably* constitutional, and vote for it, then it *is* constitutional."[119]

Conception II: The Amendment as a Limited Carve-Out from the Direct-Tax Clauses

Conception I does have a legal-realist ring of truth to it. Because hardly anyone questions the power of Congress in taxation these days, what Congress defines as constitutional is, for almost all practical purposes, what the world considers to be constitutionally acceptable. Whether the term *taxes on incomes* is judicially enforceable as a technical matter does not matter if courts are unwilling to enforce it.

Nevertheless, Conception I is not the unquestionably right way to understand the Sixteenth Amendment and the Direct-Tax Clauses. Conception I has little connection to the language of the Amendment, and it is more than a little peculiar to conclude that the Constitution permits Congress to determine the limits of its own power.

An alternative conception of the Sixteenth Amendment takes the language of the Amendment seriously. Under Conception II, Congress, in putting together the resolution that ultimately became the Amendment, accepted *Pollock* as the law of the land and then carved out a category of taxes—"taxes on incomes"—from the apportionment rule that otherwise applies to direct taxes. If *Pollock* reflected a much broader understanding of what might be a direct tax than had been true prior to 1895—and it was certainly a broader conception than the Supreme Court had outlined in Hylton v. United States (1796)—a potentially large set of direct taxes (those that are not "taxes on incomes") remains subject to apportionment. If this conception of the Amendment is appropriate, the meaning of "taxes on incomes" can be critical in determining whether a modern form of unapportioned taxation is constitutional.

On its face, the Amendment was not an unlimited expansion of the taxing power; the language does not seem to have overturned the Direct-Tax Clauses in their entirety. The Amendment was a response to *Pollock* (the two *Pollock* decisions are often referred to as the *Income Tax cases*, after all), and it is only *taxes on incomes* that the Amendment exempts from apportionment.

We do not know for sure why the Amendment took the form it did. The final language was not hammered out on the floors of the Houses of Congress, with recorded debates to guide us as to what was happening. The language was drafted in closed sessions of the Senate Finance Committee; the all-but-final version of the resolution made its first public appearance fully formed. But we do know that the committee was controlled by *Pollock*-friendly Republicans and chaired by Senator Nelson Aldrich of Rhode Island, no fan of the income tax.[120] The argument that these folks were trying to come up with language to undercut *Pollock*'s broad rationale is questionable at best.

And the language changes that occurred along the way cannot bear the weight that Professors Johnson and Ackerman would impose on them. The final language of the Amendment—"The Congress shall have power to lay and collect taxes on incomes, from whatever source derived, without apportionment among the several States, and without regard to any census or enumeration"[121]—is silent about *Pollock*. It exempts one category of taxes from apportionment, nothing more; it certainly reflects no clear attempt to undercut a broad reading of *Pollock* and thus to reinvigorate *Hylton*. Furthermore, the fact that the Senate Finance Committee removed a reference to "direct taxes" in the language of a draft resolution, something stressed by Professor Johnson, actually undercuts his position.

Johnson thinks it significant that Senator Norris Brown's original language was rejected: "Congress shall have power to lay and collect direct taxes on incomes without apportionment among the several States according to population."[122] As finalized, the Amendment makes no specific reference to direct taxation. According to Johnson, "[t]he change, rejecting Brown's language, is relevant evidence that Congress, in proposing the amendment, did not mean to treat the income tax as direct, and did not mean to make taxes that fell just outside the definition of income, as taxes that failed for want of apportionment."[123]

If anything, however, the language change points in the opposite direction. The original Brown language suggested that there might be some income taxes that are not direct (that is, there are *direct* taxes on incomes but also therefore *indirect* taxes on incomes). If a Congressman wanted to make it clear that *Pollock* was rightly decided, that an income tax is *ipso facto* a direct tax, he would have wanted to change the Brown language. Contrary to Professor Johnson's argument, the final version of the Amendment seems to be a *vindication* of *Pollock*.[124]

If "taxes on incomes" is a subset of direct taxes, it follows that the Sixteenth Amendment did not exempt all direct taxes from apportionment. As the Seventh Circuit stated in Commissioner v. Obear-Nester Glass Co. (1954), "[A]n unapportioned direct tax on anything that is not income would still, under the rule of [*Pollock*], be unconstitutional."[125]

Conception II has the Sixteenth Amendment's language and history on its side, and it also clearly represented the view of the Supreme Court in the early years after ratification of the Amendment. As is discussed in the second part of this chapter, the Court assumed that the term *incomes* had a discernable meaning and that it was not up to Congress by itself to determine whether a tax fell on "incomes." The scholarly assumption today is that the modern Supreme Court would repudiate the early cases decided under the Sixteenth Amendment, but that is only an assumption and little in recent Supreme Court history supports it.

Of course, hard categorization decisions are inevitable with a term like *incomes*. It will not be possible to develop a series of black-letter rules to determine what is and what is not "income," and some discounters of the Sixteenth Amendment have adopted Conception I because they despair of the difficulties inherent in applying a potent version of the Amendment. But interpretational difficulties do not ordinarily mean that constitutional and statutory provisions should be treated as open-ended, or otherwise meaningless. Whatever the merits of permitting a legislature to define public use or general welfare, say, without judicial review, "taxes on incomes" is a different sort of term. On its face, it defines a narrower concept, and it applies to a form of congressional power, taxation, that is inherently coercive—and that does not have the built-in protections that apply to the power of eminent domain.[126] Enforcing the restrictions of the Direct-Tax Clauses, as modified by the Sixteenth Amendment, may be messy, but it may also be what the constitutional structure requires.

THE SUPREME COURT AND THE MEANING OF "INCOMES"

The Sixteenth Amendment is not usually thought of as a limitation on governmental power, and it was hardly a staple of twentieth-century judicial controversies. The Supreme Court struck down a tax on stock dividends in Eisner v. Macomber (1920), holding that receipt of a proportionate stock dividend was not the receipt of "income" and that Congress could not tax such a stock dividend under an unapportioned "tax on incomes." But, with only a few exceptions, commentators think that case would be decided differently today,[127] and the Court soon retreated from some of its broadest statements in *Macomber*.

Nevertheless, there may be more to the case law than *Macomber* detractors think. The Supreme Court did not develop a comprehensive definition of income—it had no need to—but there are a number of respects in which post-Amendment Supreme Court jurisprudence exhibited consistency. The Amendment was explicated in a number of opinions in the two decades after ratification, and *Macomber* was not the only case in which the Court concluded, or assumed, that the term *incomes* has content. Despite the assumption by proponents of Conception I that "inherent malleability" is the law of the land, there is no evidence the current Court has a position one way or the other on that issue. (The Court has faced no "taxes on incomes" question during the term of any current justice, and no case raising that issue is on the horizon.) For what it is worth, *Macomber* has not been overruled, and it continues to be cited as if it stands for something.

The Notion of a Fixed Concept of Income

The Supreme Court understood for at least two decades after ratification of the Sixteenth Amendment that "incomes" has a meaning and that, as a result, Congress's power to define what could be covered by an unapportioned income tax was limited.

Eisner v. Macomber

In Eisner v. Macomber (1920), the issue was the taxability of a totally proportionate stock dividend—a dividend of stock from corporation to shareholder that did not change anyone's interest in the assets or earnings of the corporation. Before the distribution, Mrs. Macomber held a small percentage of the stock of Standard Oil of California; afterward, her interest was exactly the same as before.

The question was simple: Could Congress include such a stock dividend in the base of an income tax without requiring that the tax (or at least a portion of the tax) be apportioned among the states on the basis of population? That is, is a tax on a proportionate stock dividend a *tax on incomes* (or part of a *tax on incomes*) exempt from the apportionment requirement that otherwise applies to direct taxes?

The constitutional issue had not been squarely faced before, although there had been hints in Towne v. Eisner (1918), which held that the term *dividends*, as used in the Income Tax Law of 1913, did not include a stock dividend.[128] *Towne* was decided on statutory grounds, but the *Macomber* Court, in an opinion by Justice Pitney for a five-man majority, said that the district judge in *Towne*, Augustus Hand, had appropriately treated the "construction of the act as inseparable from the interpretation of the Sixteenth Amendment."[129]

In other words, Judge Hand had decided that the income reachable under the 1913 statute, when Congress had tried to exercise its full power, was identical to the constitutional concept of "incomes." Income is income. In a passage blessed in *Macomber*, Judge Hand had written, "It is manifest that the stock dividend in question cannot be reached by the Income Tax Act, and could not, *even though Congress expressly declared it to be taxable as income, unless it is in fact income.*"[130] The Sixteenth Amendment did away with apportionment for only those direct taxes that are "on incomes." (Although he agreed with the Supreme Court that "income" should have the same meaning constitutionally as statutorily, Judge Hand had a different conception of "income." He had ruled in *Towne* that a proportionate stock dividend *did* constitute income, a position the Supreme Court then rejected in *Macomber*.)

Towne had interpreted the Income Tax Law of 1913, and Congress in 1916 made it clear that it intended stock dividends to be included in the income tax base: " 'dividends' . . . shall be held to mean any distribution . . . whether in cash or in stock of the corporation."[131] Since *Towne* was a statutory interpretation case and the statute had been changed, *Towne*'s holding did not necessarily control in *Macomber*, where the constitutional issue was joined. But *Towne* had effectively determined that statutory and constitutional definitions of "income" coincided. That determination led to a clear conclusion in *Macomber:*

> [I]f . . . such a dividend is not to be regarded as "income" or "dividends" within the meaning of the Act of 1913 [the controlling statute in *Towne*], we are unable to see how it can be brought within the meaning of "incomes" in the Sixteenth Amendment; it being very clear that Congress intended in that act to exert its power to the extent permitted by the Amendment.[132]

Implicit in the above is the idea that the 1913 Congress had a good idea of the meaning of the Sixteenth Amendment. If that were not so, Congress might have been mistaken in its understanding of what the Amendment permitted, and regardless of its intentions, Congress might have exercised less than the full complement of its constitutional power. But even if the *Macomber* Court deferred excessively to an understanding of one Congress—an understanding that could have been a misunderstanding—the broader principle of *Macomber* remains: "incomes" has a meaning that we should try to discern. *Towne* was important because it considered what "income" is, and the concept does not include a proportionate stock dividend: "[T]he conclusion there reached as to the essential nature of a stock dividend necessarily prevents its being regarded as income in any true sense."[133]

Macomber also concluded that, because the Sixteenth Amendment did not exempt all direct taxes from apportionment, courts must be sensitive to that fact:

> A proper regard for its genesis, as well as its very clear language, requires also that this Amendment shall not be extended by loose construction, so as to repeal or modify, *except as applied to income,* those provisions of the Constitution that require an apportionment according to population for direct taxes upon property, real and personal.[134]

So, too, must Congress stay within the perimeters of constitutional terms:

> This limitation still has an appropriate and important function, and is not to be overridden by Congress or disregarded by the courts. [I]t becomes essential to distinguish between what is and what is not "income" . . . ; and to apply the distinction, as cases arise, according to truth and substance, without regard to form. *Congress cannot by any definition it may adopt conclude the matter, since it cannot by legislation alter the Constitution, from which alone it derives its power to legislate, and within whose limitations alone that power can be lawfully exercised.*[135]

If "incomes" means something, the remaining steps follow logically: Figure out the meaning, and apply that meaning to the case at hand.

If *Macomber* deserves criticism—and it does not deserve all the criticism it has received—it is primarily for the narrow definition of income the Court came up with. Justice Pitney discussed the mutually exclusive concepts of "capital" and "income," using the metaphor of tree and fruit. Fruit (income) is severed from the tree (capital); under an income tax, one should be taxed on the fruit and not the tree that produces the fruit. That analysis gave rise to a definition of income that controlled for decades: "the gain derived from capital, from labor, or from both combined."[136] In contrast, said Justice Pitney, a stock dividend simply divides a shareholder's capital up into more pieces, without changing the nature of her holding.[137] Taxing a stock dividend would be the equivalent of taxing unrealized appreciation (an increase in the value of property that continues to be held by the same taxpayer), and "enrichment through increase in value of capital investment is not income in any proper meaning of the term."[138]

The *Macomber* Court's conclusion that receipt of a proportionate stock dividend does not give rise to income was not unquestionably correct; there are reasons why receipt of a stock dividend from a corporation with undistributed earnings might appropriately be treated as a taxable event. (In dissent, for example, Justice Brandeis said a stock dividend is like a cash distribution followed by reinvestment—a series of events that would have been taxable.)[139] One might also question whether the *Macomber* definition of "income" was broad enough. In Commissioner v. Glenshaw Glass Co. (1955), the Court concluded that, as a statutory matter, items like punitive damages can be income even though not derived from labor or capital. Given that Congress intended the income tax to reach "all gains except those specifically exempted," *Macomber*'s definition was almost certainly narrower than the Constitution required.[140]

The particular definition adopted by the *Macomber* majority may have been incomplete, but that is not to say that the Court's project was a misguided enterprise. Modern commentators do not merely reject the outcome in *Macomber*, however; they reject the very idea of trying to define what is and what is not income.

It was in *Macomber* that in dissent Justice Holmes wrote a line that many have picked up on: "The known purpose of the [Sixteenth] Amendment was to get rid of nice questions as to what might be direct taxes."[141] Surprisingly, Holmes provided no evidence or authority to support his position—if anything, as discussed in Chapter 4, the evidence was to the contrary. And Professor Owen Fiss's narrow interpretation seems to come closer to explaining the Amendment's text: "[I]t simply removed what appeared to be a technical objection or impediment that *Pollock* had posed to the income tax."[142] But Professor Bruce Ackerman has nevertheless suggested that we should accept Holmes's understanding because of Holmes's "lived experience" during ratification.[143]

Holmes was a major figure, of course, but why we should defer, as a matter of constitutional law, to his undocumented version of history is not apparent. The ratification process was not a distant memory at the time of *Macomber*—it had been completed only seven years earlier—and the lived experiences of the *Macomber* majority, all of whom interpreted the Amendment differently, were not obviously constitutionally inferior to Justice Holmes's.

In any event, even Justice Holmes felt constrained by the language of the Sixteenth Amendment. He purported to be interpreting the word *incomes*, and to be looking for "a sense most obvious to the common understanding at the time of [the Amendment's] adoption."[144] He concluded, "I cannot doubt that most people not lawyers would suppose when they voted for [the Amendment] that they put a question like the present [the taxability of proportionate stock dividends] to rest."[145]

Holmes may have been free from doubt about the "common understanding" of the Amendment's proponents and ratifiers, but if he was wrong about what people were thinking while ratification was underway, his conclusion was wrong. Would the ratifiers really have thought that the Amendment permitted an unapportioned tax on all forms of unrealized appreciation, say, or would such a tax have been characterized as a property tax? We do not know for sure, of course, but this much can be said: It is not clear that ratification of the Amendment eliminated the need to distinguish between taxes still subject to the direct-tax apportionment rule and all other levies.

Other Cases and the Post-Amendment Congresses

The Court in *Macomber* took the term *taxes on incomes* seriously, and it was not an aberrational decision. In two cases decided shortly thereafter, Weiss v. Stearn (1924) and Edwards v. Cuba Railroad Co. (1925), the Court held that the Sixteenth Amendment had controlling effect. And there were many other cases in which the Court took for granted its power to invalidate an unapportioned tax on the ground that the tax was not one on "incomes."

In *Weiss*, the Court extended *Macomber*'s principles to corporate reorganizations. If a shareholder was cashed out, he was required to recognize any gain; no one should have thought otherwise, even with *Macomber* on the books.[146] But, in an opinion by Justice McReynolds, the Court concluded that, to the extent a shareholder maintained a stock interest in the surviving entity (a new corporation formed under the laws of the same state), *Macomber* controlled. For a shareholder who received only new stock in exchange for old stock, there was no severance of income from capital and therefore, as a matter of constitutional law, no income to be taxed.[147] Only Justices Brandeis and Holmes dissented.

In 1925, the Court decided another case in which "incomes" was deemed to mean something. *Cuba Railroad* considered the taxability of cash subsidies paid by the Cuban government to facilitate railroad construction in Cuba. Revenue officials argued the subsidies were in effect advance payments made by the Cuban government for services to be performed by the railroad. The Court concluded, however, that the payments were similar to subsidies provided to railroads in North America: "The subsidy payments were proportionate to mileage completed; and this indicates a purpose to reimburse plaintiff for capital expenditures."[148]

This conclusion had constitutional dimensions: "The subsidy payments taxed were not made for services rendered or to be rendered. They were not profits or gains from the use or operation of the railroad, and do not constitute income within the meaning of the Sixteenth Amendment":[149]

> The Sixteenth Amendment, like other laws authorizing or imposing taxes, is to be taken as written and is not to be extended beyond the meaning clearly indicated by the language used. . . . There is no support for the view that the Cuban Government gave the subsidy payments . . . merely to obtain the specified concessions in respect of rates for government transportation.[150]

The particular results in these cases, like that in *Macomber*, are certainly open to criticism, but the important point for present purposes is that the Court saw limits to the concept of income. As recently as 1961, some justices continued to do so. In James v. United States (1961), the principles of *Cuba Railroad* convinced dissenting Justice Whittaker (joined by Justices Black and Douglas) that embezzled funds could not be taxed to the embezzler in an unapportioned *income* tax:

> Equally well settled is the principle that the Sixteenth Amendment "is to be taken as written and is not to be extended beyond the meaning clearly indicated by the language used." The language of the Sixteenth Amendment, as well as our prior controlling decisions, compels me to conclude that the question now before us . . . must be answered negatively.[151]

Justice Whittaker cited *Macomber* for the proposition that Congress may not alter the definition of *incomes*, a constitutional term.[152]

In many other early cases, it was taken for granted that *taxes on incomes* had enforceable content. Sometimes the Court made that point in throwaway lines, in cases where a statute was deemed to meet constitutional requirements. For example, in Burk-Waggoner Oil Association v. Hopkins (1925), Justice Brandeis, no friend of *Macomber*, conceded that congressional power was limited: "It is true that congress cannot make a thing income which is not so in fact."[153] Brandeis made this concession when it did not matter, but he still felt it necessary to make the point.

Similarly, in Taft v. Bowers (1929), the Court stated, "Under former decisions here the settled doctrine is that the Sixteenth Amendment confers no power upon Congress to define and tax as income without apportionment something which theretofore could not have been properly regarded as income."[154] As in *Burk-Waggoner Oil*, that conception of limited congressional power did not prevent the tax at issue from being imposed, but the Court made the statement about constitutional principles because it was an accepted, nondebatable proposition.

Lots of other language supporting this conception can be found in early cases. From 1934: "The rental value of the building used by the owner does not constitute income within the meaning of the Sixteenth Amendment."[155] From 1926: "It was not the purpose or effect of that Amendment to bring any new subject within the taxing power."[156] From 1921: "[I]n determining the definition of . . . 'income,' . . . this Court has . . . approved . . . what it believed to be the commonly understood meaning of the term which must have been in the minds of people when they adopted the Sixteenth Amendment. . . ."[157] All dicta, but all reflecting a particular view about how the Amendment should be understood.

In the transition period after ratification of the Amendment, even Congress, worried about challenges that might arise if taxing statutes were aggressively drafted, recognized limitations on its own power. In general, Congress defined income conservatively—not trying to tax distributions to shareholders made out of earnings from the pre-ratification period, or to tax gain attributable to post-1913 appreciation.[158] It was feared that an income tax that reached pre-Amendment earnings or appreciation might be characterized as on property or principal—and therefore as an unapportioned direct tax unprotected by the Amendment.

Those reservations about congressional power were not universally held,[159] and Congress, as it turned out, was too cautious in its drafting. The *Macomber* Court suggested that pre-Amendment earnings could be taxed if they were realized after the Amendment was in effect.[160] But Congress's conservatism reflects a basic point about the original understanding of the Sixteenth Amendment: No one thought the Amendment was an unlimited grant of power to Congress, and hardly anyone thought "incomes" was a meaningless term.

Is Macomber *Dead?*

Of course, the recitation of old cases is of merely historical interest if *Macomber* and progeny are no longer of doctrinal importance. Professor Michael Graetz has described *Macomber* as "now archaic,"[161] and his view is consistent with that of the vast majority of modern commentators. In Union Electric Co. v. United States (2004), the Federal Circuit stated that "[t]he continued viability of that decision is open to question."[162]

The Supreme Court certainly did not give an expansive interpretation of *Macomber.* For example, in Helvering v. Bruun (1940), the government sought to tax a landlord on the value of improvements made by a lessee, in the year in which the lessee defaulted (long before the lease was scheduled to terminate). The landlord argued that, while the improvements had increased the value of his property, this was just a case of unrealized appreciation, which could not be reached as part of an unapportioned income tax because of *Macomber*. (The appreciation should have been taxed, he argued, only if and when he disposed of the land.) Without repudiating *Macomber*, the Court, in 1940, interpreted its scope narrowly, suggesting that much of the language was specific to the facts of that case:

> [Taxpayer] emphasizes the necessity that the gain be separate from the capital and separately disposable. These expressions, however, were used to clarify the distinction between an ordinary dividend and a stock dividend. They were meant to show that in the case of a stock dividend, the stockholder's interest in the corporate assets after receipt of the dividend was the same as and inseverable from that which he owned before the dividend was declared. We think they are not controlling here.[163]

If cases involving beagles are not precedents for similar cases involving terriers, it is a good indication the beagle cases are not in favor. And, although the Court strained not to reexamine *Macomber* in Helvering v. Griffiths (1943), it again hinted that *Macomber* was no longer valued. Congress had excepted from the definition of "dividends" any "distribution . . . to the extent that it does not constitute income to the shareholder within the meaning of the Sixteenth Amendment."[164] Congress apparently intended to tax whatever it could, and it punted on defining what is constitutional. With that dubious statute to enforce, the government said a proportionate stock dividend was taxable, and asked for reconsideration of *Macomber*. The Court avoided constitutional issues by finding no intent to tax such a dividend, but it also made noises, as in *Bruun*, that *Macomber* was limited to its facts.[165] Wrote frustrated dissenter William O. Douglas, "*Eisner v. Macomber* dies a slow death."[166]

The Court has let *Macomber* linger, but would-be pallbearers think Congress has pulled the plug. Congress does not seem to see *Macomber* as putting significant limitations on what can be included in the income tax base. Although proportionate stock dividends continue to be excluded from gross income—*Macomber* survives statutorily—Congress has enacted other provisions that reach unrealized appreciation in special situations. The constitutionality of those provisions seems to be taken for granted, or so the obituaries of *Macomber* say.[167]

Maybe *Macomber* has already been interred, but there are reasons to be skeptical. The case remains on the books, it does not stand by itself, and the Court continues to cite it. And the lack of challenges to Code provisions that arguably conflict with *Macomber* is not necessarily decisive. Even tax lawyers are smart enough to know that litigating a constitutional issue is to be resisted at almost all costs, and tax lawyers are often able to convert potentially unconstitutional provisions to their clients' advantages.

Even where the Court has seemed to push *Macomber* to the side, it has hinted that the case continues to have significance. In Commissioner v. Glenshaw Glass Co. (1955), for example, the Court reexamined the meaning of income—*Macomber*'s definition was too narrow—concluding that windfalls like punitive damages are income even though not derived from labor or capital. *Macomber*'s language, said the Court, "was not meant to provide a touchstone to all future gross income questions." *Glenshaw Glass* is often seen as a rejection of *Macomber*, and there is something to that view. But the 1955 Court showed respect for the old warhorse as well: "In that context—distinguishing gain from capital—the definition served a useful purpose."[168] It remained the case, the Court could be interpreted as saying, that a tax imposed on capital (rather than gain from capital) is *not* a "tax on incomes."

In Cottage Savings Association v. Commissioner (1991), the case with the most recent Supreme Court citations to *Macomber*, the Court said *Macomber* "recogniz[ed] the realization requirement,"[169] and referred to *Macomber*'s "classic treatment of realization."[170] Those words of praise for *Macomber* were tempered, however, by the Court's statement that the realization rule is "founded on administrative convenience."[171] By itself, that proposition seems to remove constitutional force from the realization concept.

The constitutional issues were not before the Court in 1991, however—the issues in *Cottage Savings* involved statutory and regulatory analysis[172]—and it is hard to tell from passing references how today's Court would rule if required to reexamine the "incomes" concept. At a minimum, the references suggest *Macomber* is not dead, and, for a Court that likes to reinvigorate once-moribund constitutional provisions, the apportionment rule and the Sixteenth Amendment could be ripe for reconsideration.

In any event, *Macomber* does not need to survive in its entirety in order for the term "taxes on incomes" to have judicially enforceable effect. A rejection of some of the broadest language in *Macomber* would not necessarily lead to the conclusion that the term *incomes* is totally without meaning, or that the Sixteenth Amendment granted unlimited taxing power to Congress. In a multitude of cases in the first half of the twentieth century, the Court consistently rejected the idea that the meaning of "incomes"—in the words of Professors Gabinet and Coffey—ought "to float freely on the shifting tides of tax theologies."[173]A twenty-first-century Court might be equally skeptical that constitutional language should be infinitely malleable.

Deference to Understanding of "Incomes" at Time of Ratification

The early cases not only concluded that "incomes" has meaning; they also concluded that the term ought to be understood as it was in 1913. In Merchants' Loan & Trust Co. v. Smietanka (1921), the Court had written that, in defining "income," it "has consistently refused to enter into the refinements of lexicographers or economists, and has approved . . . what it believed to be the commonly understood meaning of the term which must have been in the minds of the people when they adopted the Sixteenth Amendment to the Constitution."[174] If something was not understood to be income then, it should not be understood as income now. Even Justice Holmes, in his *Macomber* dissent, agreed with that basic proposition. He was interpreting the word "incomes," he said, looking for "a sense most obvious to the common understanding at the time of [the Amendment's] adoption."[175]

This does not mean that only items in fact taxed in the first post-Amendment statute can be included in the base of an unapportioned income tax. But it does mean that, in the early twentieth century, the Supreme Court thought that only items that *could* have been taxed in 1913 were properly includable in an income tax base. As the Court said in Taft v. Bowers (1929), "[T]he settled doctrine is that the Sixteenth Amendment confers no power upon Congress to define and tax as income without apportionment something which theretofore could not have been properly regarded as income."[176] Or, as the *Cuba Railroad* Court put it in 1925, "The Sixteenth Amendment, like other laws authorizing or imposing taxes, is to be taken as written and is not to be extended beyond the meaning clearly indicated by the language used."[177]

The Supreme Court thus had a fairly clear conception of the limits of the Sixteenth Amendment. The Court did not think it was within Congress's power to avoid its apportionment obligations simply by expanding the constitutional definition of "incomes."

Accounting Conventions and the Constitution

The term *incomes* in the Amendment does not necessarily mean "income" as an economist would understand the term. (Indeed, if *Macomber* is still good law, and unrealized appreciation cannot be included in the base of an unapportioned income tax, an income tax could *not* reach all economic income.) The ratifiers understood that some conventions, like annual accounting, were consistent with the Amendment, even though the conventions could, on a particular set of facts, lead to suspect results. Permitting some deviations from economic income for administrative reasons, however, does not mean the definition is open-ended. There remain limits to how Congress can define the income tax base, even if those limits cannot be set out in a way that resolves every controversy in a predictable way.

The Limits of Accounting

Some commentators have made the following argument: Whether taxpayers should be entitled to deductions or exclusions that pull items from the tax base (a deduction for amounts saved, for example) is a question of accounting and nothing more—and certainly not a matter of constitutional law. And it is possible to pick passages out of opinions to support broad congressional power in this regard. For example, the Court wrote in Helvering v. Independent Life Insurance Co. (1934), "Unquestionably Congress has the power to condition, limit or deny deductions from gross income in order to arrive at the net that it chooses to tax."[178]

Accounting matters, one by one, may not be of constitutional significance, but that is not to say that issues are necessarily subconstitutional just because someone characterizes them as "accounting" in nature. For example, consider an unapportioned gross-receipts tax—a tax that permits a business taxpayer to take no deductions for the legitimate costs of doing business. Could such a tax be a "tax on incomes"? Some lower courts have said *yes*,[179] but taxing someone with no net income under an "income" tax shatters constitutional language. Permitting this deduction or that may be a matter of accounting; deciding whether to permit *any* deductions is decidedly not a simple accounting question.[180]

If a gross receipts tax is an income tax, it must be because original understanding is to be ignored. When the Court in *Independent Life* said Congress "has the power to condition, limit or deny deductions," it was part of determining "the *net* that it chooses to tax."[181] The system as a whole is supposed to measure *net* income, as a prominent supporter of the income tax, Professor Edwin Seligman, stressed in 1911: "Income is . . . to be distinguished from mere receipts or gross revenue. . . . By income is always meant net income, as opposed to gross income. In other words, from the receipts in any enterprise we must . . . deduct the expense of the enterprise. . . ."[182] The goal of the Sixteenth Amendment was to reach higher-income, not no-income, persons, and the Income Tax Law of 1913 applied to "net income."[183] Indeed, until 1954, the term *net income* rather than *taxable income* was regularly used in the taxing statutes.[184]

Sanford & Brooks

Taxes on incomes was intended to mean taxes on *net* incomes, and a case well-known to tax lawyers, Burnet v. Sanford & Brooks Co. (1931), is, if properly understood, not to the contrary. In *Sanford & Brooks*, the Supreme Court upheld the statutory requirement that taxpayers report income on an annual basis even if annual accounting worked to convert the income tax, on a particular set of facts, into the equivalent of a gross receipts tax.

Sanford & Brooks Co. was party to a dredging contract that generated substantial losses (totaling about $176,000) from 1913 until 1916. In each year with a net loss, the company obviously paid no income tax. The company finally stopped work and sued under a breach of warranty theory, claiming the nature of the material to be dredged had been misrepresented.[185] In 1920, Sanford & Brooks recovered about $193,000 on the claim. The company paid no income tax, taking the position that the recovery should have been offset by the earlier losses. The government argued that the full amount of the recovery was taxable in 1920.

Preliminarily, the Court concluded that the losses "were not capital investments, the cost of which, if converted, must first be restored from the proceeds before there is a capital gain taxable as income."[186] That proposition was not self-evident—if the company had acquired an asset for $176,000 and then sold it for $193,000, it would have been taxed on only the $17,000 gain—but the conclusion that Sanford & Brooks had no basis to offset part of the recovery made it necessary for the Court to reach the constitutional issue.

The company argued that most of the $193,000 recovery did not represent "income" under the Sixteenth Amendment. In effect, the argument was that "income" means net income (a plausible position based on the original understanding of the Amendment) and that the time horizon for determining whether a taxpayer has net income should be extended, at least in some circumstances. If a store owner takes in $500,000 but has expenses of $500,000 in the same year, he should not be subject to an "income" tax. Sanford & Brooks Co. was in much the same position as the hypothetical store owner, if only it had been permitted to show the relationship between the revenues and the expenditures over time. And the company was harshly treated because tax rates in 1920, left over from World War I, were much higher than those in effect in the 1913 to 1916 period.[187]

Sanford & Brooks Co.'s constitutional argument was not trivial, but the Court rejected it in a summary fashion. The Amendment was not

> to be so narrowly construed. . . . The net result of the two years, if combined in a single taxable year, might still be a loss; but it has never been supposed that that fact would relieve from a tax on the first, or that it affords any reason for postponing the assessment of the tax until the end of a lifetime, or for some other indefinite period, to ascertain more precisely whether the final outcome of the period, or of a given transaction, will be a gain or a loss.[188]

While Sanford & Brooks Co. was in fact effectively taxed on gross receipts, the case is not a statement of Congress's unlimited power to define income. The Court simply recognized, as had proponents of the Sixteenth Amendment, that administrative rules are necessary for a tax to function:

> It is the essence of any system of taxation that it should produce revenue ascertainable, and payable to the government, at regular intervals. Only by such a system is it practicable to produce a regular flow of income and apply methods of accounting, assessment, and collection capable of practical operation. It is not suggested that there has ever been any general scheme for taxing income on any other basis. *The computation of income annually as the net result of all transactions within the year was a familiar practice, and taxes upon income so arrived at were not unknown, before the Sixteenth Amendment.*[189]

We are looking for the *net* result—that is what an income tax is—but taxpayers cannot be permitted to keep their books open forever: "It is not to be supposed that the amendment did not contemplate that Congress might make income so ascertained the basis of a scheme of taxation such as had been in actual operation within the United States before its adoption."[190] The Constitution does not ignore practicalities, but that is not to say that Congress can use purported accounting rules to make any levy into a "tax on incomes" exempt from apportionment.

8

What Is Left of Apportionment?: Direct Taxes That Are Not Taxes on Incomes

Until the decisions in Pollock v. Farmers' Loan & Trust Co. (1895), the opinions in Hylton v. United States (1796) defined the judicial conception of direct taxation. As described in Chapter 3, *Hylton* came to stand for two not entirely consistent propositions—that apportionment ought to be required only when it is easy to do (and when it therefore does not constrain the direct-taxing power) and that the term *direct taxes* encompasses only capitation and real-estate taxes.

Chapter 6 explained why the first *Hylton* proposition is not self-evidently correct—why, that is, the Direct-Tax Clauses perhaps *should* have important effect in cases where apportionment would be difficult. Indeed, making the enactment of direct taxes difficult was one of the purposes behind the Clauses (although obviously not all founders were happy with that goal).

The second *Hylton* proposition also has its conceptual problems. Can it really be the case that the only taxes for which apportionment might be required are capitation and real-estate taxes? As important as those two levies were in the thinking of late eighteenth-century American politicians, they are a small part of the universe of possible taxes today, when governmental sophistication in devising ways of raising revenue has grown enormously. It is counterintuitive to think that the Direct-Tax Clauses should have nothing to say about levies that were beyond the ken of the founders, but that is the way that *Hylton* is usually understood.

For that matter, some modern commentators have gone even further, arguing that *Hylton*'s second proposition gives those Clauses *too much* scope—that apportionment should no longer be required for a national tax on real estate (or a tax on wealth more generally). If those commentators are right, the Direct-Tax Clauses have no relevance whatsoever today, except for a capitation tax—which Congress might consider enacting if the Mississippi River were ever to start running backward.

It is nevertheless too early to inter the Direct-Tax Clauses. Congress has never enacted a capitation tax, but several times between 1798 and 1861 it enacted taxes on real estate (generally including slaves as well), each time providing a mechanism to ensure that the apportionment rule would be satisfied.[191] Congress took it for granted that the Direct-Tax Clauses mattered, and nothing has changed in the language of the Constitution or in judicial interpretation of the Clauses that should have contracted the Clauses' scope since that time. Moreover, in 1895 the Court in *Pollock* expanded the conception of "direct taxes" far beyond what the justices had stated in *Hylton*, concluding that an income tax (at least insofar as it reached income from property) was also a direct tax required to be apportioned among the states on the basis of population.

Pollock was significant not only for what it said about income taxes; the five-man majority also concluded that the conception of "direct taxes" that had been outlined in *Hylton* was no longer controlling. As was discussed in Chapter 4, subsequent Supreme Court cases seemed to retreat from *Pollock*'s broader interpretation of *direct taxes*, but only with the ratification of the Sixteenth Amendment did it become clear that a *tax on incomes* was not subject to apportionment. To the extent that *Pollock*'s understanding of the meaning of *direct taxes* has merit and to the extent that the Sixteenth Amendment did not repudiate that broader conception in its entirety, the Direct-Tax Clauses still have import.

This chapter considers what is left of the apportionment requirement after the Sixteenth Amendment. The constitutional language suggests that a direct tax which is not a tax on incomes should still have to be apportioned. But what taxes might today be characterized as direct? And in the universe of potentially direct taxes, which might be *taxes on incomes* exempt from apportionment under the Amendment?

The chapter begins with the clearest case for apportionment—capitation taxes; then discusses the treatment of national real-estate taxes (and, more generally, taxes on the ownership of wealth), which also ought to remain subject to the apportionment requirement; and finally considers whether other taxes, particularly those unknown to the founding generation, might fit within a reasonable definition of *direct taxes* and might also not be exempted from apportionment by the Sixteenth Amendment.

CAPITATION TAXES: STILL DIRECT AFTER ALL THESE YEARS

Whatever else is a direct tax, there can be no doubt from the constitutional language in Article I, section 9, clause 4—"Capitation, or other direct, Tax"—that a capitation tax is direct. And the meaning of *capitation tax* is generally taken for granted. Most people understand the term to refer to a lump-sum charge on each taxed person (and, if they thought about the matter at all, they would assume that a capitation tax is not a *tax on incomes*).

At the time of the founding, capitation taxes, which had been used by some states, were unpopular.[192] While expressing his unwillingness to "disarm the government of a single weapon," Hamilton expressed his "disapprobation of them" in Federalist 36.[193] But capitation taxes were thought by many to be the most likely form of direct tax. For example, the anti-federalist writer of the "Essays by a Farmer" said,

> If ever a direct tax is laid by the general government, it must, if not from necessity, at least from propriety, be laid on polls—it is the only one I believe to be practicable—there ought then to be some security that they avoid direct taxation where not absolutely indispensable. . . .[194]

It was thus in large part because of the practicality of a poll tax that many founders were worried about its oppressive possibilities.[195] Unlike the classic indirect taxes on articles of consumption, a capitation tax is difficult, if not impossible, to avoid. As the anti-federalist minority of the Convention of Pennsylvania put it in December 1787,

> The power of direct taxation applies to every individual, as congress, under this government, is expressly vested with the authority of laying a capitation or poll tax upon every person to any amount. This is a tax that, however oppressive in its nature, and unequal in its operation, is certain as to its produce and simple in its collection; it cannot be evaded like the objects of imposts or excise, and will be paid, because all that a man hath will he give for his head. This tax is so congenial to the nature of despotism. . . .[196]

An apparently equal tax can be oppressive—"*unequal* in its operation," wrote the Pennsylvania minority—because a lump-sum tax is regressive. It affects the poor more harshly than it does the rich.

Of course, even if it is taken for granted that the founders were uncomfortable with a national power to levy capitation taxes, it may not be apparent what the apportionment rule did to lessen that discomfort—as many anti-federalists pointed out. (As discussed in Chapter 2, the anti-federalists generally wanted requisitions to continue as the primary source of federal revenue, with direct taxation to be permitted only should requisitions fail.) If the term *capitation tax* refers only to a lump-sum head tax, the apportionment rule appears to be surplusage. Suppose the tax is $10 per person. A state with one million inhabitants will in the aggregate pay $10 million; a state with two million inhabitants will pay $20 million. With those numbers, there is no conceivable apportionment problem. What is the point of providing for apportionment on the basis of population for a tax that by its very nature seems to be so apportioned?[197]

In fact, the apportionment rule was not meaningless for capitation taxes in 1787. As noted earlier, one of the reasons that apportionment for a capitation tax would have had effect was the special counting rules for slaves and "Indians not taxed."[198] If a lump-sum capitation tax had been imposed, no one would have expected a slave to pay the additional tax liability associated with his (or her) being counted as three fifths of a person. That additional liability would obviously have been borne by the slave owners.

And there is yet another reason why the apportionment requirement was (and is) not necessarily meaningless for a capitation tax. It is not inherent in the idea of a tax *per capita* that each person must pay the same amount. In *The Wealth of Nations,* published in 1776 and familiar to at least a few of the founders, Adam Smith discussed capitation taxes at length, and he understood that such taxes can vary in amount from taxpayer to taxpayer.[199] He criticized capitation taxes that are "proportion[ed] to the fortune or revenue of each contributor" or are proportioned to the "rank of each contributor,"[200] but such taxes had been imposed in the past, and he did not rule them out as possibilities.

In concluding that an income tax can be a capitation tax and thus a direct tax, Adam Smith was not writing about American constitutional law, of course. And there is no evidence that any founder was trying to incorporate Smith's principles into the Constitution. But Smith's understanding does illustrate that a 1787 reference to capitation taxes should not automatically be interpreted as encompassing only lump-sum head taxes.

If a national capitation tax is really an income tax, then the Sixteenth Amendment would apply, and no apportionment would be required. But for other capitation taxes, it is *because* of the apportionment requirement that the tax, in the aggregate, would have to have the effect of a lump-sum head tax to meet constitutional requirements: a tax "proportion[ed] to the fortune" or the "rank of each contributor" could not satisfy the Direct-Tax Clauses (at least not if the assumption is that the persons on whom the tax is laid would actually have to pay the tax).

TAXES ON THE OWNERSHIP OF LAND AND OTHER PROPERTY: WEALTH TAXES

Nothing in the language of the Constitution signals to the modern reader that a real-estate tax was thought by the founders to be direct, but without exception the discussions in the Constitutional Convention were based on that assumption. Even the justices in Hylton v. United States (1796), no friends of the direct-tax apportionment rule, conceded that a tax on real estate (the 1787 version of a wealth tax) would be direct.[201] Congress thus could impose a wealth tax, but, to do so, it would have to apportion the tax. And Congress in fact did just that a number of times between 1798 and 1861, enacting *apportioned* national taxes on real estate.[202]

The understanding that a tax on the ownership of real estate was direct did not change as memories of the founding receded. In the cases decided under the Direct-Tax Clauses between *Hylton* and Pollock v. Farmers' Loan & Trust Co. (1895)—the Supreme Court held each time that the Clauses did not prohibit the unapportioned taxes at issue—the Court assumed that a real-estate tax was a direct tax.[203]

That assumption continued in *Pollock. Pollock* changed a lot of legal doctrine, and *Hylton* and *Pollock* seemed to come from different legal worlds. But the justices from the two eras were in agreement about the characterization of a tax on the ownership of real estate. Indeed, when the *Pollock* Court concluded that the 1894 income tax was direct and therefore invalid because it had not been apportioned among the states on the basis of population, the Court took *Hylton*'s characterization of a real-estate tax as a logical starting point: (1) *Hylton* had said that a real-estate tax is direct. (2) A tax on the income of real estate diminishes the value of property in the same way an *ad valorem* tax does, and therefore it ought to be thought of as a tax on real estate. (3) There is no constitutional reason to treat a tax on income from personal property differently from a tax on income from real property. (4) If income from both personal and real property was removed from the base of the 1894 income tax, which applied only to incomes over $4,000, there was almost nothing left of the tax base. (The average wage-earner did not come close to being subject to the 1894 tax.) (5) As a result, the whole unapportioned income tax had to fall.

In evaluating the income tax at issue in *Pollock*, Chief Justice Melville Fuller also looked to how shiftable (and thus avoidable) the tax was, a point derived from the original understanding of the Direct-Tax Clauses. The founders thought that a tax on the ownership of real estate was one of the quintessentially unavoidable direct taxes (as, of course, was a capitation tax). Fuller extended that principle to the ownership of personal property as well (in language that was quoted in Chapter 3):

> Ordinarily all taxes paid primarily by persons who can shift the burden upon some one else, or who are under no legal compulsion to pay them, are considered indirect taxes; but a tax upon property holders in respect of their estates, whether real or personal, or of the income yielded by such estates, and the payment of which cannot be avoided, are direct taxes.[204]

A tax on the ownership of property—on wealth—was, to the *Pollock* Court, unquestionably direct because it could not be avoided by ordinary means.[205]

Chief Justice Fuller may have had no doubt, but it is not settled today whether the ability of taxpayers to avoid a tax is dispositive in characterizing the levy as direct or indirect. In Union Electric Co. v. United States (2004), the Federal Circuit rejected taxpayer's argument that a tax on enriched uranium was automatically direct because it could not be avoided. The *Union Electric* Court could quote from Knowlton v. Moore (1900), decided only five years after *Pollock*, in which the Supreme Court had characterized as a "fallacy" the argument that a tax must be shiftable and therefore avoidable to be indirect. Although the Court in *Pollock* had been presented with "the theory of certain economists by which direct and indirect taxes are classified with reference to the ability to shift the same," wrote the *Knowlton* Court, "this disputable theory was not the basis of the conclusion of the court." As a result, the *Knowlton* Court rejected the idea that "excises which are not the essential equivalent of a tax on property generally, real or personal, solely because of its ownership, must be converted into direct taxes, because . . . they could not be shifted from the person upon whom they first fall."[206]

Avoidability may not be the be-all and end-all of direct-tax analysis, but it is a relevant factor. And the distinction between a tax on the *ownership* of property and other taxes affecting property maintained its importance in Supreme Court jurisprudence well into the twentieth century. (Indeed, although the *Knowlton* Court downplayed the significance of avoidability, it conceded, in the passage quoted above, that a levy *is* direct if it is the "essential equivalent of a tax on property generally . . . solely because of its ownership.") For example, in Bromley v. McCaughn (1929), the Court concluded that there is a significant difference between a tax on the ownership of property and the gift tax, which is imposed on the *transfer* of property. With the gift tax, said the Court, there is therefore no need for apportionment:

> While taxes levied upon or collected from persons because of their general ownership of property may be taken to be direct [citing *Pollock*], this Court has consistently held, almost from the foundation of the government, that a tax imposed upon a particular use of property or the exercise of a single power over property incidental to ownership, is an excise which need not be apportioned. . . .[207]

The result in *Bromley* was consistent with precedent treating inheritance taxes as indirect. Had the tax fallen on the ownership of property, however, there was no doubt that it would have been characterized as direct.

Although the Supreme Court has construed what constitutes a tax on ownership narrowly, as *Bromley* illustrates, no Court decision has ever repudiated the principle that a tax on the general ownership of property is direct. As late as Helvering v. Independent Life Insurance Co. (1934), the Court reiterated that time-honored conclusion in the real-estate context: "If the statute lays taxes on the part of the building occupied by the owner or upon the rental value of that space, it cannot be sustained, for that would be to lay a direct tax requiring apportionment."[208] The statement in *Independent Life* was dictum, but it was also noncontroversial. Nothing has happened in the development of the law since that time to undercut the conclusion that a tax on wealth (that is, on the ownership of property) is direct.

Professors Calvin Johnson and Bruce Ackerman have nevertheless concluded that a national tax on wealth should no longer be subject to the apportionment rule. (Wealth taxation has been seriously proposed in recent years by some commentators, including Ackerman himself, giving immediacy to the constitutional status of such a tax.)[209] Johnson makes two arguments to support that position. First, he contends that a tax on real estate (the eighteenth-century measure of wealth) should never have been understood as a direct tax. On this point, however, Johnson's position is inconsistent with the unanimity, or near unanimity, on the characterization of a land tax in 1787.[210]

In the alternative, Professor Johnson argues that the Sixteenth Amendment changed any mistaken, preexisting understanding of the constitutional nature of wealth taxes: Whatever the understanding in 1787, Johnson says the Sixteenth Amendment was intended to permit Congress to reach the nation's wealth (including real estate) with an unapportioned tax.[211] And he can quote Congressmen in the late nineteenth and early twentieth centuries who described the modern income tax as an attack on concentrations of wealth.[212] Income tax proponents in 1894 and 1909 routinely contrasted the consumption taxes they despised with taxes on wealth, and the income tax was often characterized as a tax on wealth or property.

When income tax supporters referred to taxing wealth or property, however, they were talking about reaching the "*earnings* of wealth"[213]—that is what was on the table for discussion—rather than measuring the tax by the value of a person's property. Although some Populist supporters plaintively wished it were possible to impose an unapportioned tax directly on land, following Henry George's single-tax proposal,[214] it was generally understood that such a tax would present insuperable constitutional problems.[215] (It was also a nonstarter politically.)

The language used in floor debates in 1909, on the resolution that ultimately became the Sixteenth Amendment, may have occasionally been imprecise, but it should be interpreted in context. The goal was to make an unapportioned *income* tax possible, and, as discussed in Chapter 4, Nebraska Senator Norris Brown, one of the primary proponents of the resolution, was emphatic that the Amendment should be limited to "taxes on incomes." Why would Congressmen have bothered to push for authority to also impose an unapportioned *ad valorem* tax on wealth, when such a broader point could only have complicated the prospects of ratification? Getting authority for an unapportioned income tax represented an extraordinary expansion of the national revenue power as it was; the need for still other forms of taxation was not apparent at the time.[216]

Commentators can of course reasonably argue that, whatever their form, certain types of levies are in substance taxes on incomes and, as a result, they should not be required to be apportioned.[217] For example, Professor Deborah Schenk has suggested that the Supreme Court might be convinced to see an *ex ante* wealth tax as "an income tax with a base equal to the risk-free return to certain assets,"[218] and therefore "as a tax on income within the Sixteenth Amendment."[219]

Modern recharacterizations of historically important concepts have value for many purposes, but concepts of constitutional law generally should not change with the evolution of economic theory. Whether a modern court might treat certain types of wealth taxes as taxes on incomes is not a question with a clear answer, of course—the Sixteenth Amendment has not been the subject of serious litigation for decades—but this much can be said for certain: Income taxes and wealth taxes were not viewed as constitutional equivalents when the Amendment was ratified. Professor Schenk properly notes that the Supreme Court might see her reformulation of the nature of a wealth tax "as a mere semantic change that does not cure [its] constitutional infirmity."[220] That is a serious enough concern that Congress would be taking a risky step indeed in enacting such a tax.

All of this means that a national tax on the ownership of real estate or a tax on individual wealth, including personal property, should generally have to satisfy the Direct-Tax Clauses (and, as a practical matter, it also means that such a proposed tax would be unlikely to survive the legislative process). It may nevertheless be the case that a tax on the ownership of a carefully circumscribed portion of a taxpayer's personal property would be permissible in unapportioned form, or so one appellate court has recently concluded. In Union Electric Co. v. United States (2004), the Federal Circuit thought a distinction should be drawn between a tax on the ownership of particular items of personal property and a generally applicable personal property tax. The apportionment rule, wrote the *Union Electric* court, should apply only to a "general tax on the whole of an individual's personal property."[221]

A BROADER CONCEPTION OF "DIRECT TAXES": TAXES THAT ARE NOT INDIRECT

At a minimum, the apportionment rule should still have to apply today to a capitation tax that is not a tax on incomes and to a tax on the ownership of real estate (the eighteenth-century measure of wealth)—the two categories conceded by all justices in Hylton v. United States (1796) to be direct. But the Supreme Court's decisions in Pollock v. Farmers' Loan & Trust Co. (1895) concluded that the proper conception of direct taxes is much broader than what the justices had said in *Hylton*.

By its terms, the constitutional language does not suggest that capitation and land taxes are the only forms of direct taxes. In fact, if that is what the drafters had had in mind, they could have been much more straightforward. Instead of "No Capitation, or other direct, Tax," Article I, section 9, clause 4 could simply have required apportionment for any "capitation or land tax," or something similar.

Furthermore, the conclusion that the apportionment rule applies only to capitation and real-estate taxes has the counterintuitive effect of limiting the application of a rule that was clearly intended to constrain the national taxing power to forms of taxation that were known in 1787. That cannot be the right interpretational principle if the Constitution is going to have effect in the twenty-first century.

Chapter 5, discussing the Uniformity Clause, outlined a distinction between direct taxes and indirect taxes that is consistent with the constitutional structure and with original understanding, and that also makes independent sense. While almost everyone agreed that the national government needed a direct-taxing power, if only to provide funds during emergencies when indirect-tax revenues might well decline, most founders thought that a specific constitutional limitation with teeth was required to constrain the imposition of direct taxes. Even Alexander Hamilton, no friend of limits on the national taxing power, conceded, in language quoted earlier from Federalist 21, that "[i]n a branch of taxation where no limits to the discretion of the government are to be found in the nature of the thing [i.e., direct taxation], the establishment of a fixed rule, not incompatible with the end, may be attended with fewer inconveniences than to leave that discretion altogether at large."[222]

Indirect taxes—generally taxes on articles of consumption (the "imposts, duties, and excises" subject to the uniformity rule)—contain their own protection against abuse. It is in the "nature of the thing" that they cannot be raised too high or revenue will decrease because consumption will decline.[223] In contrast, direct taxes are those levies that do not have the built-in protections against governmental abuse that are characteristic of indirect taxes. Direct taxes hit the pocketbooks of taxpayers painfully, with little if any option to shift the obligation to someone else or to otherwise avoid paying. If a levy is not indirect, it should be governed by the apportionment rule (unless it is a *tax on incomes* within the meaning of the Sixteenth Amendment). That was the original understanding, consistent with the "nature" of things: cabin the dangerous taxes and leave the safe taxes unconstrained, except for the uniformity rule and maybe, depending on what is being taxed, the Export Clause.

Indeed, in introducing the compromise which he later came to regret—a compromise that survived in the Constitution—Gouverneur Morris himself made that distinction. He agreed to limit the apportionment rule "to *direct* taxation. With regard to indirect taxes, on *exports* & imports & on consumption, the rule would be inapplicable."[224]

In 1876, Thomas Cooley, perhaps *the* nineteenth-century American authority on the law of taxation, drew a distinction that has modern resonances, but it would have been comprehensible to Gouverneur Morris as well:

> Taxes are said to be
>
> *Direct,* under which designation would be included those which are assessed upon the property, person, business, income, etc., of those who are to pay them; and
>
> *Indirect,* or those which are levied on commodities before they reach the consumer, and are paid by those upon whom they ultimately fall, not as taxes, but as part of the market price of the commodity. Under the second head may be classed the duties upon imports, and the excise and stamp duties levied upon manufactures.[225]

The *indirect taxes* are generally those that the Constitution denominated duties, imposts, and excises, and in general those are taxes imposed on articles of consumption.

The distinction between indirect taxes, which are relatively safe, and direct taxes, which are much more dangerous, gives coherence to the taxing provisions in the Constitution. The passages in *Hylton* limiting direct taxes to capitation and real-estate taxes were dicta—obviously the Court was not considering the propriety of taxes the justices could not have imagined—and they should be interpreted with that basic fact in mind. The Constitution established a system of limited government, and the limitations on the power of the national government need to be taken seriously.

An income tax is nothing like the classic forms of indirect taxation, and the Supreme Court therefore arguably got the result right in Pollock v. Farmers' Loan & Trust Co. (1895): An income tax is a direct tax as that term was originally understood.[226] Indeed, it is hard to imagine that many founders, if the matter could have been presented to them—particularly if they could have examined a copy of the Internal Revenue Code of 1986, as amended to date—would have seen the characterization of a levy like the modern income tax as a serious question. Even the staunch nationalist Alexander Hamilton, who in his heart-of-hearts probably hoped for an unlimited taxing power, would have been realistic on this point.

The Sixteenth Amendment took care of *taxes on incomes*, of course, so that even if *Pollock* was rightly decided, such a tax need not be apportioned today. But what other taxes might be subject to the apportionment rule under this analysis? The broader the definition of *direct taxes*, the more significant the meaning of *taxes on incomes* in the Sixteenth Amendment becomes: Even if a tax is direct, it need not be apportioned if it is on *incomes*.

The next part of this chapter considers the constitutional status of a direct-consumption tax, a form of levy that, because it received significant public discussion in the 1990s, ought to have its constitutional status resolved *before* Congress ever takes such a possibility seriously. An unapportioned direct-consumption tax may well be constitutional, but there are significant doubts on that score. More generally, as the last part of the chapter discusses, it should not simply be assumed that any new form of taxation would automatically be constitutional if enacted in unapportioned form.

DIRECT-CONSUMPTION TAXES: DIRECT BUT NOT ON INCOMES?

The second part of this chapter discussed why a wealth tax is likely to be treated as a direct tax but not a tax on incomes (and why a wealth tax would therefore probably have to be apportioned). Another form of taxation that has been even more seriously advanced by prominent politicians (although it had its genesis in the academic literature) is a direct-consumption tax—a tax that would be imposed directly on individuals (in a form that most taxpayers would consider indistinguishable from an income tax, with an annual return to be filed), but that would reach only the consumption component of income. (For analytical purposes, *income* is often divided into consumption and savings components: one saves the portion of income that one does not consume.) The so-called *flat tax* seriously advocated by many in the 1990s, including House Majority Leader Richard Armey, was such a tax,[227] as was the "USA (Unlimited Savings Allowance) tax," also promoted in the 1990s by Senators Sam Nunn and Pete Domenici.[228]

The critical component of the proposed flat tax was not the single rate that gave the tax its name. More fundamentally, the flat tax was structured to tax only amounts spent on consumption. (It is beyond the scope of the present volume to demonstrate why that would have been so, but it was not a proposition that was controversial to either flat-tax proponents or detractors.) The USA tax more straightforwardly would have permitted a deduction for contributions to savings in determining an individual's tax base. As with the flat tax, only the consumption component of income would have been reached: Income minus savings equals consumption.

If *Pollock* was rightly decided and an income tax was properly characterized as a direct tax, these proposed taxes would also be direct. The tax bases are different, but an income tax and a direct-consumption tax are virtually identical in the way they reach affected individuals. And under the rationale described above—a direct tax is a tax that is not indirect—the direct-consumption taxes would clearly be direct. Direct-consumption taxes would have none of the protections against governmental abuse characteristic of the classic forms of indirect taxation. A taxpayer would face no decision like that arising from a traditional indirect tax: Should I buy this item and thus bear the tax liability, or should I instead buy something else and avoid the tax?

If direct-consumption taxes are direct taxes for constitutional purposes,[229] they would therefore be exempt from apportionment only if they would qualify as *taxes on incomes* under the Sixteenth Amendment. Whether a direct-consumption tax would or would not be a tax on incomes is obviously a hypothetical question with no clear answer to be derived from case law interpreting the Amendment (of which there has been precious little in recent years). But this much can be said for sure: As discussed in Chapters 4 and 7, consumption taxes are not what the proponents of the Sixteenth Amendment had in mind.

An income tax and a consumption tax were considered fundamentally different types of taxes by the boosters of the Sixteenth Amendment. Indeed, the late nineteenth-, early twentieth-century push for an income tax, culminating in the 1913 ratification of the Amendment, was a response to the inadequacies of the consumption-tax regime, the tariffs and excise taxes, that had dominated the revenue system to that time. The point of the push for income taxation was to rechannel the national government's historical reliance on consumption taxes, not to validate new, direct forms of consumption taxation. A direct tax that reaches only the consumption component of income (or that could, in a particular year, reach *more* than current income) is quite simply not the sort of unapportioned tax that Sixteenth Amendment supporters assumed they were making constitutionally possible.

Of course, interpretational questions of this sort are unimportant if it is up to Congress to define what a *tax on incomes* is. And, as was discussed in Chapter 7, many argue that the Sixteenth Amendment effectively provides an open-ended grant of power to Congress.[230] When Congress defines what "income" is, the judiciary has no business second-guessing that judgment, or so it is argued.

But whatever the merits of generally deferring to Congress in defining what can be reached by an unapportioned tax on incomes, there should be no reason for deference where Congress does not even pretend to be defining *incomes*. Surely a rule of deference must be premised on the assumption that Congress is making a good-faith effort to meet constitutional requirements. If Congress were to enact something like the flat tax, however, Congress would know—it could not be a secret—that the revenue measure was significantly different from an income tax. Indeed, changing the nature of the revenue system was one of the most common justifications for a flat tax or some other form of direct-consumption tax. If Congress knows that it is not defining *incomes*, the case for deference should disappear.

Furthermore, those who have argued that the term *taxes on incomes* is inherently malleable, or something similar, have generally assumed that Congress would act to *broaden* the definition of income. For example, in a number of articles, Professor Marjorie Kornhauser sees *ability to pay* (as reflected in a progressive rate structure) as a defining feature of the income tax: "[T]he graduated rate has been integrally connected under U.S. tax laws to the ability-to-pay theory that underlies the income tax."[231]

> [A] progressive rate structure has been a constant feature of the income tax since 1913, when the first income tax was enacted under the Sixteenth Amendment. At that time, most of the general public, politicians and economists accepted the idea of progressivity (though they disagreed as to the appropriate rates) because it conformed to their conception of "ability to pay," which was the basis of the income tax.[232]

Professor Kornhauser's description of the critical characteristics of an income tax, as understood by the proponents of the Sixteenth Amendment, is well-supported by the historical record. And for Kornhauser, a levy that does not have ability to pay as its justificatory core is not an income tax.

Victor Thuronyi has also commented:

> An issue that has been important in the past, and may become important in the future[,] is the definition of "income". . . . [I]t may be appropriate to base the definition of income for purposes of the Constitution on tax equity. [Such a definition] would recognize that *as long as Congress is striving to impose a tax based on the relative annual financial positions of taxpayers, according to its concept of fairness, the Court should not overturn its determinations.*[233]

If Congress is not trying to do that, the inference is clear. If Congress does not define *income* in terms of the relative annual financial positions of taxpayers—and that is not what Congress would be doing with a direct-consumption tax—then Congress is not defining an income tax, and the justification for deference is gone.[234]

Of course it could turn out to be the case that a modern court would be indifferent to the income-versus-consumption-tax distinction. And it has often been pointed out that what is called an *income* tax today in the United States is really a hybrid income-consumption tax system: an income tax for some and a consumption tax for others. (To the extent that a taxpayer consumes all his income, an *income* tax effectively becomes a consumption tax.) Surely no one can expect the Supreme Court to strike down the core component of the modern American revenue system on the ground that it diverges too much from what an income tax should be. Too much is at stake.[235]

All of that may be true, and the existing income tax is probably secure from serious judicial scrutiny, except perhaps at the margins. But one might still humbly suggest that the constitutional questions here are serious enough that Congress should be hesitant in taking dramatic steps to reorient the tax system—a step like shifting from a nominal income tax to a recognized consumption tax as the centerpiece of the American revenue system. The Constitution does contain limitations on the taxing power, and the stakes are great enough that Congress ignores those limitations at its (and our) peril.

ANY OTHER TAX THAT IS NOT AN INDIRECT TAX

The above discussion suggested that an unapportioned direct-consumption tax does not fit easily within the constitutional structure that has been described to this point. A direct-consumption tax is almost certainly a direct tax, and it is not clear that it is a *tax on incomes* exempt from apportionment because of the Sixteenth Amendment. Such a tax might well survive judicial scrutiny, but the case for legitimacy is not so straightforward that the legal issues should be ignored.

Whatever the merits of the analysis for an unapportioned, direct-consumption tax, the logic outlined here applies more generally, and that is the real point of this chapter. The language of the Sixteenth Amendment does not support the proposition that the pre-*Pollock* understanding was to be resuscitated or, more broadly, that all direct taxes are exempted from apportionment. It should therefore be the case that any tax that is a direct tax but that is also not a tax on incomes is subject to the apportionment rule. At a minimum, that category continues to include capitation and wealth taxes and, it was argued above, it might also include direct-consumption taxes.

And it might include much more, including forms of taxation of which we are now unaware—the future ingenuity of revenue-raisers is likely to know no bounds—and of which the founders and the ratifiers of the Sixteenth Amendment were certainly unaware. An unapportioned tax should not be considered constitutional simply because the founders in 1787, or the Sixteenth Amendment ratifiers in the early twentieth century, could not have comprehended the tax.

9

The Export Clause

No Tax or duty shall be laid on Articles exported from any State.
—Article I, section 9, clause 5

Of the provisions in the Constitution that deal specifically with taxation, the Export Clause, included in the Article I, section 9 list of what Congress may *not* do, is the only one that has been given Supreme Court attention in the last two decades. After having been largely ignored for over seventy years, at least in important litigation, the Clause was the subject of two Court decisions in the 1990s, United States v. International Business Machines Corp. (1996) and United States v. United States Shoe Corp. (1998), both of which struck down levies on constitutional grounds.

The Export Clause is an apparently straightforward restriction on the taxing power. Of course there can be questions about application: What is a "tax or duty"? What is an "article exported"? What does it mean to say a tax is laid "on" an article? At one time, there was even a question as to whether "exportation" encompassed transfers across states lines as well as transfers to foreign countries. (The answer to that last question is *no*. United States v. Hvoslef (1915).)[236] Nevertheless, interpretational difficulties should not obscure the core principle: it is not within the power of Congress to lay a tax or duty on exported articles. Whether a tax discriminates against exports or not is irrelevant to this analysis: a nondiscriminatory tax that falls on exported articles is as invalid as a discriminatory tax that targets exports.

The prohibition is so clearly absolute that, in Marbury v. Madison (1803), Chief Justice John Marshall used the Export Clause as an example in defense of the proposition that, "[i]n some cases . . . , the constitution must be looked into by judges"—in defense, that is, of the idea that judicial review is inherent in the constitutional structure:

> It is declared that "no tax or duty shall be laid on articles exported from any state." Suppose a duty on the export of cotton, of tobacco, or of flour; and a suit instituted to recover it.

Ought judgment to be rendered in such a case? ought the judges to close their eyes on the constitution, and only see the law?[237]

Marshall obviously thought those questions were no-brainers. If such duties were to be enacted, they would be so clearly impermissible that no reasonable judge could close his eyes to the constitutional violation. And if the judiciary is going to keep its eyes open, as the *Marbury* Court concluded it must, Congress should not even try to impose such a prohibited duty.

But Chief Justice Marshall's hypotheticals were too easy to be interesting today. If they illustrated the full scope of the Export Clause, one might reasonably ask whether the Clause any longer has intellectual content. The duties hypothesized by Marshall were important concerns in the late eighteenth century, when the Southern states were worried that the new national government might try to cripple the Southern economies, but export taxation is hardly a frontburner issue these days. And even if one thinks the tax treatment of cotton, tobacco, and flour is of paramount national importance, the analysis of Marshall's hypotheticals is no more difficult now than it was at the time of the founding. Of course Congress cannot tax such products if they are in the process of being exported.

There has to be more to the Export Clause than the passage from *Marbury* might imply, and in fact Chief Justice Marshall knew that very well. Marshall's hypotheticals were developed to make the case for judicial review, not to explicate the boundaries of the Export Clause. In a later case, Brown v. Maryland (1827), which will be discussed presently, Marshall showed a far broader understanding of the Clause's scope. And the modern decisions in *IBM* and *U.S. Shoe* certainly reflect a wider understanding. When the Supreme Court takes the time to strike down the application of levies to exported goods twice within a two-year period, one has to conclude that the Export Clause still matters a great deal.

To explicate the Export Clause, this chapter first discusses the decisions in *IBM* and *U.S. Shoe*, and then, relying on earlier cases that still have validity, the next part outlines the application of the Export Clause to a number of levies that have, or can have, export implications. The third part of this chapter questions the Supreme Court's intimation that the Export Clause is unique—that its principles do not aid in understanding other constitutional provisions and that other provisions are irrelevant in interpreting the Clause. Finally, this chapter briefly discusses several provisions in a 1797 taxing statute that are used by some jurists and commentators as an indication of the original meaning of the Export Clause—a meaning that would leave the Clause with little effect—and concludes that the 1797 statute should not be read uncritically in trying to discern the original understanding of the Export Clause.

IBM AND *U.S. SHOE:* THE MODERN SUPREME COURT AND THE EXPORT CLAUSE

The founders clearly intended to prohibit a levy that takes the form "one cent per pound of flour exported." On that point, everyone agrees. And, except for some discussion about whether the Clause might prohibit an embargo, the delegates to the Constitutional Convention discussed only similarly easy cases, like those mentioned in *Marbury*. We know the Clause was meant to have real effect, however, and limiting its application to the most straightforward cases (thereby making it easy for Congress to draft around the limitation) would gut the Clause. If the purposes of the Clause are to be effectuated, it has to have greater scope than the founding debates intimated.

Over the years, the judiciary struggled to give content to the Clause. The Supreme Court evaluated quite a few levies under the Clause between 1876 and 1923, rejecting several, and then the Court seemed to give up. After its decision in A. G. Spalding & Brothers v. Edwards (1923), the Court heard no Export Clause cases until 1996. Perhaps the Court found the cases too boring (they often are), perhaps the Court despaired of developing any coherent understanding of the Clause (a good reason for despondency), or perhaps the Court simply decided, as have academic commentators, that taxation is an area in which Congress can do what it wants. Whatever the reasons for the judicial work stoppage, it ended with *IBM* and *U.S. Shoe*.

IBM: Taxes on Export Insurance

IBM was a frustrating case. At one level the result was straightforward: The 1996 Supreme Court followed a 1915 precedent holding that Congress may not impose a tax on export insurance. However, even though the Court was looking at the Export Clause for the first time since 1923, the Court managed to dodge almost all important interpretational issues, leaving the real meaning of the case up in the air.

The Purpose and Scope of the Export Clause

In *IBM*, the Court struck down what Justice Thomas called, in the opening paragraph of his opinion for the Court, a "generally applicable, nondiscriminatory federal tax on goods in export transit."[238] With the case characterized in that way by six justices, *IBM* reinforced the principle that the Clause is an absolute prohibition: a tax or duty can be forbidden by the Export Clause even if Congress does not single out exports, or a subset of exports, for discriminatory treatment.

Relying on one of the Clause's original purposes, to prevent taxation directed at the Southern states, the government had argued that the tax was constitutional precisely because it did not discriminate against exports. By its terms, however, the Clause has broader sweep, as the Court explained:

> The Government's policy argument—that the Framers intended the Export Clause to narrowly alleviate the fear of northern repression through taxation of southern exports by prohibiting only discriminatory taxes—cannot be squared with the broad language of the Clause. The better reading, that adopted by our earlier cases, is that the Framers sought to alleviate their concerns by completely denying to Congress the power to tax exports at all.[239]

That is, it was *because of* the fear of discrimination that a prohibition on all export taxation was deemed necessary in the Constitution, and that is the way earlier cases had interpreted the Clause.

In Fairbank v. United States (1901), for example, the Court had written that "[t]he requirement of the Constitution is that exports should be free from any governmental burden. The language is 'no tax or duty.' "[240] And, said the *Fairbank* Court, "the purpose of the restriction is that exportation, all exportation, shall be free from national burden."[241] The levy at issue in *Fairbank* did discriminate against exports, but in other cases, including A. G. Spalding & Brothers v. Edwards (1923), Thames & Mersey Marine Insurance Co. v. United States (1915), and United States v. Hvoslef (1915), the Court used the Export Clause to strike down nondiscriminatory taxes insofar as they applied to exported articles.

The rest of Justice Thomas's statement of the case in *IBM* assumed the conclusion, however. He characterized the tax as being "on goods in export transport," but, in form, the tax was an excise on premiums paid to certain foreign insurers (four cents per dollar of premium),[242] not a tax laid directly on exported articles. IBM challenged the levy as it applied to insurance on exports, but it was not obvious that the Export Clause has anything to do with such a levy. Simply calling the insurance tax a duty "on goods in export transport," as Justice Thomas did, seemed to leave nothing for the Court to decide.

It had been clear for over a century that a tax can implicate the Export Clause even if not levied on exported articles as straightforwardly as the duties hypothesized in *Marbury*. The critical question in a case like *IBM* ought to be how close a connection between tax and exported good is needed before there is an Export Clause problem. The *IBM* Court could have concluded that the tax on insurance premiums was a tax on an ancillary service, insurance, rather than on the exported articles—not close enough, that is, to bring the Export Clause into play. And dissenting Justices Kennedy and Ginsburg thought that was how the case should have been decided. Because the tax on premiums "taxes a service distinct from the goods and is not a proxy for taxing the goods," Kennedy wrote—a test derived from jurisprudence under the Import-Export Clause, which, among other things, limits taxation of exports by the states—"it does not fall within the prohibition of the Export Clause."[243]

In support of the proposition that the tax on insurance premiums was constitutional, Justices Kennedy and Ginsburg could point to a 1797 taxing statute that, among other things, included a stamp duty on

> any policy of insurance or instrument in nature thereof, whereby any ships, vessels or goods going from one district to another in the United States, or from the United States to any foreign port or place, shall be insured, to wit, if going from one district to another in the United States, twenty-five cents; if going from the United States to any foreign port or place, when the sum for which insurance is made shall not exceed five hundred dollars, twenty-five cents; and when the sum insured shall exceed five hundred dollars, one dollar. . . .[244]

Kennedy and Ginsburg concluded that this enactment of the Fifth Congress indicated that such a tax was consistent with the original understanding of the Export Clause. The last part of this chapter considers the constitutional merits of the 1797 Act. For present purposes, it is sufficient to note that Justices Kennedy and Ginsburg had a much too rosy view of the highmindedness of the Fifth Congress: if the 1797 Act in its entirety accurately reflected the original understanding of the Export Clause, the Clause was nearly a nullity from its inception, and that cannot be right.

The 1915 Precedent: Thames & Mersey

The Fifth Congress's constitutional expertise may have been imperfect, but Kennedy and Ginsburg's position in *IBM* ultimately did not depend on unqualified acceptance of the 1797 Act. The constitutional status of a tax that reached export insurance was not an issue with a clearly right answer derivable from constitutional text or structure. As a result, Kennedy and Ginsburg's conclusion that the tax on insurance premiums did not violate the Export Clause because it reached "a service distinct from the goods and [was] not a proxy for taxing the goods" was a plausible interpretation of the Clause. If the *IBM* Court had been writing on a clean slate, the dissenters might have carried the day.

But *IBM* was not a case of first impression, and taxpayer IBM had precedent on its side. In Thames & Mersey Marine Insurance Co. v. United States (1915), the Court used the Clause to invalidate an 1898 federal stamp tax on policies insuring against marine risks insofar as the policies related to export shipments. (The tax, designed to raise funds for the Spanish-American War, applied to insurance "upon property . . . whether against peril by sea or on inland waters," and was measured by the "amount of premium charged.")[245] The *Thames & Mersey* Court said the critical question was whether "the tax upon such policies [is] so directly and closely related to the 'process of exporting' that the tax is in substance a tax upon the exportation."[246] Determining substance depended on "the actual course of trade," and, because it could not "be doubted that insurance during the voyage is by virtue of the demands of commerce an integral part of the exportation,"[247] the Court held that the tax on insurance was forbidden by the Export Clause.

The parties in *IBM* agreed there was no fundamental difference between the tax in *Thames & Mersey* and the tax in *IBM*. As Justice Thomas put it, "A tax on policies insuring exports is not, precisely speaking, the same as a tax on exports, but *Thames & Mersey* held that they were functionally the same under the Export Clause."[248] If *Thames & Mersey* remained good law, therefore, the result in *IBM* was foreordained.

It was not clear that *Thames & Mersey* still had vitality, however, and that is why there was an issue crying for resolution in *IBM*. A lot had changed doctrinally since 1915. Courts had become much more willing to let Congress unilaterally define what can be taxed; the national power over commerce had expanded exponentially; and cases under the Import-Export Clause seemed to have contracted the judicial understanding of what constitutes a tax on exports. Furthermore, as the *IBM* dissenters noted, the *Thames & Mersey* Court had not been briefed on the relevance of the 1797 statute. It would have been possible, therefore, for the Court in 1996 to have concluded that the Court in 1915 had, through no fault of its own, misinterpreted original understanding.

With a lot of favorable authority on its side, the government asked to have *Thames & Mersey* overruled, and it is difficult to see why the Court agreed to hear *IBM* unless it was going to reconsider *Thames & Mersey.* Nevertheless, that did not happen. In one chunk of his opinion for the Court, Justice Thomas discussed *stare decisis*, rather than the merits of *Thames & Mersey*, concluding that *IBM* was not a case in which it was appropriate to reject precedent that had established a "workable" rule. Moreover, to the dissenters' dismay, Thomas said the government had not even argued that a tax on services ought to be treated as distinct from a tax on exported articles, and the Court therefore would not consider that obviously critical issue. Finally, the Court rejected the government's argument that developments after 1915 in interpreting the Commerce Clause and the Import-Export Clause were relevant to the Export Clause. Those other provisions contain no clear "textual command" like the Export Clause,[249] said the Court, and it therefore discarded the long-time understanding that the Export Clause and the Import-Export Clause should be read as a package, with mutually reinforcing goals.[250]

Chief Justice John Marshall had written, in Brown v. Maryland (1827), that "[t]here is some diversity in language [between the Import-Export and Export Clauses], but none is perceivable in the act which is prohibited."[251] The Import-Export Clause applies to "Imposts or Duties," and the Export Clause to "Tax[es] or Dut[ies]," but Marshall assumed that the process of determining whether a levy is on "Exports" or "Articles exported" should be the same under the two clauses. The *IBM* Court thought it knew better, however, apparently concluding that the Export Clause is *sui generis*: "We have good reason to hesitate before adopting the analysis of our recent Import-Export Clause cases into our Export Clause jurisprudence. . . . Meaningful textual differences exist [between the two Clauses] and should not be overlooked."[252]

After all this bobbing and weaving, none of which directly concerned the merits of *Thames & Mersey,* the Court concluded that "[r]eexamination of the question whether a particular assessment on an activity or service is so closely connected to the goods as to amount to a tax on the goods themselves must await another day."[253] As a result, what should have been the key issue in the case was not addressed. *Thames & Mersey* remained the law, but with its long-term status unclear.

Thames & Mersey was not necessarily wrongly decided, and the result in *IBM* therefore was not necessarily wrong either. Had the Court reached the merits of *Thames & Mersey* in *IBM*, it might have concluded that the tax on premiums was in fact a "proxy for taxing the goods," and that *Thames & Mersey* therefore had been rightly decided.

One can imagine at least two ways in which the Court could have come to those conclusions. First, in both cases, the taxes were measured by the amount of insurance premiums paid, a figure that correlates with the value of exported cargo. Insurance rates reflect other factors as well, of course—as the dissenters emphasized—but, all other things' being equal, the higher the value of cargo, the higher the cost of insurance, and therefore the higher any tax on premiums. If, as one commentator sympathetic to the Kennedy-Ginsburg dissent has suggested, the question should have been whether "the cost of the export service taxed correlate[d] tightly with the value of the exported goods,"[254] the Court might have answered that question *yes*.

And there was another way the *IBM* Court could have reconfirmed the result of *Thames & Mersey*. The "tight correlation" idea is an accurate restatement of the dissenters' position in *IBM*, but it is not a test mandated by the Export Clause. Nothing in the Clause requires that, for a tax or duty to be prohibited, it be tied to the value of exported articles. A one cent per shipment tax on exports is as impermissible under the Clause as a one percent tax measured by the value of the exported goods.

Had it reached the merits in *IBM*, the Court might therefore simply have concluded, as it had in *Thames & Mersey*, that "insurance during the voyage is by virtue of the demands of commerce an integral part of the exportation."[255] That is, the Court could have decided that a tax on insurance premiums is a proxy for taxing the goods—regardless of the relationship between amount of tax and value of goods and regardless of the correlation between cost of insurance and value of goods.

If the *IBM* Court had reexamined the foundation of *Thames & Mersey*, it therefore could have found the case structurally sound, under either of the above rationales, or, following Justices Kennedy and Ginsburg, it could have issued a condemnation order. It did neither. By deferring the key issue, the Court provided no guidance about how disputes should be analyzed, other than emphasizing that discrimination is irrelevant—something already known—and suggesting that the Export Clause occupies a world of its own. All that we know for sure after *IBM* is that taxes on export insurance are forbidden today, but they might not be tomorrow. Deferring consideration of a key issue for "another day," after having revived interest in the Export Clause by taking the case, was not helpful to anybody, including Congress, which must legislate in the shadow of *IBM*.

Why IBM *Is Important*

IBM was an exercise in judicial evasion, and substantively the Court seemed to do little more than leave in place a 1915 precedent, *Thames & Mersey*, on which lower courts had relied. In form, by blessing an old case, albeit in a backhanded way, the Court seemed to preserve the *status quo*.

But the fact that the Court agreed to hear *IBM* suggests that it sees a continuing role for the Export Clause, and that, by itself, was a significant development. In addition, the Court used the Constitution to repudiate the application of a tax statute, something that had not happened since the 1920s, and, in taking that step, the Court showed little deference to Congress, as the dissenters complained. Rather than presuming that application of the tax was constitutional, and looking for ways to interpret the statute in a constitutionally acceptable way, the Court left in place a 1915 case that did neither of those things. It would have been noteworthy if the Court had struck down the application of a tax after carefully reviewing the substance of the dispute; it was astonishing that the Court did so in this summary fashion.

Indeed, by adhering to *Thames & Mersey*, the *IBM* Court effectively revived a tradition of judicial scrutiny of taxing statutes that nearly all commentators assumed had disappeared forever. The Court effectively transferred to the late twentieth century the doctrines of an earlier era, when courts were much more skeptical about the taxing power.

U.S. Shoe: User Fees Are Not Taxes or Duties

Considering how badly it handled *IBM*, the Supreme Court should probably have decided to leave the Export Clause alone for another seventy years. Two years later, however, the Court revisited the Clause and again—this time after full consideration of the issues—rejected the application of a federal tax in the export context. The Court concluded that the Export Clause does not prohibit Congress from charging a "user fee," rather than a tax or duty, on those who use American ports, even if the fee may have a connection with exports.

The Harbor Maintenance Tax

In United States v. United States Shoe Corp. (1998), the Court considered whether the Harbor Maintenance Tax, as it applied to exports, was an invalid tax or duty on exported articles. In general, the HMT is an excise imposed on any "port use" ("the loading of commercial cargo on, or . . . the unloading of commercial cargo from, a commercial vessel at a port") in an amount now equal to 0.125 percent of the *value* of the "commercial cargo" involved.[256] "Commercial cargo" is "any cargo transported on a commercial vessel," including exported goods.[257]

Since there was no question that the HMT applied to exported articles, and since the Court had reiterated in *IBM* that lack of discrimination against exports does not matter for these purposes, the government was left to argue that the HMT was not a "tax or duty" at all. It was, the government said, a "charge designed as compensation for government-supplied services, facilities, or benefits,"[258] and the government pointed to authority going back to 1876 in support of the proposition that a "user fee" is not forbidden by the Export Clause.

Apparently oblivious to Export Clause concerns in enacting the HMT in 1986, Congress had called the HMT a "tax," placed it in the Internal Revenue Code, and provided that it was to be administered and enforced "as if [it] were a customs duty."[259] As embarrassing as those characterizations may have been, however, congressional acts are not invalid simply because Congress pays no attention to constitutional niceties.

What was crucial in *U.S. Shoe* was the substance of the charge: Was it in fact a tax or duty (and therefore invalid), or was it instead a charge for services or property? Were the benefits to the payor, if discernible at all, merely the more generalized ones that every taxpayer gets from paying his, her, or its share of the costs of civilization? Or did the payor receive something specific in return for its payment, as part of a value-for-value transaction similar to that which might occur in a commercial context? The HMT failed constitutionally, held the unanimous Court, because the measure of the charge, the value of the cargo, was not "a fair approximation of services, facilities, or benefits furnished to the exporters."[260] If the HMT was not part of a value-for-value transaction, it had to be a tax, not a fee. And insofar as the tax applied to exported articles, it was invalid under the Export Clause.

Taxes or Duties Versus User Fees

Reasonable people can disagree about how close the relationship should be between amount charged and the value of a specific benefit received for a charge to be treated as a user fee (and therefore not limited by the Export Clause) rather than a tax. To be a fee, said the *U.S. Shoe* Court, the HMT had to "fairly match the exporters' use of port services and facilities,"[261] but that formulation leaves wiggle room. The benefits provided by governments are often of a sort not readily available in the marketplace, making determination of a "fair match" problematic. Recognizing this difficulty, the Court has not required absolute equivalence (whatever that would mean) between value and charge for a charge to be treated as a fee. For example, in Pace v. Burgess (1876), in upholding a charge as a user fee, the Court said that

> [t]he rule by which [the amounts] are estimated may be an arbitrary one; but an arbitrary rule may be more convenient and less onerous than any other which can be adopted. . . . [H]aving due regard to that latitude of discretion which the legislature is entitled to exercise in the selection of the means for attaining a constitutional object, we cannot say that the charge imposed is excessive, or that it amounts to an infringement of the constitutional provision referred to.[262]

Inevitably, characterization is going to depend on the facts and circumstances of each case. As the Court put it in 1876, "The sense and reason of the thing will generally determine the character of every case that can arise."[263]

Courts are generally going to show deference to Congress's characterizations of its revenue-raising enactments, but a charge is not a fee just because Congress characterizes it that way. Congress had not done that with the HMT anyway, of course; it was the Department of Justice lawyers defending the HMT who argued that what Congress had called a Harbor Maintenance *Tax* was not a tax. *U.S. Shoe* was thus not a case of congressional duplicity; Congress was not trying to circumvent the requirements of the Export Clause. The Court nevertheless saw *U.S. Shoe* as an opportunity to send Congress a message, picking up language from Pace v. Burgess (1876): "[I]f we are 'to guard against . . . the imposition of a [tax] under the pretext of fixing a fee,' . . . we must hold that the HMT violates the Export Clause as applied to exports."[264]

That message was gratuitous—it had nothing to do with the actual dispute in *U.S. Shoe*—but it contained a core of good sense. Despite the tendency in popular discourse to treat all governmental exactions as indistinguishable—if a charge "looks like a duck, walks like a duck, and quacks like a duck, it's a duck" is the common refrain—all charges are not legally identical. There is a legally significant difference between the quack of a fee—a charge to get into a governmentally operated park, for example—and the quack of a more abstract levy, a tax.

To be sure, that distinction does not jump out from the founding debates or the language of the Constitution. The founders' terminology for governmental exactions was incredibly varied: "Taxes, Duties, Imposts and Excises" in Article I, section 8;[265] "Duties, Imposts, and Excises" in the Uniformity Clause;[266] "Tax or Duty" in the Export Clause[267] and in the clause limiting a levy on the "Migration or Importation" of slaves to "ten dollars for each Person";[268] "Imposts or Duties" in the Import-Export Clause;[269] and "Tax" or "Taxes" in the Direct-Tax Clauses.[270] Most of these provisions have a core of good sense, but it is doubtful that each term standing alone had a precisely understood meaning. There is overlap among the terms—"imposts," "duties," and "excises" are "taxes," for example, at least for some purposes—and cases generally have not turned on fine distinctions among the terms, even when they might exist.

Nevertheless, none of these terms works in context if understood to include garden-variety governmental charges for services or other benefits. How, for example, can Congress apportion a fee for services among the states on the basis of population, as it would have to if the fee were a direct "tax"? Should the Export Clause or the Import-Export Clause really be interpreted to preclude an appropriate governmental body from charging those who use ports and harbors? And if a federal charge is imposed for use of a particular port, what would it mean to require that the charge be "uniform" throughout the United States? Surely the Constitution cannot require that the same fee be charged for services provided in every U.S. port, regardless of the value (or the cost) of the services. Presumably one of the reasons the fee-tax distinction does not appear in the founding debates is that the founders, when discussing provisions dealing with taxation, were not talking about charges for specific benefits.

The distinction between a fee and a tax also has support in older Supreme Court cases construing the Export Clause. For example, the stamp tax upheld in Pace v. Burgess (1876) (a case on which the Court relied in *U.S. Shoe*) was determined to have been "compensation given for services properly rendered" and hence not a tax or duty.[271] Congress had enacted an excise tax on tobacco, generally thirty-two cents per pound, but with an exemption for tobacco intended for exportation. Exported tobacco was instead required to have a twenty-five cent stamp affixed to each package, regardless of the package's size or value.[272]

The taxpayers in *Pace* argued that the charge for the stamp on exported tobacco was itself a forbidden tax or duty on exports, but the Court characterized the charge as, in effect, a user fee. Unlike the tax in *U.S. Shoe*, the charge "bore no proportion whatever to the quantity or value of the package on which [the stamp] was affixed."[273] *Ad valorem* levies like the HMT thus should not be characterized as user fees for these purposes: If a harbor usage *fee* is going to be measured by value, it should be the value of the benefit provided (presumably determined by the amount or manner of harbor use), not the value of the goods being shipped. Furthermore, the stamps in *Pace* had a payment-for-services flavor: they were intended to prevent fraud, and the proceeds from the stamps were used to fund the administrative mechanism necessary to police the excise tax. In short, said the Court, "A stamp may be used, and, in the case before us, we think it is used, for quite a different purpose [than a tax or duty]: indeed, it is used for the very contrary purpose,—that of securing exemption from a tax or duty."[274]

The critical distinction enunciated in *U.S. Shoe* was that between a tax or duty and a user fee. The Court did not have to consider whether user fees are the only permissible charges on exportation or whether Congress has the power to enact still other types of levies without running afoul of the Export Clause. The Clause effectively divides the universe of levies into taxes and duties, which cannot fall on exported articles, and everything else. Does the "everything else" include any charge that is not a user fee (and that is also not a tax or duty)? This much can be said: No court has yet uncovered a permissible charge on exports that is not a user fee, and it is unlikely that any future court will have the occasion or desire to seek such a creature.

One final point is worth making about user fees. Two commentators, Professors Claire Kelly and Daniela Amzel, have recently argued that the "user fee exemption" endorsed in *U.S. Shoe* is "mythical."[275] Although Kelly and Amzel think the result in the case was right—the HMT was properly struck down as it applied to exported articles—the Court would have come to the wrong result if it had concluded that the HMT was, in fact, a user fee. In their view, any governmental charge that burdens exports, including a user fee, is invalid under the Export Clause.

The Kelly-Amzel thesis goes too far. By its terms, the Export Clause prohibits only "Tax[es] or dut[ies]" on exported articles, terminology that does not encompass all conceivable governmental charges. In addition, as suggested earlier, a distinction between user fees and taxes seems to be inherent in the text and structure of the Clause, and the Court in *Pace* purported to be interpreting constitutional text. Other nineteenth-century cases explicating other constitutional provisions similarly distinguished user fees from the governmental exactions specifically referred to in the Constitution.[276]

To diminish the precedential value of *Pace*, Kelly and Amzel reinterpreted the decision, suggesting that it was not based on the taxes-fees distinction. Instead, they wrote:

> [T]he Court in *Pace* found that the tax fell outside of the Export Clause's prohibition not because it was not a "revenue raising exaction" under the Taxing Power or fell into some mythical user fee exception under the Export Clause, but because the exaction was not laid upon articles exported and bore no relationship to those articles.[277]

Perhaps *Pace* could have been decided using an alternative rationale—some later cases came to that conclusion[278]—but that is not what the *Pace* Court did. It is impossible to read the short opinion and see it as standing for anything other than the distinction between a tax or duty and a user fee. Indeed, the Court ended its opinion with the statement that "[t]he court being of the opinion that the charge for the stamps . . . *was not a tax or duty within the meaning of the [Export] clause* . . . , it is unnecessary to examine the other questions that were discussed in the argument of the cause."[279]

The Significance of U.S. Shoe

The *U.S. Shoe* Court reaffirmed that not all governmental charges affecting exportation are limited by the Export Clause, and that in itself was a significant conclusion. As it did with *IBM*, the Court applied old precedent to a modern controversy: What the Court said about the Export Clause in Pace v. Burgess (1876) has continuing significance today. Furthermore, in *U.S. Shoe*, the Court left no doubt that the old precedent was the law now and in the future. The Court blessed *Pace* in a way that it would not bless *Thames & Mersey* in *IBM*.

As was true in *IBM*, however, the Court emphasized the uniqueness of the Export Clause. In other contexts, the government argued, the Court had characterized some flat and *ad valorem* levies as user fees, even though the charges bore no necessary, or even arguable, relationship to the value of benefits received.[280] But, wrote Justice Ginsburg, those cases "involved constitutional provisions other than the Export Clause, . . . and thus do not govern here." "*IBM* plainly states," wrote Ginsburg, "that the Export Clause's simple, direct, unqualified prohibition on any taxes or duties distinguishes it from other constitutional limitations on governmental taxing authority."[281] *U.S. Shoe*'s analysis, significant though it was for the Export Clause, was to be confined to that Clause. The third part of this chapter considers the merits of that proposition.

INTERPRETATIONAL ISSUES AFTER *IBM* AND *U.S. SHOE*: NEW LIFE FOR OLD CASES

At first glance, the Court did not seem to do anything dramatic in either *IBM* or *U.S. Shoe*. It pointedly avoided reevaluating a 1915 case in *IBM* and then relied on an 1876 precedent in *U.S. Shoe.* If the Court had heard the disputes in 1916, the results would presumably have been the same as they were in the late 1990s.

But it is *because* of the time warp that the results in the two cases were striking. While the conclusion that the Export Clause is alive and well would not have been noteworthy in 1916, it certainly was in 1996 and 1998. Moreover, by leaving a 1915 precedent in place, and by explicitly relying on an 1876 decision, the Court in effect told us to start retrieving a lot of other old Export Clause cases that, as far as many students of taxation were concerned, had been transferred to the intellectual equivalent of off-site storage. The following discussion outlines the learning of those old cases.

The Required Relationship Between a Tax or Duty and "Articles Exported"

The founders were smart men, and we should not infer from their failure to discuss all issues at mind-numbing length that the Export Clause should be limited to taxes and duties imposed directly on exported articles. Such an interpretation would have made the Clause a dead letter and, although many founders did not favor the Clause, they understood that it was supposed to have real effect. Indeed, that is why many opposed it.

On the other hand, it also makes no sense to try to find Export Clause issues in every levy that can be tangentially tied, by an imaginative lawyer, to exportation. There need to be some principles, even if they cannot be converted into bright-line rules, to distinguish taxes or duties that are levied "on" exported articles from those that are not. In 1996, in *IBM*, the Court said that its "cases have broadly exempted from federal taxation not only export goods, but also services and activities closely related to the export process. At the same time, we have attempted to limit the term 'Articles exported' to permit federal taxation of pre-export goods and services."[282] That is a pretty good description of the state of Export Clause jurisprudence.

The following discussion summarizes the understanding of several issues under the Export Clause—the inapplicability of the Clause to taxes of general application; the potential application of the Clause to some levies that, although nominally not imposed on exported goods, are closely tied to such goods; the question of when a good is treated as entering the stream of exportation—that is, the point in time after which Congress may no longer impose a tax or duty on the good; and the interpretive principle that ought to be applied in doubtful situations to determine whether a levy falls on exported articles.

Taxes of General Application

The cases are clear that a tax of general application does not violate the Export Clause as long as the tax's connection with exportation is sufficiently attenuated. At a minimum, this category includes a generally applicable income tax and a generally applicable excise on pre-export goods or services.

Generally Applicable Income Tax

A tax that reaches the income of an exporter in exactly the same way it reaches the income of any other taxpayer is consistent with the Export Clause. In W. E. Peck & Co. v. Lowe (1918), the Court held that an exporter could be subject to a corporate income tax, which applied to the "entire net income arising or accruing from all sources during the preceding calendar year."[283] As imposed, the income tax had no particular connection to exportation: "It is not laid on income from exportation because of its source, or in a discriminative way, but just as it is laid on other income. . . . [W]hat is taxed—the net income—is as far removed from exportation as are articles intended for export before the exportation begins."[284] (One can infer that a tax imposed *only* on exportation income or on the income of exporters would therefore not be permitted.)

To make the point another way: Liability under the corporate income tax was not attributable to exportation *per se*, but to the success of the enterprise (measured by net income). And the fact and level of the tax would have been exactly the same if none of the income had derived from exportation.

That, to be sure, is not a totally satisfactory explanation as to why a generally applicable income tax should not be constrained by the Export Clause. A tax on exported articles does not become acceptable just because it is imposed in a nondiscriminatory way, and a tax that reaches the income of a successful exporter burdens the exporter in a very real sense: he has fewer dollars after taxes than would otherwise be the case.

But, at some point, the connection with exportation is not close enough to implicate the Export Clause. One reason a generally applicable income tax should be constitutionally acceptable is that it does not necessarily apply to someone engaged in exporting. For someone who is not successful—someone, that is, with no net income—the income tax does not come into play at all, an indication of how tenuous the connection is between a tax on income and the process of exportation. The connection is there, but it is not strong enough.

Of course no one can say for sure what the founders would have thought about corporate income taxes. There was no well-developed conception of an income tax in 1787, and, for that matter, there was no conception of corporations. Nevertheless, if a generally applicable income tax were treated as falling on exported goods—and were, as a result, considered unconstitutional insofar as it applied to the export income of a taxpayer—then any tax that reaches someone involved in exportation, however tangentially, could have constitutional problems. That result would arguably give the Export Clause too much effect. The Clause was intended to be a real limitation within its sphere, but not to be the primary check on the taxing power.

Generally Applicable Excise on Pre-Export Goods or Services

The reference in *W. E. Peck* to "articles intended for export before the exportation begins" picked up on a line of cases, discussed in more detail below, that tried to determine the point at which goods ought to be treated as "articles exported."

If, for example, a tax is imposed once a good is on a ship ready to head overseas, there is no question: the tax is on "articles exported," within the meaning of the Export Clause.

At the other extreme, a tax imposed at the time of manufacture is generally acceptable, even if it is known that some of the goods will eventually be exported and even if, in fact, the tax winds up falling both on the goods that are exported and those that are not. (For this purpose, "manufacture" ought to be understood broadly, and not be limited to industrial goods. For example, an excise on agricultural products imposed while the goods are still on the farm should be treated in the same way as goods taxed while still at the factory.) This was what Justice Thomas, in *IBM*, referred to as "federal taxation of pre-export goods and services,"[285] permissible under the modern understanding of the Export Clause. (A tax on "services" would not be covered by the Export Clause in any event, unless the services are integrally related to, or are surrogates for, "articles exported.")

The "pre-export goods" exemption from the Export Clause was first articulated in Turpin v. Burgess (1886), which relied, in part, on a contemporaneous case interpreting the Import-Export Clause. The Court explained the rationale for the exemption in Cornell v. Coyne (1904):

> The true construction of the constitutional provision is that no burden by way of tax or duty can be cast upon the exportation of articles, and does not mean that articles exported are relieved from the prior ordinary burdens of taxation which rest upon all property similarly situated. The exemption attaches to the export and not to the article before its exportation.[286]

At the time of manufacture a good is not yet an "exported article," and Congress may therefore impose an excise on the manufacture of widgets without violating the Export Clause.

As with a generally applicable income tax, there is a connection with exportation at an abstract level: under the Supreme Court's understanding, a good that is ultimately exported may be subject to taxation. But if a tax or duty is to be prohibited, the Export Clause requires a closer, more concrete relationship between levy and exported good than results from the mere possibility of future exportation. The line between permissible and impermissible levies may not be bright, but it is a boundary that must be policed as well as possible.

In any event, the difficult cases that arise at the margin should not hide the basic principle at work here: if a tax is imposed at the time of manufacture and is not directed at exportation *per se*, there should be no problems under the Export Clause.

Taxes on Exportation Disguised as Taxes of General Application

None of this is to say, however, that an income tax or an excise on manufactured goods is automatically safe under the Export Clause. If a tax is targeted at exports, it ought to fail the Clause regardless of its other characteristics. For example, if an excise on manufacturing applied only to goods that were to be exported, even though in form it might appear to be a neutral, pre-exportation tax, it should be invalid. An excise would also be flawed if the rate applicable to exported goods were higher than for other articles. As is generally true in American tax law, substance ought to control in characterizing a levy under the Export Clause.

Similarly, if a tax applied to the income of exporters only, and not to that of other business persons—or if income from exportation were taxed at a higher rate than other income—a court should see the tax as burdening exportation and hence as falling on "articles exported." Such a tax would be like a levy hypothesized by Chief Justice Marshall in Brown v. Maryland (1827).

Marshall's examples of export taxation in *Marbury* were ridiculously simple, and therefore noncontroversial, but in *Brown*, Marshall showed a sophisticated sense of substance-over-form in discussing a hypothetical occupational tax that would fall only on exporters: "Would government be permitted to shield itself from the just censure to which this attempt to evade the prohibitions of the constitution would expose it, by saying that [the occupational tax on exporters] was a tax on the person, not on the article, and that the legislature had a right to tax occupations?"[287] In his 1833 *Commentaries*, Justice Story also took for granted that such an occupational tax would be invalid: "The prohibition extends not only to exports, but to the exporter. Congress can no more rightfully tax the one, than the other."[288] The tie between the tax and any particular exported good might be minimal with such an occupational tax, but the link between the tax and exportation would be so strong that the tax should fall.

Taxes on Goods and Services Related to Exportation

Chief Justice Marshall's dictum in *Brown v. Maryland* was an early indication that courts ought to apply substance-over-form principles to determine whether a tax or duty is on articles exported. One case in which such principles must apply, unless the Export Clause is to be a nullity, is when Congress imposes a tax on an unquestioned surrogate for "articles exported." And it is also appropriate to see some "integrally related services" as so closely intertwined with exported goods that a tax on the services ought to be treated as a tax on the goods.

Taxes on Surrogates for Exported Goods

There is little doubt that the Export Clause should prevent Congress from imposing taxes on clear surrogates for exported goods, such as bills of lading. Nevertheless, Congress did just that several times, beginning in 1797,[289] and the legitimacy of such a tax was not tested until Fairbank v. United States (1901).

The Court in *Fairbank* evaluated a stamp tax, imposed at a rate of ten cents, that applied to, among other things, "[b]ills of lading . . . for any goods, merchandise, or effects, to be exported from a port or place in the United States to any foreign port or place."[290] (Bills of lading for domestic shipping were subject to only a one cent tax.)[291] The provision was part of the same 1898 Act that created another Export Clause issue in *Thames & Mersey.*

The amount of the tax was not measured by the value of the goods shipped, but nothing in the Export Clause limits the Clause's scope to taxes or duties measured by value. The Court looked to the tax's effect—"a stamp duty on a bill of lading is in effect a duty on the article transported"[292]—and came to the obvious conclusion: Congress could not burden exports through a tax on exported articles, and that is exactly what it had done here, albeit surreptitiously.

Chief Justice Roger Taney had made a similar point in Almy v. California (1860), a case interpreting the Import-Export Clause:

> [A] tax or duty on a bill of lading, although differing in form from a duty on the article shipped is in substance the same thing; for a bill of lading, or some written instrument of the same import, is necessarily always associated with every shipment of articles of commerce from the ports of one country to those of another.[293]

Fairbank was nevertheless a controversial case, with four dissenters accepting the government's argument that the tax was really on the bills of lading, which were not "articles exported." Adopting an incredibly formalistic position, Justice Harlan wrote that "stamp duties were imposed specifically for and in respect of the vellum, parchment or paper upon which was written or printed a bill of lading for goods or merchandise to be exported to foreign countries."[294] The dissenters relied in part on the fact that a similar levy had been imposed in 1797 (discussed later in this chapter), inferring that the founding generation thought such a tax was consistent with the Constitution. But because this interpretation would have left the Export Clause with almost no effect, *Fairbank* had to be decided the way it was. As the *Fairbank* majority explained, "[W]hen the meaning and scope of a constitutional provision are clear, it cannot be overthrown by legislative action, although several times repeated and never before challenged."[295]

Taxes on Integrally Related Services

In other cases, the Court had to consider levies that were not as closely tied to particular goods as was a tax on bills of lading. In two cases in particular, the Court effectively decided that if a tax reaches a service that is critical to exportation, so that one cannot realistically untangle the service from the goods, the Export Clause ought to forbid the tax.

One example is Thames & Mersey Marine Insurance Co. v. United States (1915), the case relied on by the Court in *IBM*. Exporting valuable goods without insurance is almost inconceivable, making insurance "an integral part of the exportation."[296] As a result, a tax on insurance premiums was "so directly and closely related to the 'process of exporting' that the tax is in substance a tax upon the exportation"[297]—a conclusion validated, in a backhanded way, in *IBM*.

A similar analysis was applied in United States v. Hvoslef (1915), a companion case to *Thames & Mersey*. Like *Thames & Mersey*, *Hvoslef* involved a tax imposed under the 1898 Act as it applied to certain "charter parties"—generally contracts for the lease of vessels—for carrying cargo from the United States to foreign ports.[298] And it involved yet another levy with ties to the 1797 Act, which also included a tax on charter parties.[299]

The amount of tax was based on the tonnage of the vessel, not on the value of the cargo carried, but that fact is not relevant under the Export Clause. Instead of imposing a tax directly on exported goods, Congress had slapped a levy on the ships carrying the goods, or, perhaps more precisely, on the paperwork associated with arranging for the ships.

It is difficult to imagine anything more "integrally related" to exportation: "The charters were for the exportation; they serve no other purpose. A tax on these charter parties was in substance a tax on the exportation; and a tax on the exportation is a tax on the exports."[300] The tax did not discriminate—the levy applied to all charter parties, regardless of whether the ships went to other countries—but the Export Clause is an absolute prohibition. At bottom, the Court concluded that it was necessary to reject the tax if the Export Clause was to be protected:

> This prohibition . . . is designed to give immunity from taxation to property that is in the actual course of such exportation. . . . This constitutional freedom, however, plainly involves more than mere exemption from taxes or duties which are laid specifically upon the goods themselves. If it meant no more than that, the obstructions to exportation which it was the purpose to prevent could readily be set up by legislation nominally conforming to the constitutional restriction but in effect overriding it.[301]

If there was any question at all in *Hvoslef* about the substance of the tax on charter parties, it arose when only part of a vessel's cargo was destined for exportation. Even then, however, the Court decided that the Export Clause applied: "Whether the contract of carriage covers a small lot, or a partial cargo, or an entire cargo . . . can make no constitutional difference."[302] Since the tax was based on the vessel's tonnage, rather than the value or weight of the cargo, that result was hardly surprising. A tax on a vessel carrying goods for export, or on the arrangements for the vessel, was in substance a tax on the cargo, including the exported articles.

When Has a Taxed Good Entered the Stream of Exportation?

Fairbank, Thames & Mersey, and *Hvoslef* considered whether taxes that did not fall directly on goods nevertheless ought to be treated as reaching articles exported. At a minimum, that should be true when the tax falls on a clear surrogate for the goods or when the "integrally related" test is satisfied. In still other cases, the Supreme Court had to decide whether a tax that was unquestionably on goods ought to be treated as falling on *exported* goods.

The following discussion considers the treatment of, in order, pre-export goods, goods that are unquestionably in the process of exportation, and goods that fall between the two polar cases. How these principles would apply to national taxation of modern e-commerce—if, for example, Congress were to consider imposing a tax on the downloading of electronic products—is not at all clear. That is probably the major Export Clause issue of the future.

Pre-export Goods

Despite the Export Clause, Congress may impose a generally applicable tax on goods, or on the manufacture of goods, even if some of the goods wind up being exported, as long as the tax attaches before the goods have entered a stream of commerce that is heading toward exportation. That is what the *IBM* Court called "federal taxation of pre-export goods and services,"[303] or a "nondiscriminatory 'pre-exportation assessment.' "[304]

For example, an excise that applies at the time of manufacture to all widgets, whether they will be exported or not, is constitutionally permissible. Suppose identical widgets A and B are manufactured simultaneously in Massachusetts. It turns out that A heads for Mississippi and B for England, but it could just as well have been the other way around. As long as the tax applies before the fungible widgets leave the factory, the tax is not foreclosed by the Export Clause; it is not a tax on articles exported.

And the principle is broader than that. Suppose widgets are, in general, manufactured for use both inside and outside the United States, but a particular manufacturer produces widgets only for exportation. An excise applied to those to-be-exported widgets would be permissible so long as it applied to all manufacturers of the widgets—those who export everything they produce, those who do not export at all, and those who export only some of their product.

This principle is illustrated by Cornell v. Coyne (1904), in which the Court, over two dissents, held that a one cent per pound manufacturing tax on filled cheese could be imposed on all such ersatz cheese,[305] including stuff to be exported. The tax had nothing specifically to do with exporting: "Subjecting filled cheese manufactured for the purpose of export is casting no tax or duty on articles exported, but is only a tax or duty on the manufacturing of articles in order to prepare them for export." Just because they are exported later, articles are not "relieved from the prior ordinary burdens of taxation which rest upon all property similarly situated. The exemption attaches to the export and not to the article before its exportation."[306]

The result in *Cornell* followed the stated rationale of Turpin v. Burgess (1886). In *Turpin*, the Court reaffirmed the result in Pace v. Burgess (1876)—the case that first analyzed user fees under the Export Clause—and added an alternative justification for *Pace*'s result.

The statute in *Turpin* was precisely the same one involved in *Pace*. It imposed a stamp levy on tobacco marked for export at a lower rate than would otherwise have applied.[307] *Turpin* was decided just ten years after *Pace*, and it appears that the Court decided to hear the new case only because, in the meantime, Congress had repealed the levy.[308] Maybe, it was argued, the repeal showed that Congress had conceded the stamp charge's constitutional problems.

The Court did not buy the concession argument, however. The repeal was not a "concession by Congress that the charge for the stamp was an export tax," said the Court,[309] or even if the repeal were interpreted that way, "it would only be the opinion of one Congress opposed to that of another."[310] Once it decided that repeal did not affect how the statute should be interpreted, the Court could simply have reaffirmed its analysis in *Pace*. For reasons that are not clear, however, it did not do that. Instead, without repudiating the reasoning in *Pace*, the Court added a new justification for the result. The stamp tax, it said, was not imposed "by reason or because of [the goods'] exportation or intended exportation, or whilst they are being exported": "[A] general tax, laid on all property alike, and not levied on goods in course of exportation, nor because of their intended exportation, is not within the constitutional prohibition."[311]

Therefore, even if *Pace*'s stated rationale did not hold up—and the Court specifically refused to say any such thing—the result would have been exactly the same. The levy was valid: "In the present case, the tax (if it was a tax) was laid upon the goods before they had left the factory. They were not in course of exportation; they might never be exported; whether they would be or not would depend altogether on the will of the manufacturer."[312]

It is possible to get a pretty good sense of what the Court meant about pre-export levies in both *Turpin* and *Cornell*, but the Court left a troubling loose end in *Turpin*. One of the striking things about the Court's opinion is that it did not connect with the facts. Whatever the merits of permitting a "general tax, laid on all property alike, and not levied . . . because of [the good's] intended exportation," that was not the situation in the case. The levy at issue in *Turpin* and *Pace did* single out goods to be exported. The charge for tobacco was generally thirty-two cents per pound, but exported tobacco was instead required to have only a twenty-five cent stamp affixed to each package.[313] With such a differential rate structure, the total amount a producer owed Uncle Sam could not be determined until the producer had decided which tobacco was to be exported, and which was not.

Does *Turpin* therefore mean that, despite the Export Clause, a tax directed at exported goods can be levied on goods that have been set aside for exportation, as long as the goods are still at the factory? The language of the opinion—*not levied . . . because of [the good's] intended exportation*—suggests the answer to that question is *no*, but the result of the case is otherwise. To be sure, the charge for the stamp affixed to exported tobacco in *Pace* and *Turpin* was *lower,* indeed much lower, than would otherwise have been the case; exported goods therefore were not being singled out for discriminatorily unfavorable treatment. But lack of discrimination is not supposed to matter under the Export Clause. Since the cases discussing the irrelevance of discrimination came after *Turpin*, however, maybe the *Turpin* result depended on an understanding of the Clause that was repudiated in *Fairbank* and other cases.

The authority is not clear, but it seems that a tax that applies specifically because articles have been designated for exportation should not be treated as on "pre-export goods"—wherever the goods are located when the tax attaches and regardless of whether the tax on goods to be exported is less than, equal to, or greater than any tax on other goods. As meritorious as *Turpin*'s rationale may have been in the abstract, it should not have applied to the facts of *Turpin*. That said, however, *Turpin* is cited these days for the proposition that a "nondiscriminatory 'pre-exportation assessment'" is permissible.[314] If *Turpin* is really an example of such an assessment, then a tax that falls on goods set aside for exportation is valid, as long as the goods have not "left the factory," and, presumably, as long as the tax rate for exported goods is no higher than for other goods.

In the Stream of Exportation

As *Turpin* and *Cornell* concluded, Congress may tax goods at the pre-export stage without violating the Export Clause. At the other extreme, once articles have entered the stream of commerce that leads inexorably to exportation, Congress may not impose a tax on the articles. That is what the Export Clause is all about.

For example, an excise applied only to widgets that have been set aside for exportation should be invalid. An even clearer case: if the widget is already on a ship (or airplane) bound for England at the time the tax attaches, no one would doubt that the tax violates the Export Clause insofar as it applies to the exported goods, even if all shipped widgets—those going to other countries and those staying within the U.S.—are subject to the tax.

At the (Wide?) Margin: Spalding

Except in the polar cases, where a good is still at the manufacturing stage or is already on a vessel headed to another country, determining whether the good is an "article exported" is not easy. (Indeed, how computer software developed in the United States to be downloaded in another country would be treated for these purposes may require divine revelation—should Congress contemplate trying to tax such software.) Even if a purportedly bright-line rule were adopted that would confine the Export Clause to cases like those in Marshall's *Marbury* hypotheticals—for example, a tax laid directly on flour—there can still be questions about whether, or when, the flour is being exported. If Congress is going to tax goods, or surrogates for goods, or services integrally related to goods, there is no way to eliminate characterization questions of that sort.

A. G. Spalding & Brothers v. Edwards (1923), the Court's last Export Clause case before *IBM*, illustrates the difficult line-drawing that is inevitable. At issue was the constitutionality of a wartime tax imposed on "baseball bats, . . . balls of all kinds . . . sold by the manufacturer, producer, or importer,"[315] as that tax applied to baseball equipment that would ultimately wind up in Venezuela. A Venezuelan purchaser enlisted the efforts of a commission merchant to acquire equipment on its behalf and have the equipment shipped. The commission merchant did just that, arranging for Spalding to deliver the goods to a carrier, at which point title passed. Spalding was paid by the commission merchant and the merchant was paid later by the ultimate purchaser.

If the equipment had still been "in process of manufacture" at the time the tax attached, the tax would have been valid, under the authority of *Turpin* and *Cornell*. In contrast, Justice Holmes wrote for the Court, "no one would doubt that [the bats and other equipment] were exempt after they had been loaded upon the vessel for Venezuela and the bill of lading issued."[316]

The problem was that the *Spalding* facts fell between those two extremes. The tax liability was not on the manufacture, but it was also not on goods loaded for overseas shipment. The Court had to decide which of the two polar cases the facts were closer to, and Justice Holmes concluded, with a decided lack of certainty, "It seems to us that the facts recited are closer to the latter than to the former side, and that the export had begun."[317]

Manufacture alone would not have been treated as a "step in exportation," but this tax was on the *sale* of equipment—closer to the export stage. Moreover, although baseball bats manufactured in the United States were not ordinarily headed overseas, in this case, as Holmes put it, "[t]he transaction from start to finish was understood and intended by [Spalding and the commission merchant] to be for the purpose of exporting the goods to [the Venezuelan buyer]."[318] If all of that were not enough, "[t]he overt act of delivering the goods to the carrier marks the point of distinction between this case and *Cornell v. Coyne* [the filled-cheese case]."[319]

Some might see arbitrariness in this line-drawing, and Justice Holmes admitted as much: "[W]e have to fix a point at which, in view of the purpose of the Constitution, the export must be said to begin. As elsewhere in the law there will be other points very near to it on the other side, so that if the necessity of fixing one definitely is not remembered any determination may seem arbitrary."[320] Even hard cases need to be decided, but the harder the case, the easier it is to conclude that the case should have been decided differently.

Spalding was not clear-cut, but neither was the result arbitrary. Justice Holmes prescribed a way to decide difficult Export Clause cases. His reference to the "overt act of delivering the goods to the carrier" was coupled with a principle which justified treating that event as critical: to have the Export Clause come into play "at any later point would fail to give to exports the liberal protection that hitherto they have received; of which an example may be seen in *Thames & Mersey*."[321]

Applying the Export Clause to Doubtful Cases: "Liberal Protection"

The cases described above advance some reasonably consistent principles about the necessary relationship, if the Export Clause is to apply, between a tax or duty and exported articles. If Congress is aggressive in enacting taxes that have export implications, however, courts will face tough judgment calls. For that matter, Congress also faces uncertainty in evaluating the likelihood that a proposed tax could face a legitimate Export Clause challenge. What to do?

The founders intended the Clause to be a real restriction on Congress's power, and it should be interpreted in a way that ensures it has effect. Moreover, that is the way other constitutional restrictions on the taxing power used to be interpreted, until modern conceptions of congressional plenary power gained currency, and that is the way Justice Holmes concluded that the Export Clause should be applied in *Spalding*. With the Export Clause, we are no longer in the plenary-power era: courts after *IBM* and *U.S. Shoe* have an obligation to police the Clause.

The bottom line in *Spalding* was this: If there is doubt about whether a tax falls on exported articles—if there is uncertainty as to where, on the continuum between manufacture and overseas transport, a particular tax attaches to goods—the doubt should be resolved in a way that protects the principles of the Export Clause. That is the *liberal protection* Justice Holmes was talking about.

A common argument today is that it is too onerous to tell whether a levy has suspect effects. The difficulty of determining whether a tax or duty ought to be treated as falling on exported articles is not imaginary, and therefore, the argument goes, the constitutional limitation should not be applied, except in the most straightforward, noncontroversial situations.

That was one of Justice Kennedy's points in his *IBM* dissent. He suggested that it was going to be a real chore, in most cases, to determine how a tax on insurance premiums relates to exportation, and therefore courts should not even have to try. If that reluctance leaves the Export Clause applying to nothing but *Marbury*-like hypotheticals and therefore leaves Congress with a basically unconstrained power to burden exportation, so be it.

That cannot be the right interpretational principle. The idea that constitutional limitations ought to be applied only when they are easy to apply gives away the store. The older cases, of which *Spalding* is one, suggest another, reasonable way a limitation might be applied: if there is doubt about whether a particular levy attaches closer to the manufacturing stage or the transport stage, the doubt should be resolved *against* the levy. To give "liberal protection" to the Export Clause is, in effect, to create a default rule, and the default position is that a tax is *not* valid unless its legitimacy can be demonstrated.

Providing liberal protection to exported articles is not merely a matter of courts' getting it right in interpreting the Export Clause. For a legislator contemplating a proposed piece of tax legislation, a similar rule should apply: if there is doubt about whether the Export Clause would forbid a proposed tax, that doubt should be resolved against the proposal. If courts are going to defer to Congress's implicit determination that enactments are constitutional—and that is still likely to happen, despite *IBM* and *U.S. Shoe*—then Congress should legislate with a good sense of what the Constitution, including the Export Clause, requires.

IS THE EXPORT CLAUSE REALLY UNIQUE?

In both *IBM* and *U.S. Shoe*, the Supreme Court discussed the Export Clause as if it were unique. The Court rejected the importation of principles from other constitutional provisions into its analysis of the Export Clause, and it also suggested that Export Clause principles should be confined to the analysis of that provision. Among other things, the Court specifically rejected the application of jurisprudence developed under the Import-Export Clause—the provision restricting *states'* power to tax exports—to disputes arising under the Export Clause. In the strongest statement of this interpretational posture, Justice Ginsburg wrote, in *U.S. Shoe*, "*IBM* plainly states that the Export Clause's simple, direct, unqualified prohibition on any taxes or duties distinguishes it from other constitutional limitations on governmental taxing authority." And, if that were not clear enough, she rejected the idea that authority "involv[ing] constitutional provisions other than the Export Clause [should] govern" in an Export Clause dispute.[322]

The Clause does speak in a direct and relatively unqualified way, but it is not unique in that regard. If by fiat the Court creates an impenetrable barrier around the Clause, that is the way things will be, of course, at least for a while. But it will be difficult for the Court to maintain that position in an intellectually coherent way. There are at least three respects in which the Export Clause should not be treated as *sui generis*.

What Is a Levy "on" Exports?

The language of the Export Clause is strong, but treating the Clause as if it occupies its own legal universe, particularly for purposes of determining whether a levy falls on exported goods, is a marked break with tradition. For decades the assumption had been that the Import-Export Clause, restricting state authority, and the Export Clause, restricting national authority, ought to be interpreted in tandem. The Export Clause forbids a national "tax or duty" on "articles exported"; the Import-Export Clause generally forbids state "duties" on "exports" without congressional consent. In 1827, in a passage quoted earlier, Chief Justice John Marshall wrote that "[t]here is some diversity in language [between the Import-Export and the Export Clauses], but none is perceivable in the act which is prohibited."[323]

The term *tax or duty* is broader than *duty*, obviously, so that the prohibition under the Export Clause might very well be broader than that under the Import-Export Clause, as the Court concluded in *IBM* and *U.S. Shoe*. Moreover, the Export Clause contains a direct "textual command" (emphasized in *IBM*),[324] and it is an "unqualified prohibition" (language from *U.S. Shoe*).[325] Neither is as clearly true with the Import-Export Clause.

Although the Export Clause therefore arguably prohibits more than the Import-Export Clause does, it should also be true that the Export Clause would, at a minimum, prevent Congress from enacting the sorts of levies on exports that states are forbidden to enact. It should therefore be possible to glean from Import-Export Clause jurisprudence some of the state levies that, if they were to be considered by the national government, would fail the Export Clause.

Chief Justice John Marshall could think of no good reason for having two different bodies of law on what is, at bottom, a single issue: when is a levy treated as falling on exported goods? For that matter, the post-Marshall Supreme Court said the same thing, repeatedly, when it was hearing Export Clause cases on a regular basis. It was not until 1996 and the decision in *IBM* that the Court said the two provisions might reasonably be interpreted in different ways.

How could it have happened that the Supreme Court, after not hearing an Export Clause case in more than seventy years, suddenly rejected the time-honored understanding that the Export Clause and the Import-Export Clause have a core of common meaning? Perhaps some of the justices who favored treating the Export Clause as if it were *sui generis* might have been uncomfortable with questioning the national taxing power. Overturning a revenue statute was unusual enough in the late twentieth century; doing so twice in two years was extraordinary. Justice Ginsburg's opinion in *U.S. Shoe*, which stressed the unique nature of the Export Clause, was written by someone who had already shown her distaste for an expansive interpretation of the Clause in *IBM*. Cabining the Export Clause, as her opinion for the Court in *U.S. Shoe* did, may have been a form of damage control.

Another explanation is possible. In the years between 1923 and 1996, the Court was deciding cases under the Import-Export Clause and ignoring the Export Clause. The Import-Export Clause became increasingly permissive as the Court, for whatever reason, became less willing to see state prerogatives limited by the Clause. For one thing, even though the Import-Export Clause does not say so, the Court had stated that, if a tax did not "relate[] to the value of the goods, [it was not] taxation upon the goods themselves."[326] And the Court had hinted, without resolving the question directly, that a state levy was invalid under the Import-Export Clause only if it discriminated against imports or exports.

At the same time, the Court was hearing no Export Clause cases, and no one was paying attention to the fact that the rules being applied under the Import-Export Clause were becoming far removed from what had been traditionally understood to apply under the Export Clause. Because the two clauses are directed at different sovereigns, cases do not require analyzing the two provisions simultaneously.

Under the circumstances, a divergence in principles was not surprising; indeed, it was probably inevitable. The Court started with two bodies of law governed by a common core of principles but then focused judicial effort on only one of the bodies of law. At the end of seventy years, the original principles may have been stretched out of shape in the active area. Notwithstanding *stare decisis*, the cumulative effect of several decades' worth of incremental changes can be dramatic.

Only in 1996, when the Court revisited the Export Clause after a long hiatus, did it become apparent that the two lines of cases were no longer compatible. If, in the interests of conformity, the Court in 1996 had applied the full complement of modern Import-Export Clause jurisprudence to the analysis of the Export Clause, there would have been little left of the Export Clause. Applying permissive rules to the interpretation of a Clause that, by its terms, is not at all permissive simply would not have worked. To preserve a significant role for the Export Clause, the Court therefore had to break the historical connection between the two clauses, or so one might hypothesize.

Breaking the connection may therefore have made sense under the circumstances, but Chief Justice Marshall was still right that the clauses should be interpreted consistently. Whether the Court can get to that result is another question, however. If conformity is to be reachieved, the Court will need to reexamine the principles it has developed in the last few decades under the Import-Export Clause. And in reexamining the Import-Export Clause, the Court will have to be sensitive to Export Clause doctrines—even though that Clause will not be directly implicated in an Import-Export Clause case.

What Is a Tax?

It is not automatically the case that the term *tax* and its variants have to mean the same thing throughout the Constitution, but conformity in meaning should be used as a starting point and abandoned only if absolutely necessary. Variation in the meaning of a term in a single legal document, especially a Constitution, is something to be resisted, not endorsed.

Export Clause cases should therefore provide useful guidance on what distinguishes a tax from other governmental exactions. For example, there is no obvious reason why the understanding that a user fee is not a *tax or duty* under the Export Clause, reaffirmed by the Supreme Court in *U.S. Shoe*, should not be extended to the interpretation of other taxing provisions in the Constitution. Those provisions also do not work if interpreted to include user fees, and we do not need a full explanation of what, if anything, distinguishes a *tax* from the multitude of other terms used in the Constitution to distinguish between a *tax* and a *user fee*.

For example, suppose Congress delegates to an administrative agency the power to set the fees for services provided by the agency—such as fees for processing patent applications. And suppose the administrative agency sets a charge that greatly exceeds any amount that can reasonably be viewed as a fee. The amount of the excess (and maybe the whole charge) might be recharacterized as a *tax*—the learning in *U.S. Shoe* as to what is and what is not a *tax* should be relevant to that determination—and, if so, there are legitimate questions about the authority of an administrative agency to impose such a charge on its own. Regardless of how broad the federal taxing power is, it is not clear that Congress can delegate that power to an administrative agency.

Review of Tax Statutes Generally

Perhaps the biggest question that arises from the Court's efforts to cabin Export Clause jurisprudence is this: Is the Court's willingness to review taxing statutes, and to direct other courts to do the same, limited to the Export Clause? And if the answer to that question is *yes*, we should wonder why that should be so.

In *IBM* and *U.S. Shoe*, the Court struck down taxing statutes on constitutional grounds, something that had not happened since the 1920s. Treating the Export Clause as unique may have been intended, by at least some justices, to leave the remainder of the congressional taxing power generally unconstrained by judicial review.

But why should the Court interpret the Export Clause expansively and other limitations on the taxing power narrowly? Justice Ginsburg in *U.S. Shoe* pointed to the Export Clause's being an "unqualified prohibition" as one reason for treating the Clause as different from other tax provisions in the Constitution,[327] and in *IBM*, Justice Thomas noted the clear "textual command" of the Clause as a distinguishing factor.[328] But the Export Clause is not fundamentally different, in either respect, from other limitations on the national taxing power.

The Export Clause *is* "unqualified" in a way—when it applies, it is a command without reservations—but the Clause applies only to levies on "articles exported," a fairly significant qualification. In any event, compare the Export Clause to the Direct-Tax Clauses discussed in Chapter 6, which absolutely prohibit direct taxes that have not been apportioned on the basis of respective state populations, or the Uniformity Clause, discussed in Chapter 5, which absolutely prohibits duties, imposts, and excises that are not geographically uniform.

In fact, the form of the Direct-Tax Clause in Article I, section 9 is *identical* to the form used for the Export Clause: "No Capitation, or other direct, Tax shall be laid" versus "No Tax or Duty shall be laid." If the Export Clause contains a clear "textual command," so too does that Direct-Tax Clause. If Congress were to enact an unapportioned direct tax—an unapportioned, national real-estate tax would be the clearest case—or a duty on imports that was not uniform, a court should be just as willing to reject the levy as the Supreme Court was in *IBM* and *U.S. Shoe*.

Nevertheless, one can infer from the majority opinions in both *IBM* and *U.S. Shoe* that the Court is unlikely to be as vigorous in enforcing other limitations on the taxing power as it was with the Export Clause. Maybe the Clause is so peculiar that we should draw no grand conclusions about the Supreme Court's willingness to hold taxing statutes, outside the export context, to constitutional requirements. That may be the case, but it is not obvious why it should be so.

AN AFTERWORD ON INTERPRETING THE EXPORT CLAUSE: THE 1797 ACT

One particular piece of early legislation, enacted in 1797, has assumed significance in the debates about interpreting the Export Clause. The 1797 Act contained a number of provisions that are at least questionable under the Clause, and defenders of modern legislative initiatives have pointed to the Act, which was never evaluated by a court, as a definitive interpretation of original understanding. In particular, the government made that argument in *IBM* because the 1797 Act contained a tax on export insurance that was substantively similar to the tax evaluated, and ultimately rejected, in *IBM*.

The 1797 Act contained quite a few provisions that were constitutionally suspect, however, and at least one provision was so constitutionally infirm that it should have been laughed out of Congress. Viewing the Act as an accurate indication of the original understanding of the Export Clause is questionable, if not clearly wrong.

Congress entitled the 1797 statute "An Act laying Duties on stamped Vellum, Parchment and Paper," suggesting that duties were being laid on documents, rather than associated goods.[329] Among other things, the 1797 Act imposed a tax of ten cents on "[a]ny note or bill of lading, for any goods or merchandise to be exported, if from one district to another district of the United States, not being in the same State"; or, if the goods were "to be exported to any foreign port or place," the tax was twenty-five cents.[330] The Act thus taxed bills of lading for "goods to be exported to any foreign port or place" at a rate higher than that applicable to domestic bills.

Does a tax that clearly burdens exportation become constitutionally acceptable if levied on paperwork associated with exported articles instead of on the articles themselves? The late eighteenth century was a more formalistic time than today, to be sure. But the 1797 tax was the equivalent of taxing the air surrounding an exported article, and it does not take much sophistication to see that if such a tax is not prohibited by the Export Clause, the Clause is a nullity. The Clause would prohibit only the most obvious sort of taxes on exports, and thus give free rein to Congress to avoid its limitations.

Indeed, that is the way the Supreme Court later characterized a similar tax enacted in 1898. In United States v. Fairbank (1901), discussed earlier, the Supreme Court struck down the 1898 tax as violating the Export Clause and refused to defer to the Fifth Congress's constitutional understanding. The substance of the tax was apparent (although four justices dissented): "[A] stamp duty on a bill of lading is in effect a duty on the article transported."[331]

The 1797 Act also contained a tax on export insurance, of the sort that was invalidated in Thames & Mersey Marine Insurance Co. v. United States (1915) and later in *IBM*, and a tax on charter-parties, similar to that rejected in 1915 in *Hvoslef*. These two levies may have raised harder questions under the Export Clause than did the levy on bills of lading, but the Supreme Court in 1915 had little difficulty in finding violations of the Export Clause in both cases: The services were integrally related to exportation.

Whatever the merits of deferring to the constitutional interpretations of the very earliest Congresses, by the time the Fifth Congress came along, the Federalists were on their last legs, trying to hold on to power; paying attention to constitutional niceties was not given primacy. And opponents of the 1797 levies had no realistic hope of successfully challenging the taxes in court; the Supreme Court's performance in Hylton v. United States (1796) should have made that obvious. The *Hylton* Court, made up of Federalists sympathetic to a Federalist government, did not view itself as a check on the other branches of government in a way we have come to expect today.

* * * * *

One might argue that this chapter has been much ado about nothing or what should be nothing. Maybe it is time for the Export Clause simply to disappear from the Constitution. The fears of sectional strife that gave rise to the Clause are weaker in 2004 than they were in 1787, and even if that were not true, it is doubtful that without the Export Clause we would see such strife reflected in discriminatory taxation of exports. Furthermore, the Clause has its embarrassing history. Although something like the Export Clause would probably have wound up in the Constitution anyway, the Clause did have an unfortunate connection with slavery.

Besides, the Export Clause is a peculiarly limited protection against abuse of the national taxing power: when it applies, it has great effect, but it applies only within a narrow context. As sources of revenue largely unknown to the founders have come to dominate the national taxing system—the income tax in particular—a limitation on the national power to tax exports may seem to be an anomaly.

As if all of that were not enough to call into question the significance of the Export Clause, Congress can often avoid Export Clause issues by relying directly on its regulatory powers under the Commerce Clause (powers that have expanded exponentially over the last two centuries). Suppose Congress wishes to prohibit exports of a particular good. A confiscatory tax on the export of the good could have a prohibitory effect, but such a tax would face Export Clause scrutiny. (If the Clause would not forbid such a levy, it would have to be because a court might characterize a measure intended to raise little or no revenue as something other than a "tax or duty.")[332] In contrast, if Congress has the power under the Commerce Clause (or some other constitutional provision) directly to forbid exportation of the good, no Export Clause issue would be raised.[333]

Nevertheless, there are still reasons to care about the Export Clause. The Clause may not be the most significant provision in the Constitution, but it remains important for at least three reasons. First, the Clause is not going to disappear in the near future. Second, the Supreme Court in *IBM* and *U.S. Shoe* took the Clause seriously, which means that the rest of us have to as well. Finally, and most important, the Court showed in those two cases that it is now willing, at least occasionally, to evaluate the constitutional merits of a federal revenue statute. If the Export Clause is not unique in its fundamentals, the long-time assumption that the judiciary will keep its collective hands off the national revenue system may no longer be justified.

10

The Rest of the Story

This chapter discusses some remaining constitutional issues associated with taxation. If there is a unifying principle here, it is that the topics, all having to do with taxation, have not been dealt with in the first nine chapters. In effect, this chapter is a series of discrete essays that fill in gaps in the preceding material.

The chapter begins with a discussion of the borrowing power under the Constitution, which was understood to be closely tied to the power to tax. The second part considers two as-yet-unaddressed constitutional provisions that, by their terms, are clearly tax-related—one of which is of only historical interest (clarifying the authority of Congress to tax the importation of slaves), while the other may have a modicum of contemporary relevance (the Origination Clause). The third part discusses some potential limitations on the taxing power that arise, or may arise, under general constitutional doctrines (such as intergovernmental immunity and the doctrine of enumerated powers—an issue that is ordinarily characterized as one of taxation versus regulation) or from constitutional provisions that, on their faces, do not seem to have a tax connection (the Due Process Clause, the Takings Clause, and the Compensation Clause). The fourth part addresses an issue alluded to earlier in the book: did the requisitions power survive ratification of the Constitution? Finally, the chapter ponders the proper way to interpret ambiguous constitutional provisions relating to taxation.

THE BORROWING POWER

The Congress shall have Power . . . To borrow Money on the credit of the United States.—Article I, section 8, clause 2

All Debts contracted and Engagements entered into, before the Adoption of this Constitution, shall be as valid against the United States under this Constitution, as under the Confederation.—Article VI, clause 1

The power to borrow was understood by the founders, Federalists and antifederalists alike, as "inseparably connected with that of raising a revenue," as

St. George Tucker wrote in 1803 (and Justice Joseph Story quoted, without specific attribution, in 1833).[334] The taxing and borrowing powers are both critical to funding government.

Under Article IX, clause 5 of the Articles of Confederation, the Continental Congress was entitled "to borrow money or emit bills on the credit of the United States." Since repayment of borrowed funds ultimately depended on the compliance of the states, however—how else would borrowed amounts be repaid except with requisitioned funds?—the national government had difficulty borrowing. As St. George Tucker wrote in 1803, "[N]ot possessing any revenue independent of the states, their loans were obtained with difficulty, and very rarely in time to answer the purposes for which they were intended."[335] Benjamin Franklin had had some notable successes arranging war loans from the French government, but Franklin could not be cloned and his influence was difficult to institutionalize. Just as most founders thought it was necessary to replace (or supplement) the requisitions process with a real national power to tax individuals, the founders generally thought it was necessary for the national government to have a real power to borrow money—a power that could not be interfered with by the states.[336]

One step in making the new nation creditworthy was to make it clear that national obligations would be honored—that creditors would not be harmed because of changes in the form of government. Article VI of the Constitution accordingly required the new government to treat as valid all "debts contracted" by the United States under the Articles of Confederation. This provision, which actually precedes the Supremacy Clause in the text of Article VI, was not successfully challenged at the Constitutional Convention, although there was brief discussion of a few issues. Some questioned the need for the Clause (was the United States not already legally bound by the actions of its agents under the Articles?),[337] and some worried that the new government would be dragged down by excessive debt. George Mason of Virginia argued, for example, that the word "shall" provided no flexibility to the government if repayment became a problem.[338] (He stressed this point at the Virginia ratifying convention as well.) Pierce Butler of South Carolina complained the Clause would "compel payment as well to the Blood-suckers who had speculated on the distresses of others, as to those who had fought & bled for their country."[339] Finally, some delegates contended that state debts incurred while the Articles were in effect should become national obligations, a position attractive to the most debt-laden states, but resisted by others.[340]

To govern the future borrowing of the national government, the Committee of Detail at the Convention originally prepared language that was largely copied from the Articles of Confederation. It would have given Congress the power "To borrow Money, and emit bills on the credit of the United States."[341] The first part of this proposal, dealing with the general power to borrow, was relatively noncontroversial. In one of his 1788 essays, anti-federalist Brutus did express fear of too much debt: "I can scarcely contemplate a greater calamity that could befal [*sic*] this country, than to be loaded with a debt exceeding their ability ever to discharge."[342] But there was no serious opposition at the Convention to the idea that the national government needed to be able to borrow money. Besides, since this was a power the Continental Congress had had, at least in theory, under the Articles of Confederation, the Constitution did not seem to have increased national power in this regard.

The national government had to have the power to borrow if only because, in time of war, tax revenues might be insufficient to pay the government's bills. Justice Story explained:

> This power seems indispensable to the sovereignty and existence of a national government. Even under the confederation this power was expressly delegated. . . . Though in times of profound peace it may not ordinarily be necessary to anticipate the revenues of a state; yet the experience of all nations must convince us, that the burthens and expenses of one year, in time of war, may more than equal the ordinary revenue of ten years. Hence, a debt is almost unavoidable, when a nation is plunged into a state of war. . . . Indeed, this recourse becomes the more necessary, because the ordinary duties upon importation are subject to great diminution and fluctuations in times of war; and a resort to direct taxes for the whole supply would, under such circumstances, become oppressive and ruinous to the agricultural interests of the country.

Even in peacetime, Story noted, "exigencies may occur, which render a loan the most facile, economical, and ready means of supply, either to meet expenses, or to avert calamities, or to save the country from an undue depression of its staple productions." He pointed to the Louisiana Purchase as "a striking illustration of the economy and convenience of such arrangements."[343]

Although the straightforward power to borrow was noncontroversial, the Committee of Detail's draft raised hackles with its reference, picked up from the Articles of Confederation, to the power to "emit bills on the credit of the United States." The opposition to this power, which was ultimately successful, came from some of those friendliest to the idea of a strong national government. On August 16, Gouverneur Morris moved to strike the words "and emit bills" from the clause.[344] As reported by James Madison, Morris said that, "[i]f the United States had credit such bills would be unnecessary: if they had not unjust & useless."[345]

"Emit[ting] bills" is definitely not twenty-first century language. What the founders were arguing about was the propriety of permitting the national government to issue paper money. The basic borrowing power, which survived in the Constitution, was understood in its traditional sense: you get something, and you promise to pay it back. As James Madison later explained, "The obvious meaning of the power to borrow money, is that of accepting it from, and stipulating payment to those who are *able* and *willing* to lend."[346]

In contrast, printing money to fund the activities of the United States was understood, by at least some of the founders, to be a fundamentally different exercise. To the skeptics, the fact that the Continental Congress had explicitly had the power to "emit bills," and had used that power, was not reassuring. The experience under the Articles was to be rejected, not celebrated.

It was founders who became Federalists, and in some cases strong Federalists, who spoke most forcefully against the issuance of paper money. Pennsylvanian James Wilson said that "[i]t will have a most salutary influence on the credit of the U. States to remove the possibility of paper money. This expedient can never succeed whilst its mischiefs are remembered. And as long as it can be resorted to, it will be a bar to other resources."[347] Who is going to lend money to the United States if he might be repaid in greenbacks, rather than real money? And Gouverneur Morris feared that "[t]he Monied interest will oppose the plan of Government, if paper emissions be not prohibited."[348]

Oliver Ellsworth of Connecticut, a more equivocal Federalist, "thought this a favorable moment to shut and bar the door against paper money. . . . By withholding the power from the new Governt. more friends of influence would be gained to it than by almost any thing else—Paper money can in no case be necessary—Give the Government credit, and other resources will offer—The power may do more harm than good."[349]

Surprisingly, it was some prominent anti-federalists-to-be who supported the power to issue paper money, if only because the needs of the future were unknown. Virginian George Mason, for example, generally no friend of expansive national power, spoke in favor of retaining the language from the Articles of Confederation: "Though he had a mortal hatred to paper money, yet as he could not foresee all circumstances, he was unwilling to tie the hands of the Legislature. He observed that the late war could not have been carried on, had such a prohibition existed."[350] And Mason thought the power to print paper money would not exist unless it were specifically provided for in the Constitution.

Fellow Virginian Edmund Randolph, a mild supporter of the Constitution, agreed that the government's hands should not be tied: "[N]otwithstanding his antipathy to paper money, [Randolph] could not agree to strike out the words, as he could not foresee all the occasions that might arise."[351] Besides, stressed John Francis Mercer of Maryland (and Virginia), why cut off support from proponents of paper money—people like him? Mercer, who became an anti-federalist, said it "was impolitic . . . to excite the opposition of all those who were friends to paper money. The people of property would be sure to be on the side of the plan, and it was impolitic to purchase their further attachment with the loss of the opposite class of Citizens."[352]

Morris's motion nevertheless prevailed overwhelmingly, nine states to two, and the reference to emitting bills was eliminated from the Borrowing Clause.[353] In state ratification conventions, some anti-federalists ridiculed the deletion of the power to emit bills because, they said, the Constitution had lodged all sorts of dangerous powers in Congress. At the Maryland convention in 1788, for example, anti-federalist Luther Martin explained that opponents of the Morris motion at the Constitutional Convention had reasonably urged, that it would be improper to *deprive* the Congress of that *power*; that it would be a novelty unprecedented to establish a government which should not have that authority—That it was impossible to look forward into futurity so far as to decide, that events might not happen that should render the *exercise* of such a power *absolutely* necessary—And that we doubted, whether if a war should take place it would be *possible* for this country to *defend* itself, without having recourse to *paper credit*, in which case there would be a *necessity* of becoming a *prey* to our *enemies*, or *violating* the *constitution* of our government. . . .

Nevertheless, Martin added sarcastically,

a majority of the convention, being wise beyond every event, and being willing to risque any political evil rather than admit the *idea* of a paper emission, in any *possible* case, refused to *trust* this authority to a government, to which they were *lavishing* the most *unlimited* powers of taxation, . . . they *erased* that clause from the system.[354]

No explicit power to "emit bills" was thus provided in the Constitution, and the power to issue paper money also appears to be suspect under the language of Article I, section 8, clause 5, which grants Congress the power to "*coin* Money" and "regulate the Value thereof." In 1787, the founders understood the term *coin* literally, to refer to hard currency. But the founders did not think that they were prohibiting the use of all commercial paper, such as promissory notes, by the government. Madison's notes on the Convention indicate that Virginia voted for the Morris motion because Madison himself "became satisfied that striking out the words ['emit bills'] would not disable the Govt from the use of public notes as far as they could be safe & proper; & would only cut off the pretext for a paper currency and particularly for making the bills a tender either for public or private debts."[355] A paper currency was not to be used, but the national government was not forbidden to use paper in connection with its legitimate borrowing.

Whatever the merits of the old distinction between borrowing *per se* and issuing paper money, the importance of the distinction disappeared long ago. Despite its suspect status under the language of the Constitution, paper money has a long history in the United States, and the power of the national government to issue paper money was definitively resolved in the *Legal Tender Cases* in the 1870s.[356] Whether the power to issue greenbacks is ultimately one of borrowing or one of "coining money" does not seem to matter. Under one theory or another, Congress can issue paper money, even though the original understanding was to the contrary.

Does the Borrowing Clause constrain Congress in any meaningful way? Few issues under the Clause have reached the courts, and the Supreme Court has therefore had almost no opportunity to explicate the borrowing power. Nevertheless, the answer to that question is pretty clearly *no*. Any borrowing presumably has to be for constitutionally acceptable purposes, but, if a constitutional question is raised in that context, it will be about the legitimacy of the expenditure, not the source of the funds. In any event, most national borrowing occurs without any specification of how the borrowed dollars will be used.

The reference in the Borrowing Clause to the "credit of the United States" has also had no limiting effect on congressional power. In practice, that language seems to describe a market-based limit—the government obviously can borrow only if its credit is good enough to do so—not a legal one. Even then, the creditworthiness of the United States is likely to be reflected in the interest rate that the government must pay, not in the ability to borrow *per se*. If it came to pass that the United States could not borrow at all because of its poor credit rating, the meaning of the Borrowing Clause would be the least of the nation's worries.

Finally, Congress may not alter the terms of existing obligations without providing compensation for "actual loss." Perry v. United States (1935). For example, if Congress were to decide to pay back only fifty cents on the dollar, a damaged lender would clearly be entitled to compensation. But this limitation, such as it is, does not preclude the effective reduction in the burden of the obligation through inflation—inflation that reduces the economic cost of repayment. In that respect, a lender to the government bears the same risk as a lender to any other entity: an increase in prevailing interest rates will reduce the value of the note the lender holds.

TWO FINAL, SPECIFICALLY TAX-RELATED CONSTITUTIONAL PROVISIONS

Two clearly tax-related provisions in the Constitution have not been addressed to this point in the book, and each deserves brief consideration. The Origination Clause was intended to govern the procedures for enacting tax legislation, although its practical effects have turned out to be minor at best. And, under the first clause of Article I, section 9, the power of Congress to tax the importation of slaves was protected during a period when Congress could not altogether prohibit importation.

The Origination Clause

All bills for raising Revenue shall originate in the House of Representatives; but the Senate may propose or concur with Amendments as on other Bills.
—Article I, section 7, clause 1

The Origination Clause can be traced to an English requirement that money bills must commence in the House of Commons; it was intended to ensure that "power over the purse" lies with the legislative body closer to the people. The Clause was one of several provisions meant to cabin the national revenue power created under the Constitution, and it was part of a compromise between large and small states, helping to temper the large states' unhappiness with equal representation in the Senate.

At the Constitutional Convention, Elbridge Gerry of Massachusetts posited "that the people ought to hold the purse-strings";[357] he was afraid that the Senate would become an aristocratic body because of its small size, its selection by legislatures rather than election, and the six-year term of office. He accordingly proposed a provision that would have required all "money bills" (including appropriations) to originate in the House, and would have given the Senate no power to amend.

The strongest proponents of national power opposed an Origination Clause in any form, if only because the Clause seemed to be pointless. For example, James Wilson of Pennsylvania argued that, "[i]f both branches were to say yes or no, it was of little consequence which should say yes or no first."[358]

The form of the Origination Clause that survived the debates was closer to Wilson's vision than to Gerry's. The Clause was restricted to bills for raising revenue, and the Senate was given the amendment power (which, Gerry thought, gutted the provision).

Although dramatically weakened from Gerry's conception, the Origination Clause still did not seem to be meaningless. James Madison, not a supporter of the Clause at the Convention, gave it a generous interpretation in Federalist 58:

> The House of Representatives cannot only refuse, but they alone can propose the supplies requisite for the support of the government. . . . This power over the purse may, in fact, be regarded as the most complete and effectual weapon with which any constitution can arm the immediate representatives of the people, for obtaining a redress of every grievance, and for carrying into effect every just and salutary measure.[359]

Whether Madison really meant what he wrote, or whether he was merely puffing to sell the Constitution, it is impossible to know. In any event, the Origination Clause has had little effect. Most revenue bills have their intellectual genesis in the Treasury Department, not in Congress, and it is hard to imagine how Congress could be prevented from adopting such proposals if it wished to do so. Furthermore, in practice the Senate's power to amend is generally understood to be so broad that the Senate can replace the entire text of a bill that technically originates in the House. What "originates" in the House may be nothing but the number attached to a piece of tax legislation.

The understanding that the Clause is a nullity reflects practice, however, not necessarily doctrine. In its most recent Origination-Clause case, United States v. Munoz-Flores (1990), a divided Supreme Court rejected the argument that origination issues are automatically nonjusticiable political questions: A plaintiff with standing may pursue a claim that a revenue statute improperly originated in the Senate. In *Munoz-Flores*, the Court did not get to the larger issues, concluding that a bill to impose a user fee, where raising revenue was a secondary concern, was not a "bill for raising revenue" for Origination-Clause purposes. Supreme Court consideration of the Clause must therefore await another case where a taxpayer subject to an unquestioned revenue statute can raise serious questions about the statute's origin.

Taxing the Importation of Slaves

The Migration or Importation of such Persons as any of the States now existing shall think proper to admit, shall not be prohibited by the Congress prior to the Year one thousand eight hundred and eight, but a Tax or duty may be imposed on such Importation, not exceeding ten dollars for each Person.
—Article I, section 9, clause 1

Article I, section 9 contains limitations on congressional power, and the limitation in clause 1—preventing Congress from restricting the importation of slaves until 1808—was important in getting the Southern states' support (particularly that of North Carolina, South Carolina, and Georgia) for the Constitution. The Southern states feared that, without a specific limitation, Congress might be understood to have the power to forbid importation—under the Commerce Clause or some other grant of power in Article I, section 8. (Indeed, the cutoff of the prohibition in 1808 implied that Congress would have the power to prohibit importation at that point. And, in United States v. *The William* (1808), a district judge wrote that, "under the power to regulate commerce, Congress would be authorized to abridge it [i.e., commerce] in favor of the great principles of humanity and justice. Hence the introduction of a clause . . . as to interdict a prohibition of the slave trade, until 1808.")[360]

Clause 1 is not entirely restrictive, however. It temporarily prevented Congress from prohibiting the importation of slaves (and maybe more), but it did not preclude Congress from imposing a tax or duty on the importation of "persons." Such a tax or duty would have made importation of slaves less profitable and, as a result, less likely. Opponents of slavery were not happy that importation was going to be permitted for a minimum of twenty more years, but at least the power to tax represented a mild attack on the peculiar institution, or so it was argued. Given the practicalities of nation-building, slavery opponents probably could not have hoped for more. The power to tax was a "partial prohibition; it was all that could be obtained," James Wilson reported to the Pennsylvania ratifying convention in December 1787.[361]

Not all slavery-skeptics viewed the "Tax or duty" passage positively, however. Roger Sherman of Connecticut, for example, objected at the Constitutional Convention because the language "acknowledg[ed] men to be property, by taxing them as such under the character of slaves."[362] James Madison added that "it would be wrong to admit in the Constitution the idea that there could be property in men. The reason of duties did not hold, as slaves are not like merchandise, consumed. &c."[363]

Sherman's remark triggered a discussion as to whether the power to tax was really intended to discourage importation of slaves. Nathaniel Ghoram of Massachusetts answered *yes*, and George Mason added that "[n]ot to tax will be equivalent to a bounty on the importation of slaves."[364] Sherman was not persuaded, however. He responded that "the smallness of the duty shewed revenue to be the object, not the discouragement of the importation."[365]

Did the passage permitting a tax or duty add anything to the congressional powers that would have existed anyway? Under the general grant of taxing power in Article I, section 8, clause 1, Congress could tax imports, as long as the Uniformity Clause was satisfied. ("Imposts" and "Duties" are specifically enumerated in that provision.) Is the importation of a slave any different, for purposes of taxation, from the importation of tea? So understood, the "Tax or duty" passage in section 9, clause 1 does not seem to be a grant of power. It merely clarified that the restriction on congressional power outlined in that provision was not intended to extend to the taxing power otherwise available, except by capping the amount of an allowable tax or duty.

Read in that way, however, as not restricting the basic power to tax imports, the "Tax or duty" clause seemed to do exactly what its critics complained of: It treated "persons" as conceptually no different from barrels of whiskey. Congress could slap a duty on the importation of either category of "property." But interpreting the passage as countenancing property in men may be reading too much into language that, by its terms, was not limited to the importation of slaves. Here, as elsewhere in the Constitution, the founders were careful not to use explicit references to slaves and slavery, and Gouverneur Morris noted that "as the clause now stands it implies that the Legislature may tax *freemen* imported."[366] Responding to Morris, George Mason provided a reason for using language that would include more than slaves: "[T]he provision as it stands was necessary for the case of Convicts in order to prevent the introduction of them."[367] That was helpful, but Mason's answer was still not fully responsive to Morris's point. The language seemed to include much more than slaves and convicts. Why the reference to *persons?*

All of which suggests that the passage, although it existed only because of slavery, may have backhandedly confirmed that Congress had the power to tax any "persons" entering the United States. Congress, that is, could impose a tax on immigrants generally, with slaves merely a subset of that broader class. Sherman and Madison had complained that the passage conceptualized slaves as property, but the language need not be understood in that way.

In any event, no tax on the importation of slaves ever emerged from Congress. (Direct taxes on real estate, which generally applied to slaves as well, were enacted more than once, beginning in 1798, and they were properly apportioned, as required by the Direct-Tax Clauses. But these taxes were not directed only at slaves—given the way apportionment works, a slaves-only tax would have been politically impossible—and they had nothing to do with importation.) Indirect taxes on importation of slaves were suggested several times between 1798 and 1804, but the proposals failed, for various reasons, including a fear that discussion of the proposals would inevitably reopen arguments about whether slaves were properly characterized as persons or property.[368]

TAXING ISSUES UNDER OTHER CONSTITUTIONAL DOCTRINES AND PROVISIONS

Chapters 5 to 9 dealt with limitations on the taxing power specifically provided for in the text of the Constitution. With the Uniformity Clause, the Direct-Tax Clauses, and the Export Clause, the boundaries of the limitations may not always be clear, but there is no question that those clauses are related to the taxing power.

This part considers some limitations, or potential limitations, on the taxing power derived from constitutional provisions that make no reference to taxation. In particular, it considers intergovernmental immunity (a once-powerful doctrine derived from concepts of federalism that are implicit in the structure of the Constitution); the relationship of taxation and regulation; the limited relevance of the Due Process Clause and the Takings Clause to taxation; and the extent of any restriction on the national government's power to tax federal judges under the Compensation Clause.

Intergovernmental Immunity

For a long time it was assumed that Congress could impose no taxes on state and municipal governments, on employees or instrumentalities of those governments, and, in some cases, on other private parties that contracted with those governments. This limitation on congressional power was attributed to principles of federalism and was usually characterized as a matter of "intergovernmental immunity." The doctrine of intergovernmental immunity has fallen on hard times in recent years, however, probably with good reason. This section discusses the rise and fall of the doctrine and the question of what, if anything, is left of it.

The Supreme Court articulated the current state of intergovernmental immunity law in South Carolina v. Baker (1988), in a passage that contrasts the extent to which states cannot tax the federal government to the similar, but not identical, rules running in the other direction:

> States can never tax the United States directly but can tax any private parties with whom it does business, even though the financial burden falls on the United States, as long as the tax does not discriminate against the United States or those with it whom it deals. . . . A tax is considered to be directly on the Federal Government only "when the levy falls on the United States itself, or on an agency or instrumentality so closely connected to the Government that the two cannot realistically by viewed as separate entities." . . . The rule with respect to state immunity is essentially the same, . . . except that at least some nondiscriminatory federal taxes can be collected directly from the States even though a parallel State tax could not be collected directly from the Federal Government.[369]

Thus, despite old case law to the contrary, Congress's power to tax those who contract with state and local governments (including employees of those governments) is now unconstrained, except by constitutional limitations like the Uniformity Clause that would apply in any event to the national taxing power. The constitutional rules governing "direct" taxation of state and local governments are less clear, but it appears that such a national tax is also likely to be upheld, even if the tax reaches what historically might have been considered an essential governmental function.

In this discussion of intergovernmental immunity, the terms *direct* and *indirect* are used quite differently from the way they are used for purposes of determining the *direct taxes* subject to the apportionment rule. The distinction drawn in the intergovernmental immunity context is between a tax actually levied on the state or municipality (*direct* taxation), and a tax that in form is levied on someone else (an employee of the government, say), although the state or local government may bear some or all of the economic burdens of the national levy (*indirect* taxation).

Indirect Taxation

The early cases that limited the national power to impose taxes having indirect effects on the states (or on subdivisions of states) relied on two basic assumptions. First, it was thought that, if the national government were allowed to tax a person or entity under contract with a state government, the state's ability to exercise its constitutional powers would be impeded. Second, it was thought that a tax on something associated with such a contract was the equivalent of a tax on the government itself.

Those rationales no longer have vitality. The following subsections discuss indirect taxation in several contexts that once gave rise to significant litigation, including the taxation of salaries of government employees and the taxation of interest paid on government bonds. The power of the national government to impose such indirect taxes is now understood to be unimpeded, except by the generally applicable limitations on the national taxing power.

Salaries of Government Employees

Salaries paid to state and municipal officials were thought for decades to be constitutionally protected against federal taxation. It was not until the late 1930s that this always-anomalous understanding was put to rest.

In Collector v. Day (1870), the Supreme Court held that the Civil War federal income tax could not reach the salaries of state employees. The Court relied on Dobbins v. Commissioners of Erie County (1842), a case rejecting a state tax on the salary of officers of the federal government, to invalidate a federal tax on the salary of state probate judges. Just as a state may not interfere with the federal government's exercise of its constitutional powers by taxing a federal employee, the Court reasoned, the federal government cannot interfere with a state's exercise of its constitutional authority by taxing a state employee.[370] Although the federal government is supreme, for purposes of taxation, the Court saw equality of sovereignty as the ideal.[371] And the Court stressed Chief Justice Marshall's great dictum in McCulloch v. Maryland (1818): "[T]he power to tax is the power to destroy."[372]

Day reigned for decades, but the end of *Day* effectively came in 1938. In Helvering v. Gerhardt (1938), the Supreme Court did not explicitly overrule *Day*, but over two dissents, it interpreted the holding narrowly, finding an exception to the intergovernmental immunity rule for state employees working on a nonessential, proprietary government project. The Court held that the national government could tax the income of such employees for two reasons. First, the Court said, the people of the states are represented in Congress and, when Congress acts to tax a state entity, the people are in essence voting to tax themselves.[373] That reason may not have been fully persuasive, but the Court added a second justification for upholding the tax: Congress's constitutional authority to tax should be limited only as necessary to preserve state sovereignty, and the purpose behind the intergovernmental immunity limitation—to "protect the States from curtailment of the essential operations of government which they have exercised from the beginning"—was not implicated in *Gerhardt*.[374]

Concurring in *Gerhardt*, Justice Hugo Black wrote that a distinction between essential and nonessential governmental operations would be impossible to maintain,[375] and he was proven right almost immediately. In Graves v. New York (1939), decided less than a year later, the Court explicitly overruled *Day*: A tax on the salary of a governmental employee is not a tax on the government, regardless of the nature of the employee's services.[376] In particular, the Court concluded that "[t]he theory . . . that a tax on income is legally or economically a tax on its source, is no longer tenable."[377] The state would not be harmed by a tax on its employees, even if the employees were engaged in essential governmental operations, and there was no reason why state employees should be exempt from the obligation, shared by other working people, to pay for benefits provided by the national government.[378]

Justice Frankfurter's concurring opinion in *Graves* nicely identified the transition in thinking from *Day* to *Graves*. He attributed the old understanding to an overemphasis on a "seductive cliché" from *McCulloch* ("Failure to exempt public functionaries from the universal duties of citizenship to pay for the costs of government was hypothetically transmuted into hostile action of one government against the other"),[379] and to the false assumption that a state government must be immune from federal taxation just because the federal government was immune from state taxation. That assumption was not based on the "actual workings of our federalism," but was rather a "pernicious abstraction" of it.[380] Under the constitutional structure, there is not absolute symmetry: the federal government can impose some taxes on states that the state governments would not be permitted to levy on the national government. As the Court later explained in South Carolina v. Baker (1988), "[S]tate immunity arises from the constitutional structure and a concern for protecting state sovereignty whereas the federal immunity arises from the Supremacy Clause."[381]

Interest on Government Bonds

Interest on state and municipal bonds is generally exempt from federal income taxation under today's version of the Internal Revenue Code (in section 103), and it was thought for many years that such a result was constitutionally mandated as well. Indeed, the Supreme Court, in Pollock v. Farmers' Loan & Trust Co. (1895), had said just that. The exemption continues, but not because of constitutional law.

The first case to exempt state and municipal bond interest from the federal income tax base was United States v. Railroad Co. (1872), a case arising under the Civil War income tax. As in the cases exempting salaries of state employees, the Supreme Court in *Railroad Co.* assumed that such a tax was a threat to the sovereignty of the state. Justice Hunt wrote, "If they may be taxed lightly, they may be taxed heavily; if justly, oppressively. Their operation may be impeded and may be destroyed, if any interference is permitted. Hence, the beginning of such taxation is not allowed."[382]

In *Pollock*, the Court reasoned that a tax on bond interest was equivalent to a tax on the bond itself. To support that point, the Court cited several cases holding that a tax on a derivative was equivalent to a tax on the referenced item or process: Dobbins v. Commissioners of Erie County (1842), holding that a tax on federal bond interest was the equivalent of a tax on the federal bond; Almy v. California (1861), holding that a duty on a bill of lading was a duty on the goods that the bill represented; Cook v. Pennsylvania (1878), holding that a tax on income of an auctioneer was a proxy for taxing the auctioned goods; and Philadelphia Steamship Co. v. Pennsylvania (1887) and Leloup v. Port of Mobile (1888), holding that a tax on income received through interstate commerce was effectively a tax on interstate commerce. The *Pollock* Court accordingly concluded that a federal tax on interest from a state or municipal bond would unconstitutionally interfere with the sovereignty of the state or a state subdivision.

As discussed in Chapter 4, Governor Charles Evans Hughes resisted having New York ratify the Sixteenth Amendment until he had been reassured that the Amendment was not intended to affect intergovernmental immunity. He was told that the Amendment, which became effective in 1913, was intended to overturn what the *Pollock* Court had said about apportioning income taxes, not what it had said about federal taxation of state and municipal bond interest.

Nevertheless, the latter aspect of *Pollock* was regularly criticized, and finally, in South Carolina v. Baker (1988), the Court eliminated any constitutional basis for exempting interest on state and municipal bonds. (The dispute arose in *Baker* because of a provision in Internal Revenue Code section 103 excepting interest on certain unregistered bonds issued by states from the tax exemption otherwise provided.) The Court concluded that a federal tax should be considered to fall on a state government for these purposes only "when the levy falls on the [state] itself, or on an agency or instrumentality so closely connected to the Government that the two cannot be realistically viewed as separate entities."[383]

In contrast, a tax should not be treated as falling on a state government when it is levied on a private party with whom the state does business, even if the economic burden of that tax falls on the state in whole or in part.[384] The fact that taxing interest on state bonds would inevitably raise the cost of a state's borrowing is therefore irrelevant for these purposes.

Other Historically Important Exemptions

In the course of ruling on the constitutional status of interest on state and municipal bonds, the Supreme Court in South Carolina v. Baker (1988) noted and relied on a number of cases that had rejected once-vibrant applications of the intergovernmental immunity doctrine.[385] For example, Helvering v. Mountain Producers Corp. (1938) had overturned an exemption from federal taxation of the net income from leases of state government lands; Oklahoma Tax Commission v. Texas Co. (1949) had held that a state tax on income derived from an Indian lease was constitutional; and Alabama v. King & Boozer (1941) and James v. Dravo Contracting Co. (1937) had overturned exemptions of a sales tax and a gross income tax, respectively, associated with government contracts. Many of these cases involved state (rather than federal) taxation, but the significance of the cases runs in both directions. With indirect taxation, the intergovernmental immunity doctrine seems to be a dead letter.

Direct Taxation

McCulloch v. Maryland (1818) held that states cannot tax the federal government directly[386]—the Supremacy Clause controls—and this proposition has not been seriously questioned since. According to the Supreme Court in South Carolina v. Baker (1988), a tax is considered "on" the federal government when it is laid on the government itself, or "on an agency or instrumentality so closely connected to the Government that the two cannot realistically be viewed as separate entities."[387] To what extent the federal government may tax the government of a state directly is less certain, but given *Baker*'s statement that "at least some nondiscriminatory taxes can be collected directly from the States,"[388] such an exercise of federal power is not altogether precluded.

For some potential levies, the constitutional issues are only theoretical because Congress does not seek to tax state and local governments directly. In Internal Revenue Code section 115(1), for example, Congress has excluded from the federal income tax base "income derived from any public utility or the exercise of any essential governmental function and accruing to a State or any political subdivision thereof." If Congress does not tax income from an essential governmental function, the constitutionality of such a tax cannot be tested in court.

Professors Bittker and Lokken note that the statutory "language by negative inference suggests that proprietary or 'nonessential' functions and the activities of state-owned corporations may give rise to taxable income."[389] Moreover, the Code reaches the "'unrelated business income' of state colleges and universities,"[390] also suggesting that income from nonessential functions of state instrumentalities is potentially taxable—or at least suggesting that Congress thinks such income may be taxed consistent with constitutional requirements. (Congress of course might be wrong about the limits of its own power.)

The distinction reflected in the Internal Revenue Code between essential governmental functions and fundamentally proprietary functions was at one time critical in determining whether direct federal taxes on state governments were constitutional.[391] However, just as that distinction fell by the wayside in the indirect taxation context, it was repudiated in New York v. United States (1946) and several later cases.

The distinction may have been problematic—hence its demise—but no generally accepted test has appeared to take its place. A plurality opinion in Massachusetts v. United States (1978) set out what a few Supreme Court justices apparently thought should be the test, but the test proposed by the *Massachusetts* plurality has yet to be adopted by the full Court.

Massachusetts involved a "flat fee" aircraft registration "tax" that was imposed on a helicopter owned by the Commonwealth of Massachusetts. The plurality opinion noted two reasons for narrowing intergovernmental immunity: The scope of the federal government's power to tax should be limited only as necessary to preserve the vertical separation of powers, and the political process is generally adapted to check the federal government's exercise of its tax power if it overly burdens the states.[392] From those principles, the plurality reasoned that "[w]here the subject of tax is a natural and traditional source of federal revenue and where it is inconceivable that such a revenue measure could ever operate to preclude traditional state activities, the [federal] tax [laid directly on a state] is valid."[393] The aircraft registration fee, the full Court concluded, was valid.

The proposed two-part test has something to be said for it, and part of the analysis may have been implicitly blessed, in a somewhat different setting, by the full Court. In Garcia v. San Antonio Metropolitan Transit Authority (1985), the Court said that limits on Congress's Commerce Clause power should be "tailored to compensate for possible failings in the national political process."[394] That is, to the extent that the political process can guard against constitutional violations, courts should be reluctant to strike down exercises of the commerce power. One scholar has said that this rule might apply to Congress's taxing power as well.[395]

None of this is unquestionably "the law," however, in the intergovernmental immunity context. The opinion in *Massachusetts* was merely that of a plurality, and, in addition, the *Massachusetts* Court mixed up a couple of issues, thereby further weakening the persuasive power of the proposed test. Applying its "rule," the plurality had concluded "that taxes that operate as user fees may constitutionally be applied to the States,"[396] and the Court as a whole upheld the application of the charge. But, as discussed in Chapter 9, dealing with the Export Clause, for at least some purposes user fees are not treated as taxes at all and are therefore not subject to constitutional limitations that apply to "taxes."

If a charge is a legitimate user fee—a reasonably calculated charge for specific goods or services received—it is not clear that the doctrine of intergovernmental *tax* immunity should be relevant to analyzing the charge. Sovereign entities are not exempt from paying their bills. Can a state seriously argue that it should not have to pay for goods and services just because the provider was the federal government? Once the *Massachusetts* Court had decided that the "flat fee" was in fact a user fee, there should have been nothing else to decide.

The confusion in the cases should not affect the analysis of most levies, however. Despite some uncertainty about the boundaries of intergovernmental immunity as it applies to direct taxation of states and municipalities, the direction of the law is clear: the presumption is strongly against limiting congressional taxing power. There may be some federal taxes that cannot constitutionally be imposed directly on states and municipalities, but if so, they are few and far between.

Taxation and Regulation

When it was thought that the Commerce Clause and other grants of power in Article I, section 8 were much more limited in scope than is assumed today, a commonly litigated issue was whether Congress could circumvent otherwise applicable limitations by imposing taxes (or what purported to be taxes) instead. Does the power to tax provide Congress with a way to regulate subject matter that is not covered by the other, specific grants of power in section 8? Or, to put the question another way: does the taxing power provide a route to federal regulation of activities that were intended to be within the purview of the states? By adjusting the amount of a tax, and by creating regulatory structures to enforce a tax, Congress could often get effects equivalent to direct regulation. Indeed, if the amount of a "tax" is high enough, the taxed activity will disappear altogether (except perhaps in illegal forms)—the ultimate form of "regulation."

As congressional power increased in the twentieth century, however—with the Commerce Clause in particular becoming an apparently boundless grant of power—the issue of taxation versus regulation receded into the background. If Congress has the power to regulate a particular activity anyway, it does not seem to matter whether Congress uses a purported tax as a means to carry out its legitimate powers.

One might think that, if the Supreme Court returns to an old-fashioned conception of the Commerce Clause—and United States v. Lopez (1995) was one small step in that direction—it could matter once again whether Congress can use the taxing power as a method of regulating something that would otherwise be outside its power. But even if the Commerce Clause were to return to its pre-New Deal conception, a court is unlikely, except in extraordinary circumstances, to second-guess Congress's exercise of the taxing power.

It is true that the Supreme Court did occasionally conclude that a charge was not really a tax (and that the enactment at issue was otherwise outside congressional power), as in the Child Labor Tax Case (Bailey v. Drexel Furniture Co., 1922). But even before the New Deal, cases of that sort were exceptional. In general (and to the dismay of some Supreme Court justices), the Court has bent over backward not to challenge levies that Congress had characterized as taxes.

For example, in McCray v. United States (1903), the Court considered federal taxes on margarine. In an 1886 act, Congress provided for taxing yellow margarine at ten cents per pound, while margarine of other colors (that is, margarine that was less attractive and therefore less likely to affect sales of butter) was taxed at only one-quarter cent per pound. Occupational taxes similarly varied depending on the type of margarine. The purpose behind the taxes was clear—to make margarine less competitive with butter—but the Court refused to look behind the form of the statute. The Court quoted an 1888 opinion to the effect that "[t]he judicial department cannot prescribe to the legislative department limitations upon the exercise of its acknowledged powers. The power to tax may be exercised oppressively upon persons; but the responsibility of the legislature is not to the courts, but to the people by whom its members are elected."[397]

Sonzinsky v. United States (1937), a New Deal–era case, contains some of the best known, and most far-reaching, language about deference to congressional characterizations. In *Sonzinsky*, the Court ruled on the constitutionality of a license tax on dealers in firearms. The National Firearms Act defined "firearms" in such a way that it picked up certain disfavored weapons (like sawed-off shotguns), and the obvious purpose of the Act was to gain federal control over those weapons. Sonzinsky challenged the constitutionality of the statute, arguing that the levy was "not a true tax, but a penalty imposed for the purpose of suppressing traffic in a certain noxious type of firearms, the local regulation of which is reserved to the states."[398] It was assumed that Congress's exertion of direct regulatory power over such firearms was questionable—hence the use of the taxing power.

In a unanimous opinion, the Supreme Court upheld Congress's exercise of the taxing power in these circumstances. And the Court provided an amazingly generous interpretation of that power:

> [A] tax is not any the less a tax because it has a regulatory effect, . . . and it has long been established that an Act of Congress which on its face purports to be an exercise of the taxing power is not any the less so because the tax is burdensome or tends to restrict or suppress the thing taxed.

The levy looked like a tax. It produced "some revenue," and a little bit was enough. As in *McCray*, the Court refused to question congressional motives:

> Inquiry into the hidden motives which may move Congress to exercise a power constitutionally conferred upon it is beyond the competency of courts. . . . They will not undertake, by collateral inquiry as to the measure of the regulatory effect of a tax, to ascribe to

Congress an attempt, under the guise of taxation, to exercise another power denied by the Federal Constitution.[399]

The formalism embodied in such cases has occasionally prompted vigorous dissents. For example, in United States v. Kahriger (1953), the Supreme Court upheld the constitutionality of an occupational tax on those engaged in the business of accepting wagers even though, as the majority admitted, the revenue generated was "negligible."[400] Dissenting Justice Frankfurter complained: "[W]hen oblique use is made of the taxing power as to matters which substantively are not within the powers delegated to Congress, the Court cannot shut its eyes to what is obviously, because designedly, an attempt to control conduct which the Constitution left to the responsibility of the states, merely because Congress wrapped the legislation in the verbal cellophane of a revenue measure."[401]

But shut its eyes is what the Court did in *Kahriger* and many other cases—including those involving taxes on narcotics (United States v. Doremus, 1919)[402] and marijuana (United States v. Sanchez, 1950).[403] Marchetti v. United States (1968) and Grosso v. United States (1968) overruled *Kahriger* on issues relating to the constitutionality of registration and information requirements under a wagering tax statute; the rules were held to violate the constitutional privilege against self-incrimination. But the legitimacy of the taxing power as a method of regulating the suspect activities was consistently upheld.[404]

The Supreme Court has generally deferred to Congress in this area, but occasionally the Court has looked behind a congressional characterization of a levy as a tax. The best known example is the Child Labor Tax Case (Bailey v. Drexel Furniture Co., 1922). Congress had blatantly used a purported "tax" (ten percent on the net profits of businesses "knowingly" employing children in violation of the terms of the statute) as a way to get around an earlier Supreme Court decision, Hammer v. Dagenhart (1918), which had held that Congress did not have the power to regulate child labor.

Writing for the Court, Chief Justice Taft concluded that the usual deference to Congress in taxation did not apply when the levy was not a tax "on its face," but was instead a penalty. The *scienter* requirement attached to the "tax" was itself evidence that this was a penalty. "[P]rovid[ing] a heavy exaction for a departure from a detailed and specified course of conduct in business," said the Court, was not consistent with the exercise of the taxing power.[405] Presumably some members of the Court were irritated too by Congress's unseemly haste in trying to use the taxing power to get effects that the Court had just told Congress could not be achieved through direct regulation.

The narrow holding of the *Child Labor Tax Case* is no longer relevant because the Court subsequently overruled *Hammer* making it clear that Congress has the power to regulate child labor. And the *Child Labor Tax Case* was unusual in the extent to which it evidenced judicial skepticism of the taxing power. But the case does demonstrate that there could be some charges that are not actually taxes—and that would be invalid if Congress does not otherwise have the power to regulate the "taxed" activity. Congress's power is very broad, but it is not limitless.

Due Process

[N]or shall any person . . . be deprived of . . . property, without due process of law. —Amendment V

Under the Fifth Amendment, a person may not be deprived of "property" without "due process of law." Although taxation by its very nature deprives people of "property," the Due Process Clause has had little, if any, effect on the taxing power.

In A. Magnano Co. v. Hamilton (1934), the Supreme Court rejected a Due Process Clause challenge to a selective state sales tax of 15 cents per pound of margarine (where the arguable effect of the tax was going to be destruction of the taxpayer's business). *Magnano* involved a *state* tax, but Justice Sutherland noted the judicial reluctance to see the Due Process Clause as limiting the taxing power of *any* government:

> Except in rare and special circumstances, the due process of law clause contained in the Fifth Amendment is not a limitation upon the taxing power conferred upon Congress by the Constitution. . . . That clause is applicable to a taxing statute . . . only if the act be so arbitrary as to compel the conclusion that it does not involve an exertion of the taxing power, but constitutes, in substance, the direct exertion of a different and forbidden power, as, for example, the confiscation of property.[406]

It is hard to imagine a congressional taxing enactment so blatantly defective that it would reach Justice Sutherland's threshold, and it is hard to find many due process claims taken seriously in litigated cases involving taxation. Flighty tax protesters routinely characterize revenue provisions as arbitrarily leading to the confiscation of property (as well as violating the Uniformity Clause, the Direct-Tax Clauses, and the legal equivalents of the kitchen sink). But, at bottom, the position advanced by protesters is typically little more than that an unwanted tax is a violation of due process, and courts summarily reject such claims. The perceived unfairness of a taxing statute is not enough, by itself, to violate the Due Process Clause.

Of course, if Congress were to impose a tax that reached only American citizens of a particular race, or a tax that reached only men or only women, the tax would be struck down on due process grounds. But these hypotheticals, like the confiscation-of-property possibility raised by Justice Sutherland, are far removed from the real world. Such taxes would unquestionably be invalid, but there is no possibility that Congress would consider them to begin with—or so one hopes. (The next part of this chapter discusses a related, and similarly otherworldly issue—the circumstances in which a tax might be treated as a "taking" of property, requiring compensation to the harmed party.)

The one area in which it is possible to imagine the Due Process Clause's potentially having serious application is with taxing statutes that have negative, retroactive effects: is a taxpayer deprived of property without due process of law if his tax bill increases as a result of a statutory change, and the change applies to a period preceding the date of enactment?

A change in the law that applies only prospectively is of course not even arguably a Due Process Clause violation. The possibility of statutory amendments always makes planning more difficult, but changes with prospective effect are inevitable in a complex society. A taxpayer might plan on the assumption that the top income tax rate will remain at 35 percent, say, but if Congress pushes the rate up to 40 percent for future years, the Due Process Clause is not implicated. The Constitution does not guarantee that a particular version of the Internal Revenue Code will remain in effect in perpetuity.

But changes with negative, retroactive effects—where taxpayers planned their affairs not on the basis of an assumed future version of the Code, but on the basis of an actual *current* version—are arguably different phenomena. For example, if a taxpayer engaged in apparently tax-favored behavior in 2003, but in 2004 Congress took away the tax benefit he had relied upon—and made the change effective for taxable year 2003—the taxpayer is going to feel aggrieved, and with some justification.

Courts have nevertheless been unwilling to see *constitutional* violations in tax enactments that have retroactive effects. For example, in United States v. Carlton (1994), the Supreme Court upheld, against a Due Process Clause challenge, the retroactive addition of a qualification for an estate-tax deduction—a qualification that was enacted in 1987 but was effective for 1986. The retroactive change made it less likely that an estate would qualify for the deduction, and the change occurred after it was too late for the executor of an affected estate to rearrange the estate's affairs to get the benefit of the redefined deduction. The result may have seemed harsh, but, for constitutional purposes, none of that mattered. And in fact the result was not as harsh as it might have seemed initially. The statutory change in *Carlton* was a congressional attempt to close an unintended loophole in the statute; no one has a due process right, one might argue, to take advantage of slips of a drafter's pen.

To this point, the Supreme Court has considered only cases where retroactive effects did not exceed one taxable year (what the *Carlton* Court referred to as a "modest period of retroactivity")[407], and in general, the retroactive changes evaluated by courts have been made for defensible reasons. As the *Carlton* Court explained (quoting from a prior, non-tax case), "Provided that the retroactive application of a statute is supported by a legitimate legislative purpose furthered by rational means, judgments about the wisdom of such legislation remain within the exclusive province of the legislative and executive branches. . . ."[408] Taxpayers may understandably complain about retroactive amendments that affect them adversely, but their complaints should be directed to Congress, not to the courts.

Some commentators think that enactments with more egregious, retroactive effects—retroactivity of more than a year, for example—might well be held to violate the Due Process Clause. No one knows for sure, however, and one might hope that we will never know. The best protection against grossly unfair statutory changes is Congress's good sense in not pushing the limits of its power.

Taxation and Takings

[N]or shall private property be taken for public use without just compensation.
—Amendment V

Given that Congress unquestionably has the power to impose taxes, no one can seriously argue that taxation *per se* should be treated as a taking of property that would require the government to pay compensation. If takings doctrine were to apply to every tax imposed, the taxing power would be a nullity. As Professor Eric Kades has explained in an influential recent article, "Requiring compensation for taxation would immediately bankrupt the state, as the state would have to return immediately all tax receipts to meet this compensation duty."[409] What would be the point of Congress's imposing a levy to raise one dollar if Congress were then required to compensate the taxed persons to the extent of that dollar?

The exercise of the taxing power thus must be understood as something other than the taking of property, at least in ordinary circumstances. That is not to say, however, that absolutely anything would be permitted under the guise of taxation. Professor Kades again: "[T]he label 'tax' confers no immunity to the principles of the Takings Clause."[410] Even the most vigorous proponents of a strong national government recognize that the takings doctrine imposes limits on congressional power. For example, Professor Bruce Ackerman has stated that "[u]nder the constitutional regime inaugurated by the New Deal, there are no significant limits on the national governments's taxing, spending, and regulatory power where the economy is concerned—other than the requirement that government compensate owners if their property is taken for public purposes."[411] Professor Ackerman's reference to takings was probably directed more at exercises of direct regulation than at taxation, but his point remains valid.

It is nevertheless hard to come up with realistic examples to illustrate the application of the Takings Clause in a taxation context. An income "tax" of 100 percent imposed on a single individual almost certainly would be treated as a taking of property, not a tax,[412] but how could such a purported levy ever get through Congress? Absurd hypotheticals do not give rise to decided cases, and the case law provides little guidance about the boundary between taxation and takings.[413]

As a result, there are no universally accepted principles to delineate the difference between a tax and a taking. The one absolutely clear point is that courts are not inclined to see takings in the operation of taxing statutes. A few serious commentators, most notably Professor Richard Epstein, have urged that the takings doctrine should be reinvigorated in taxation. For example, Epstein has argued that the progressive rate structure of the income tax is unconstitutional because it takes the property of the highest-income persons to a disproportionate extent.[414] But Epstein's theoretical arguments do not reflect current judicial understanding, and Epstein has lamented that "[t]he proposition that all taxes are subject to scrutiny under the eminent domain clause receives not a whisper of current support."[415]

Modern case law is sparse, but some principles have nevertheless been posited in the literature as potentially important in distinguishing a legitimate tax from a taking. Professor Kades has summarized classical thinking as follows:

> [T]he classical view on the tax/takings line recognized the fundamental similarity between the two mechanisms, and developed a three-step test to distinguish them. First, this doctrine determined whether the burden fell on many (tax-like) or few (takings-like). Second, it tried to further delineate this many/few distinction by declaring that taxes must fairly apportion burdens. Finally, realizing that a large gray area remained, classical doctrine militated that courts should strike down tax legislation as a taking only in the most extreme cases of disproportionate impact.[416]

A nineteenth-century New York court, in Griffin v. Mayor of Brooklyn (1851), nicely summarized the first two points: "Taxation operates upon a community or upon a class of persons in a community and by some rule of apportionment. The exercise of eminent domain operates upon an individual, and without regard to the amount, or value extracted from any other individual, or class of individuals."[417] And the great nineteenth-century jurist Thomas Cooley emphasized point two: there is no taking if "the burdens . . . fall ratably upon all who in justice should bear them."[418]

Other commentators have derived similar, arguably relevant factors. Taxes are general obligations, usually to be satisfied with payments of money, while a taking operates on particular property of a particular taxpayer. And with a taking, the injured party is compensated directly, generally in cash. In contrast, an "injured" citizen must look for "compensation" for the payment of his tax dollars to the more generalized protections provided to citizens.

The distinctions described above ring true to varying extents, but they are for the most part the products of academic inquiry rather than judicial decision-making. And that probably will continue to be the case. Whatever the principles that should be applied, courts are unlikely to determine that a purported tax gives rise to a governmental obligation to compensate.

The Compensation Clause and the Taxation of Federal Judges

> ***The Judges, both of the supreme and inferior Courts, shall hold their Offices during good Behaviour, and shall, at stated Times, receive for their Services, a Compensation, which shall not be diminished during their Continuation in Office.***
> —Article III, section 1, clause 2

The issue has a narrow focus, but, for those affected, the application of the Compensation Clause to the taxation of federal judges has been controversial, occupying the time of the Supreme Court as recently as 2001. The question is obvious: does Congress have the power to impose (or extend) a tax that would reach already-sitting federal judges, or should such a tax be forbidden because it would diminish their "compensation"? (A tax in place at the time new judges take office ought not to be limited under any interpretation of the Compensation Clause; such a tax would not be a diminishment of compensation occurring "during [the judges'] Continuation in Office." But, as discussed below, the Supreme Court took a contrary position for a while in Miles v. Graham (1925).)

In Hatter v. United States (2001), the Supreme Court held that the Compensation Clause permits Congress to apply "a generally applicable, nondiscriminatory tax to the salaries of federal judges, whether or not they were appointed before enactment of the tax."[419] Although that conclusion had not been clearly stated in earlier cases, it was consistent with the way commentators had interpreted the development of twentieth-century Compensation Clause jurisprudence.

In *Hatter*, the Court also held, however, that bringing the federal judiciary into the Social Security system, and thus imposing the Social Security wage tax on sitting judges who had previously been exempt from the tax, was discriminatory and was therefore a violation of the Clause. Surprising though that conclusion may have been—the Compensation Clause matters, or so it seemed—the Clause is unlikely to have significant future effect, as will be discussed at the end of this section.

Purposes of the Compensation Clause

The Compensation Clause was intended to help protect federal judges from external pressures, particularly those from Congress and the President, that might keep the judges from acting impartially. The Supreme Court wrote, in United States v. Will (1980), "The Compensation Clause has its roots in the longstanding Anglo-American tradition of an independent Judiciary. A Judiciary free from control by the Executive and Legislature is essential if there is a right to have claims decided by judges who are free from potential domination by other branches of government."[420]

A guaranteed job would mean little if a judge's compensation could be tied to the content of his decisions. As Justice Story wrote in 1833, "Without [the Compensation Clause], the other [provision], as to the tenure of office, would have been utterly nugatory, and indeed a mere mockery."[421] How impartial would a judge be if he knew that Congress might adjust his salary downward when he did not decide cases in the congressionally desired way or that Congress might give him a bonus when he acted as desired? In the first sentence of Federalist 79, Alexander Hamilton emphasized that, "[n]ext to permanency in office, nothing can contribute more to the independence of the judges than a fixed provision for their support."[422]

In theory, taxes could unconstitutionally diminish an otherwise "fixed provision for . . . support." For example, a tax directed only at the judiciary (or at specific judges) would clearly violate the Compensation Clause. For that matter, a facially neutral statute motivated by a congressional desire to influence the judiciary (if that bad motive could be demonstrated) would probably fail constitutional requirements.

But taxes so obviously aimed at the judiciary are almost impossible to imagine in modern times. The litigated issues have generally involved the treatment of taxes of general application as they affect federal judges. With such taxes, it is much more difficult to see that the Compensation Clause should play any role at all.

The founders did not discuss income taxation in 1787, of course, but there is nothing in the founding debates to suggest that federal judges were to be automatically exempt from the taxes that the founders did expect to be imposed, such as duties on imports, the burden of which was assumed to be borne by consumers. And the direct taxes on real estate enacted between 1798 and 1861—apportioned to meet the requirements of the Direct-Tax Clauses of the Constitution—contained no exemptions for federal judges, even though such taxes would obviously have "diminished" the economic position of any judge subject to the tax.

One might argue that generally applicable real-estate taxes and duties on imports are not limited by the Compensation Clause because they do not directly relate to "compensation," as that term is generally understood—salary, fringe benefits, that sort of thing. But surely the Clause would be implicated if a national real-estate tax were applicable only to federal judges; at least in some hypothetical circumstances, "compensation" must be interpreted to refer to the judges' overall economic positions if the purposes of the Clause are to be effectuated. The reason that judges should not be constitutionally exempt from national real-estate taxes and duties on imports is not that the judges' "compensation" is unaffected; it is that taxes of general application do not affect judicial independence.

The Compensation Clause as Applied to Taxation

Litigation about the relationship between the Compensation Clause and taxation did not occur until the twentieth century, but the antecedents of those later disputes can be found in the nineteenth century. When Congress enacted the Civil War income tax, Chief Justice Taney protested to the Secretary of the Treasury against applying the tax to judges: "The act in question, as you interpret it, diminishes the compensation of every judge three per cent, and if it can be diminished to that extent by the name of a tax, it may in the same way be reduced from time to time at the pleasure of the legislature."[423] Taney's position received a sympathetic response soon after the war's end. In 1869, Attorney General Hoar issued an opinion stating that a tax on judicial salaries would violate the Compensation Clause.[424] Four years later, the government refunded the taxes paid by federal judges.[425]

Twentieth-Century Litigation

The reluctance to tax federal judges carried over to a new century. In the first post–Sixteenth Amendment income tax statute, the compensation of federal judges was specifically exempted.[426] Feeling its way because the boundaries of the Amendment were unclear and not wanting to invite constitutional challenges, Congress drafted the Income Tax Law of 1913 conservatively, not seeking to tax many items that might have been within congressional power.

Wartime revenue needs overcame congressional caution, however, and, in the Revenue Act of 1918, Congress extended the tax base, "including in the case of the President of the United States [and] the judges of the Supreme and inferior courts of the United States . . . the compensation received as such."[427] A federal judge appointed to the bench in 1899, long before the effective date of the Act—and long before the Sixteenth Amendment—challenged the application of the Revenue Act to him, culminating in the Supreme Court's decision in Evans v. Gore (1920).

In *Evans*, the Supreme Court concluded that the tax was invalid under the Compensation Clause. Despite a dissent from Justice Holmes (who thought the tax would have been valid anyway, but who also suggested that the Sixteenth Amendment, with its reference to "incomes . . . from whatever source derived," should have removed any doubt), the majority opinion reads as if there were no question about the right result. Justice Van Devanter concluded in effect that no diminution in compensation means no income tax on judicial salaries, regardless of whether the tax reaches other government officials and regardless of whether it applies generally. The Court did not explain what the danger to judicial independence was from such a tax.

The Court in *Evans* had not seemed to rely on the fact that the judge was already sitting when the Revenue Act of 1918 went into effect, but some commentators suggested that fact might have been crucial to the result in the case. If a judge assumes office when a tax is already on the books, so that he can take the tax into account in calculating his future economic position, how can he claim that his compensation has been diminished during his continuance in office? In Miles v. Graham (1925), the Supreme Court nevertheless concluded that such a judge was also protected from federal income taxation.

Judge Graham's appointment was effective September 1, 1919, after the Revenue Act of 1918 was in place. So, asked Justice McReynolds, "[d]oes the circumstance that [Graham's] appointment came after the taxing act require a different view concerning his right to exemption?"[428] The answer (for all but dissenting Justice Brandeis) was *no:*

> The words and history of the clause indicate that the purpose was to impose upon Congress the duty definitely to declare what sum shall be received by each judge out of the public funds and the times for payment. When this duty has been complied with, the amount specified becomes the compensation which is protected against diminution during his continuance in office.[429]

The applicable statute said Judge Graham should be paid $7,500 and that, said Justice McReynolds, meant he should be left with $7,500 after taxes.

The result in *Miles* was short-lived, however. The Court again considered the Compensation Clause in O'Malley v. Woodrough (1939). In the Revenue Act of 1932, Congress had provided that the statutory term *gross income* would include compensation of "judges of courts of the United States taking office after June 6, 1932."[430] Fitting within that defined category, Judge Woodrough brought suit, reasonably arguing that, under *Miles*, the tax could not be applied to him.

Judge Woodrough lost, and the difference between the Court's analysis in 1939 and the two cases from the 1920s is the difference between day and night. The Court concluded that the tax did not affect judicial independence, and the justices were obviously irritated that Woodrough was seeking to avoid obligations applicable to ordinary citizens. Justice Frankfurter wrote,

> To suggest that [the tax] makes inroads upon the independence of judges who took office after Congress had thus charged them with the common duties of citizenship, by making them bear their aliquot share of the cost of maintaining the Government, is to trivialize the great historic experience on which the framers based the safeguards of Article III, § 1.[431]

Nevertheless, Justice Frankfurter said nothing directly about the continuing vitality of *Evans*, and he could not even bring himself to say that *Miles* had been overruled. Frankfurter wrote only that "to the extent that what the Court now says is inconsistent with what was said in *Miles v. Graham*, the latter cannot survive."[432]

Miles had clearly been rejected, however, and because *Miles* rested exclusively on *Evans*, the repudiation of *Miles* necessarily eviscerated *Evans* as well. This interpretation was confirmed in United States v. Will (1980), where the Court noted the obvious: "Because *Miles* relied on *Evans v. Gore*, *O'Malley* must also be read to undermine the reasoning of *Evans*."[433] But "undermining" is not the same as "overruling," and the Court was forced to hear yet another tax-related, Compensation-Clause case, Hatter v. United States (2001), to remove any residual doubt about the validity of taxes of general application that fall on federal judges.

Hatter v. United States

Judge Terry Hatter and several other federal judges sued in 1989, challenging the application to them of the wage taxes that fund the Social Security old-age, survivors', and disability insurance (OASDI) program and the Medicare insurance program. Prior to 1983, most federal employees, including judges, were exempt from Social Security taxes because of retirement systems established by the federal government on their behalf. But a 1982 tax act subjected federal judges to the Medicare tax,[434] and the Social Security Amendments of 1983 imposed the OASDI wage tax on the judges.[435] Hatter and the other judges were already on the bench when the wage taxes became effective—hence the claim that their compensation had been unconstitutionally diminished.

With the statutory changes, Congress was trying to increase revenue for the Social Security system, not to attack the judiciary, and the changes also imposed the wage taxes for the first time on several other federal officials, including the President, the Vice President, cabinet members, and members of Congress. At bottom, the changes merely required treating most government officials in the same way other American citizens had been treated for decades.

Since the Court had not explicitly overruled *Evans*, the lower courts in *Hatter* had followed that case. With only Justice Thomas dissenting, however (and two justices not participating), the Supreme Court tossed the last shovelful of dirt on *Evans's* grave: "We now overrule *Evans* insofar as it holds that the Compensation Clause forbids Congress to apply a generally applicable, nondiscriminatory tax to the salaries of federal judges, whether or not they were appointed before enactment of the tax."[436] Not surprisingly, the Court, over the dissents of Justices Scalia and Thomas, upheld the application of the Medicare tax to federal judges.

But the Court also held, with all seven participating justices in agreement, that the extension of the OASDI tax to judges sitting in 1983 was in fact discriminatory, and therefore invalid. That result seemed to indicate that the Compensation Clause still has life in the taxation context. As will be discussed presently, however, the holding on the OASDI tax is unlikely to have significant future effect.

Taxes of General Application. The most important part of *Hatter* was the repudiation, once and for all, of the core of Evans v. Gore (1920) and the acceptance of the proposition that the Compensation Clause affects only those taxes that discriminate against the judiciary.

As Justice Breyer wrote for the Court, "In our view, the Clause does not prevent Congress from imposing a 'non-discriminatory tax laid generally' upon judges and other citizens, . . . but it does prohibit taxation that singles out judges for specially unfavorable treatment."[437] The Court had decided, in United States v. Will (1980), that Congress may not reduce judicial salaries, even if done as part of a nondiscriminatory cost-cutting move.[438] But, with taxation, the only concern is whether there has been discrimination against the judiciary in a way that might damage judicial independence:

> [T]here is no good reason why a judge should not share the tax burdens borne by all citizens. We concede that this Court [in *Will*] has held that the Legislature cannot *directly* reduce judicial salaries even as part of an equitable effort to reduce *all* Government

salaries. . . . But a tax law . . . affects compensation indirectly, not directly. . . . [The] prophylactic considerations that may justify an absolute rule forbidding direct salary reductions are absent here. . . . In practice, the likelihood that a nondiscriminatory tax represents a disguised legislative effort to influence the judicial will is virtually nonexistent. Hence the potential threats to judicial independence that underlie the Constitution's compensation guarantee cannot justify a special judicial exemption from a commonly shared tax, not even as a preventive measure to counter those threats.[439]

The OASDI Tax and Discrimination. The Court in *Hatter* did, however, find a constitutional problem with the extension of the OASDI tax to sitting federal judges. The Court concluded that judges were generally hit harder by 1983 Act changes than were other government officials. Federal judges, and (with an exception or two) only federal judges, had increased tax obligations from the changes, with no compensating benefits.

That result was discriminatory, said the Court, even though there was no evidence that Congress was acting to single out the judiciary for unfortunate consequences, and the effect of the legislation was merely to bring the judiciary into the broadly applicable Social Security system. Justice Breyer explained:

The Government also argues that there is no evidence here that Congress singled out judges for special treatment in order to intimidate, influence, or punish them. But this Court has never insisted upon such evidence. To require it is to invite legislative efforts that embody, but lack evidence of, some such intent, engendering suspicion among the branches and consequently undermining that mutual respect that the Constitution demands. . . . Nothing in the record discloses anything other than benign congressional motives. If the Compensation Clause is to offer meaningful protection, however, we cannot limit that protection to instances in which the Legislature manifests, say, direct hostility to the Judiciary.[440]

Of course a tax that openly discriminates against the judiciary should be forbidden—the danger to judicial independence from such a tax is obvious—but Justice Breyer was less than persuasive in contending that extending the OASDI tax was similarly dangerous. Is it really possible that Congress—a group of 535 very independent, very voluble people—could ever take an action motivated by hostility without leaving traces along the way?

The Court's analysis of the OASDI tax also ignored the context in which Congress had been legislating. After *Hatter*, we know that the OASDI taxes could constitutionally have been imposed on federal judges at the same time they were imposed on other Americans. But the 1935 Congress that established the Social Security system knew nothing of the sort. At that time, *Evans* was the law, and Congress legislated accordingly. When the Court's understanding of the Compensation Clause changed dramatically, however, Congress had no way to adjust. Once the judges were exempt, because the Court had initially misunderstood the Compensation Clause, Congress could not extend the taxes to sitting judges without having the extension characterized as discriminatory. The Supreme Court had put Congress in a Catch-22 situation.

The Future Effect of the Compensation Clause on Taxation

Whatever the merits of the Supreme Court's consideration of the OASDI tax in *Hatter*, however, that analysis should have little or no effect on the subsequent treatment of taxation under the Compensation Clause. A *Hatter*-like set of facts, involving the repeal of an already existing tax exemption for federal judges, cannot arise again: no similar exemption remains on the books, and Congress is unlikely to exempt federal judges from any other generally applicable tax in the future. Moreover, as Justice Breyer noted in *Hatter*, the likelihood that a facially nondiscriminatory tax could represent an attack on the judiciary is "virtually nonexistent."

With *Evans* overruled, no longer can anyone seriously argue that federal judges are constitutionally exempt from a generally applicable income tax or from an increase in rates under a generally applicable income tax. Although Justice Thomas, in a two-sentence dissent in *Hatter*, wrote that the "Court was correct in *Evans v. Gore* . . . when it held that any tax that reduces a judge's net compensation violates Article III of the Constitution,"[441] that statement was far removed from the common understanding of the last several decades. And it was rejected by the six other justices sitting in *Hatter*.

All of this leaves the Compensation Clause to prohibit only those taxes that clearly discriminate against judges, and serious congressional consideration of discriminatory taxes would be difficult to imagine even if there were no Compensation Clause. The Clause, therefore, seems unlikely ever again to constrain the national taxing power.

One caveat is necessary, however. What the *Hatter* Court said about nondiscriminatory taxes is consistent with the historically understood rationale for the Compensation Clause, to protect judicial independence. But the Court has suggested that the Clause has a second purpose as well. The Court stated in United States v. Will (1980),

> As well as promoting judicial independence, [the Clause] ensures a prospective judge that, in abandoning private practice—more often than not more lucrative than the bench—the compensation of the new post will not diminish. Beyond doubt, such assurance has served to attract able lawyers to the bench and thereby enhances the quality of justice.[442]

This self-serving pronouncement is not derived from discussions of the founding era, and, whatever its merits in policing the Compensation Clause in non-tax contexts (of which *Will* was an example), it ought to have no effect on evaluating the legitimacy of a tax that affects the population as a whole. Nevertheless, if the Court takes seriously this open-ended justification for preserving the economic positions of federal judges, it is possible that, in special circumstances, a tax that does not affect judicial independence may still be treated as violating the Compensation Clause.

REQUISITIONS AND THE CONSTITUTION

A question that has no clear answer, and probably will never have a clear answer, is whether it is now within Congress's power under the Constitution to issue requisitions to the states, as was done, often unsuccessfully, under the Articles of Confederation. Since the Constitution was intended to increase national power, perhaps it should be interpreted as also having preserved the powers of the national government that existed (at least in theory) under the Articles, including the power to issue requisitions.

To the extent that anyone thinks about this question at all, however, the conventional wisdom is that requisitions died with ratification of the Constitution. The Constitution itself makes no mention of requisitions, and, it is generally assumed, the silence was deliberate. As discussed in Chapter 2, several attempts by anti-federalists to preserve requisitions as the initial step in revenue-raising failed, and the inference usually drawn from that failure is that the power to tax individuals through direct and indirect taxes superseded the unhappy requisitions process.

As a practical matter, the conclusion that requisitions are dead is probably right. It is difficult to imagine today's Congress seeking to raise money by sending revenue directives to state governments. Such a step would be controversial politically and, in any event, there are other, more efficient ways for Congress to raise revenue—the income tax, for example.

But to say that requisitions are not politically palatable or economically necessary is not to say that they are unconstitutional. Despite the founders' rejection of requisitions as a primary revenue source—on that point there can be no doubt—it is not at all clear that, as a matter of law, the requisitions power expired with the Constitution.

In fact, many in the founding generation thought that requisitions survived ratification of the Constitution. For anti-federalists, survival of requisitions remained a fervent hope. The hope may seem to have defied logic, given the anti-federalists' failure to obtain the constitutional language they wanted, but all that had been rejected was the use of requisitions as a mandatory prerequisite to invoking the direct-tax power. There had been no specific rejection of requisitions *per se*.

Furthermore, it was not only anti-federalists who saw continued life for requisitions. Permitting the federal government to tax individuals directly, circumventing the states, added to national power and is thus perfectly consistent with the general understanding of the Constitution's purposes—to increase the power of the national government at the expense of the states. If the requisitions power had been taken away, however, the Constitution would have shrunk national power in an important respect—a counterintuitive result. And it is not at all obvious that the extension of power over individuals logically required a contraction of power over the states.

This last point has assumed importance in recent Supreme Court jurisprudence under the Tenth Amendment. For example, Justice Stevens wrote in dissent in New York v. United States (1992): "Nothing in . . . history suggests that the Federal Government may not also impose its will upon the several States as it did under the Articles. The Constitution enhanced, rather than diminished, the power of the Federal Government."[443]

In Federalist 36, Alexander Hamilton, the most nationalistic of all nationalists, left no doubt that he thought Congress could issue requisitions under the Constitution:

> It has been very properly observed by different speakers and writers on the side of the Constitution that if the exercise of the power of internal taxation by the Union should be judged beforehand upon mature consideration, or should be discovered on experiment to be really inconvenient, the federal government may forbear the use of it, and have recourse to requisitions in its stead. By way of answer to this, it has been triumphantly asked, Why not in the first instance omit that ambiguous power and rely upon the latter resource? Two solid answers may be given. The first is that the actual exercise of the power may be found both convenient and necessary; for it is impossible to prove in theory, or otherwise than by experiment, that it cannot be advantageously exercised. The contrary, indeed, appears most probable. The second answer is that the existence of such a power in the Constitution will have a strong influence in giving efficacy to requisitions. When the States know that the Union can supply itself without their agency, it will be a powerful motive for exertion on their part.[444]

Hamilton disagreed with the anti-federalists that indirect and direct taxes should be used only if and when requisitions failed, because the country needed to try new, more efficient forms of revenue-raising. But he thought that requisitions remained as an important backup to the power to tax individuals.

There is also some support in *The Federalist* for the idea that the direct-tax apportionment rule, although it did not mandate requisitions, was consistent with the continued use of a requisitions process. (Indeed, some anti-federalists explicitly stated that the apportionment rule should be interpreted as preserving a system of requisitions-in-disguise.) The census would determine each state's share of the total to be raised through direct taxation, and the federal government could give the order to each state for so many dollars. Each state could then decide how to satisfy that obligation—perhaps even deciding what and when to tax.

The most extensive description is found in Madison's Federalist 44. If a direct tax is imposed—unlikely, but possible—the tax collectors will ordinarily be state officials because they will be collecting an amount equal to the state's direct-tax quota, just as was true under the requisitions system:

> [I]t is probable that this power [of collecting internal as well as external taxes] will not be resorted to, except for supplemental purposes of revenue; that an option will then be given to the States to supply their quotas by previous collections of their own; and that the eventual collection, under the immediate authority of the Union, will generally be made by the officers, and according to the rules, appointed by the several States.[445]

To be sure, Madison was not writing about a full-fledged requisitions system: the states as states would participate only if they elected to, and Madison assumed that the dollars involved would not exceed the states' already existing revenue capacities. But the similarities to the requisitions system are there.

Perhaps the strongest evidence that requisitions survived under the Constitution, at least in the minds of many in the founding generation, is found in debates leading to the enactment of the first direct-tax statute, finalized in 1798. In a 1796 report on direct taxation, prepared at congressional request, Treasury Secretary Oliver Wolcott suggested three possible approaches that could be followed: Congress could specify the objects of taxation; Congress could elect to tax whatever items the states were already taxing directly; or Congress could have the states determine what to tax, make the actual collections, and turn over the appropriate amounts to the federal government.[446]

Different participants in the policy-making process had different views about the merits of each of Wolcott's possibilities, but none apparently saw constitutional constraints on any of the choices. Wolcott himself, for example, rejected reliance on state systems on practical, not constitutional, grounds—because that possibility "partakes of the system of requisitions . . . , which utterly failed under the late Confederation, and to remedy which, was one great object of establishing the present Government."[447] But Representative Joseph B. Varnum of Massachusetts defended the method, also obviously assuming its constitutionality:

> The several States being convinced that the authority of the General Government would be exercised if the money was not furnished by the time prefixed, they would in all probability make the remittance; but if any State should fail of doing it, this Government would make the assessment on the inhabitants of the delinquent States. . . .[448]

While the House Ways and Means Committee finally recommended directly taxing land, improvements, and slaves under a national system—the form of direct taxation eventually adopted[449]—the Committee had originally proposed that the federal statute should incorporate state law, and the full House initially accepted that proposal.[450]

After reviewing the legislative history of the 1798 direct-tax statute, Professor David Currie concluded that no one saw "any constitutional impediment to laying taxes that differed from one state to another, or to delegating to the states authority to define and collect federal taxes."[451] No one, that is, saw a constitutional prohibition against ordering the states to play a central role in the national revenue system.

In 1813 it was still assumed that the states had a role to play. A short-lived wartime direct-tax statute enacted that year delegated significant responsibility to the states. The statute went so far as to apportion the tax liability throughout the United States on a county-by-county basis, but "each state may vary, by an act of its legislature, the respective quotas imposed by this act on its several counties and districts, so as more equally and equitably to apportion the tax."[452] Moreover, the statute provided that the *states* were to pay their quotas to the Treasury, with a discount of up to fifteen percent if a state made payment on a timely basis.[453]

The idea that the Constitution permits requisitions, or something like requisitions, survived well beyond the founding era. The instances of explicitly direct taxation are few, but the Supreme Court's majority opinion in the second decision in Pollock v. Farmers' Loan & Trust Co. (1895), which held that an unapportioned income tax was unconstitutional, confirmed that at least some justices thought a role could be played by the states under a direct-tax regime. Chief Justice Melville Fuller wrote that, if a state wanted to serve as a buffer between the national government and its citizens, as Madison had suggested in Federalist 44, it could do so:

> [The states] did not grant the power of direct taxation without regard to their own condition and resources as states; but they granted the power of apportioned direct taxation, a power just as efficacious to serve the needs of the general government, but securing to the states the opportunity to pay the amount apportioned, and to recoup from their own citizens in the most feasible way, and in harmony with their systems of self-government.[454]

The states, that is, could decide whether to position themselves as intermediaries between the states' residents and the national direct-tax power that would otherwise extend directly to those residents.

Like James Madison in Federalist 44, Chief Justice Fuller described an arrangement that differs in some details from the requisitions system used under the Articles of Confederation. But the Fuller opinion indicates that the idea of something like requisitions had not died a century after the ratification of the Constitution. Regardless of whether a system of requisitions is a good idea—most founders thought not, and it is all but inconceivable that such a system could be seriously advanced today—requisitions are not necessarily unconstitutional.

THE EFFECT OF AMBIGUITY IN UNDERSTANDING TAXING PROVISIONS IN THE CONSTITUTION

Few constitutional provisions that affect serious issues are so clear in application that they decide all conceivable questions without doubt. Interpretation is required with the taxing provisions in the Constitution, just as with other clauses.

How then should cases be resolved when there are significant factors pointing in different directions? How, for example, should we decide whether a tax is a "direct tax" or whether, even if it is a direct tax, it is exempted from the apportionment requirement because it is a "tax on incomes"? Or—another example—how should we decide whether a tax or duty falls *on* exported articles?

No single conception of "direct taxes" or "Articles exported" will be accepted by all commentators, including those who believe the historical record matters and who carefully study that record. Taxation issues in Philadelphia were caught up in the slavery question, and the focus in discussions was not always on the right definitional issues. It is also true that the founders had different understandings of the scope of many constitutional provisions;[455] a disagreement in the debates about limits on the taxing power is not surprising.

Nevertheless, the same sorts of things could be said about most, if not all, important constitutional provisions—if by "important" we mean often discussed. (Some constitutional provisions are not heavily discussed precisely because there is little or no dispute about their application.)[456] Noting the disagreement, the uncertainty, the possibility that the meaning may have been left "deliberately ambiguous"[457]—as Professor Jack Rakove has suggested—should be the beginning, not the end, of the process. With the Direct-Tax Clauses, ambiguity has been used as a justification for ignoring the Clauses altogether, or for latching onto Hylton v. United States (1796) as the best that we can do in interpreting the Clauses. But surely disregarding ambiguous clauses is a curious way to deal with what is, after all, the fundamental political and legal document of our country. When confronted with a real-world question about the "precise meaning" of a constitutional provision—Rufus King asked such a question about "direct taxes" at the Constitutional Convention and received no answer—judges, legislators, and even constitutional commentators do not have the luxury of not answering.

Even if we decide that the original meaning of the Direct-Tax Clauses is irretrievably lost in the antiquarian mists—and that the meaning of "incomes" in the Sixteenth Amendment is also hopelessly uncertain—we must decide what to do with those conclusions. Does doubt about the scope of congressional power mean that we should presume that the power exists? Or ought we to conclude that, if there is indeed serious doubt about the extent of congressional power, we should err on the side of restricting that power? To put those questions in modern terms, what is the default rule?

The Supreme Court has periodically indicated that it will not look closely at congressional power to impose taxes, because of the "reluctance of this Court to enlarge by construction, limitations upon the sovereign power of taxation by Article I, Section 8, so vital to the maintenance of the National Government."[458] The default rule has therefore generally been one of deference to Congress, but why should that be so?

A related question is how to interpret the validity of forms of taxation that were not discussed in late-eighteenth-century America because they were unknown. How should we interpret silence in the founding debates, when only silence could have been expected? As Professor Edward McCaffery has noted,

Tax would no doubt have played a much greater role in *The Federalist Papers* if they were being written today. . . . Madison's days were simpler ones, in which no one could possibly imagine the massive tax systems of the post-World War II era, where taxes take up one-third and more of national economies.[459]

Professor Sidney Ratner has argued that "[s]ince taxes on personal and corporate income, gifts, inheritances, and excess profits were not in existence in 1787, it is impossible to state dogmatically what the founders and the ratifiers of the Constitution would have thought of these taxes."[460] Fair enough. But is the default principle that the founders could not have meant to prohibit or limit a taxing power that they could barely imagine? Or is the appropriate principle that additional manifestations of taxing power, the classifications of which might not be clear under the constitutional categories, should have to satisfy limitations that were drafted, in part, because of concern about congressional abuse? The Court in *Pollock* suggested an answer different from the prevailing view today: "A direct tax cannot be taken out of the constitutional rule because the particular tax did not exist at the time the rule was prescribed."[461]

Of course, one could reasonably argue, as did the dissenters in *Pollock*, that by 1895, *Hylton* had come to define the constitutional landscape in the direct-tax area, and it should have been left unchallenged for that reason—even if the case was demonstrably wrong in some respects. The doctrine of *stare decisis* is not merely a matter of convenience; it has principle behind it.[462] And prudence might counsel us not to return to first principles if the country has moved so far away from those principles that recapturing them would be impossible. For example, paper money is here to stay even though—as discussed in the first part of this chapter—it was originally intended to be forbidden, and no constitutional amendment has dealt with that issue.[463]

Justice Edward Douglass White wrote in his dissent in the first *Pollock* decision that the Direct-Tax Clauses could not have been understood by the founders in a single way: "Those who accepted the compromise viewed the word 'direct' in different lights and expected different results to flow from its adoption. This was the natural result of the struggle which was terminated by the adoption of the provision as to representation and direct taxes."[464] White suggested that this disagreement—or what would have been disagreement had the matter been fully discussed—pointed toward accepting the 1796 *Hylton* analysis in 1895: "[I]f such difference existed, it is certainly sound to hold that a contemporaneous solution of a doubtful question, which has been often confirmed by this court, should not now be reversed."[465]

But a revival of careful scrutiny of congressional tax enactments today would be considerably less earth-shattering than was *Pollock* more than a hundred years ago, when the Court rejected much of the conventional judicial wisdom of the nineteenth century. And Congress has it within its own power to limit judicial scrutiny of tax statutes by interpreting its own powers narrowly; the most clearly constitutional route for Congress is not to take the national revenue system in entirely new directions.

In fact, after the Sixteenth Amendment, revival of careful scrutiny would have far less significant effects than *Pollock* had. Modern government would not come to a grinding halt if some traditional notions were reinvigorated. With the Amendment on the books, it is not as though the national government is going to be bereft of revenue sources. At worst, the government would be left with the forms currently available, with perhaps a few constitutional challenges at the margins. No one but the craziest of tax protesters can have serious doubts today about the constitutionality of an unapportioned income tax—at least as long as Congress makes a serious attempt to define "income" and does not try to hide a non-income tax in the guise of a "tax on incomes."

In any event, twice in the 1990s the Supreme Court struck down tax statutes as they applied to exports. In this one area of taxation, where the Export Clause is implicated, the Court seems to be paying attention to constitutional limitations on the taxing power. If that is so with the Export Clause, is it clear that it should not be so with other limitations on the taxing power?

Notes to Part II

1. *Knowlton,* 177 U.S. at 84.

2. Nelson Lund, "The Uniformity Clause," *University of Chicago Law Review* 51 (1984): 1193, 1216 n.103 (citing *Ptasynski,* 462 U.S. at 77 & n.5, 78, 85).

3. David P. Currie, *The Constitution in Congress: The Federalist Period, 1789–1801* (Chicago, University of Chicago Press, 1997): pp. 60–61.

4. *Ptasynski,* 462 U.S. at 80–81 (quoting 1 Joseph Story, *Commentaries on the Constitution of the United States* (Thomas Cooley ed., Boston: Little Brown, 1873) (1833) § 957).

5. Lund, *Uniformity:* pp. 1194–95 (emphasis added).

6. Boris I. Bittker, "Constitutional Limits on the Taxing Power of the Federal Government," *Tax Lawyer* 41 (1987): 3, 10.

7. *Knowlton,* 178 U.S. at 83–106.

8. *Head Money Cases,* 112 U.S. at 594.

9. *Head Money Cases,* 112 U.S. at 583–84.

10. *Head Money Cases,* 112 U.S. at 589–90.

11. *Head Money Cases,* 112 U.S. at 594.

12. *Head Money Cases,* 112 U.S. at 595.

13. *Head Money Cases,* 112 U.S. at 595 (citation omitted).

14. *Head Money Cases,* 112 U.S. at 594.

15. *See Knowlton,* 178 U.S. at 83–84.

16. *Knowlton,* 178 U.S. at 86.

17. *Knowlton,* 178 U.S. at 87.

18. *Knowlton,* 178 U.S. at 95–106.

19. *Knowlton,* 178 U.S. at 87–89.

20. James Wilson, "Speech" (State House, Oct. 6, 1787) [hereinafter *October 1787 Speech*], *in Friends of the Constitution: Writings of the "Other" Federalists 1787–1788* (Colleen A. Sheehan & Gary L. McDowell eds., Indianapolis: Liberty Fund, 1998) [hereinafter *Friends*]: pp. 102, 106.

21. *See Knowlton,* 178 U.S. at 89.

22. *Knowlton,* 178 U.S. at 89.

23. Pub. L. No. 96–223, 94 Stat. 229.

24. *Head Money Cases,* 112 U.S. at 594.

25. *Ptasynski,* 462 U.S. at 84.

26. *Ptasynski,* 462 U.S. at 84 (citing *Knowlton,* 178 U.S. at 106); *see also* Lund, *Uniformity:* p. 1203 n.46 (criticizing *Ptasynski* Court's interpretation of *Knowlton*).

27. Lund, *Uniformity:* p. 1206.

28. Lund, *Uniformity:* p. 1203.

29. *Ptasynski,* 462 U.S. at 85 (citing *Regional Rail Reorganization Act Cases,* 419 U.S. at 160–61).

30. Lund, *Uniformity:* p. 86.

31. *Ptasynski,* 462 U.S. at 85–86

32. *Ptasynski,* 462 U.S. at 84.

33. U.S. Const. Art. I, § 8, cl. 4.

34. *See Regional Rail Reorganization Act Cases,* 419 U.S. at 156–61.

35. *Regional Rail Reorganization Act Cases,* 419 U.S. at 160–61.

36. Lund, *Uniformity:* p. 86.

37. In Patton v. Brady (1902), the Supreme Court concluded that a levy on tobacco and snuff was an excise because it was imposed "on an article manufactured for consumption, and imposed at a period intermediate [*sic*] the commencement of manufacture and the final consumption of the article." *Patton,* 184 U.S. at 618. Although many taxes on the ownership of property were historically understood to be direct, the Federal Circuit concluded, in Union Electric Co. v. United States (2004), that "an excise tax (in contradistinction to a direct tax) is a tax imposed on the acquisition, ownership, or use of particular kinds of property that falls short of being a general tax on the whole of an individual's personal property." *Union Electric,* 363 F.3d at 1304.

38. *The Federalist No. 21,* at 142 (Alexander Hamilton) (Clinton Rossiter ed., New York: Mentor Books, 1961).

39. *The Federalist No. 12,* at 93 (Alexander Hamilton) (Clinton Rossiter ed., New York: Mentor Books, 1961).

40. *The Federalist No. 35,* at 212 (Alexander Hamilton) (Clinton Rossiter ed., New York: Mentor Books, 1961).

41. *The Federalist No. 35,* at 212.

42. James Wilson, "Speech" (Pa. Convention, Dec. 4, 1787), in *Friends:* pp. 231, 245.

43. *The Federalist No. 21,* at 142.

44. "Essays of Brutus V," *New York Journal* (Dec. 13, 1787), *reprinted in* 2 *The Complete Anti-Federalist* (Herbert J. Storing ed., Chicago: University of Chicago Press, 1981): pp. 388, 392–93.

45. *See, e.g.,* "Essays of Brutus I," *New York Journal* (Oct. 18, 1787), *reprinted in* 2 Storing, *Complete:* pp. 363, 366 ("[W]hen the foederal government begins to exercise the right of taxation in all its parts, the legislatures of the several states will find it impossible to raise monies to support their governments.").

46. Debating the merits of a constitutional amendment that would have made requisitions the primary revenue source, Elbridge Gerry referred in 1789 to the possible "annihilation of the State Governments." 1 *Annals of Congress* 776 (Joseph Gales ed., 1834).

47. 3 Jonathan Elliot, *The Debates in the Several State Conventions on the Adoption of the Federal Constitution* (Philadelphia: J. B. Lippincott Co., 1836): p. 253 (June 11, 1788).

48. *Hylton,* 3 U.S. (3 Dall.) at 173 (Chase, J.); *Hylton,* 3 U.S. (3 Dall.) at 181 (Iredell, J.).

49. 2 Story, *Commentaries* § 948, at 420–21.

50. U.S. Const. Art. I, § 8, cl. 1.

51. U.S. Const. Art. I, § 8, cl. 1.

52. U.S. Const. Art. I, § 9, cl. 5.

53. U.S. Const. Art. I, § 9, cl. 1.

54. U.S. Const. Art. I, § 10, cl. 2.

55. U.S. Const. Art. I, § 2, cl. 3; U.S. Const. Art. I, § 9, cl. 4.

56. *Pollock,* 157 U.S. at 557.

57. *See* Dwight W. Morrow, "The Income Tax Amendment," *Columbia Law Review* 10 (1910): 379, 412.

58. *Brushaber,* 240 U.S. at 18–19.

59. *See* Act of Aug. 5, 1861, Ch. 45, 12 Stat. 292; Act of Mar. 5, 1816, Ch. 24, 3 Stat. 255; Act of Feb. 27, 1815, Ch. 60, 3 Stat. 216; Act of Jan. 9, 1815, Ch. 21, 3 Stat. 164; Act of Aug. 2, 1813, Ch. 37, 3 Stat. 53; Act of July 14, 1798, Ch. 75, 1 Stat. 597.

60. Calvin H. Johnson, "Purging Out *Pollock*: The Constitutionality of Federal Wealth or Sales Taxes," *Tax Notes* 97 (2002): 1723, 1725.

61. *See, e.g.,* Arthur C. Graves, "Inherent Improprieties in the Income Tax Amendment to the Federal Constitution," *Yale Law Journal* 19 (1910): 505, 515 ("The qualification of direct taxes is the only provision in the entire Constitution which appears twice in that instrument. This fact ought to teach us to hold it in still higher regard and to respect the more the earnestness and intent of the framers who placed it there.").

62. *See* Act of June 2, 1924, Ch. 233, 43 Stat. 253.

63. Bittker, *Constitutional:* p. 10.

64. N. Trickett, "The Income Tax: Is It Constitutional? A Rejoinder," *American Law Review* 29 (1895): 73, 75.

65. Act of July 14, 1798, Ch. 75, 1 Stat. 597.

66. A capitation tax is specifically denominated a direct tax in Article I, section 9, clause 4, and a lump-sum head tax would seem to be geographically uniform today. Even with a lump-sum head tax, however, the apportionment rule would not have been surplusage when the special counting rules for slaves and "Indians not taxed" were still in effect.

67. Calvin H. Johnson, "Barbie Dolls in the Archeological Dig: Professor Johnson Responds," *Tax Notes* 100 (2003): 832, 840.

68. Johnson, *Barbie Dolls*: p. 838.

69. Johnson, *Barbie Dolls*: p. 838.

70. Owen M. Fiss, *History of the Supreme Court of the United States: Troubled Beginnings of the Modern State, 1888–1910* (New York: Macmillan Pub. Co., 1993): pp. 88–89.

71. *See, e.g.,* Johnson, *Purging*: p. 1727; Bruce Ackerman, "Taxation and the Constitution," *Columbia Law Review* 99 (1999): 1, 54.

72. *See* U.S. Const. Art. I, § 9, cl. 5.

73. 4 *Annals of Congress* 730 (1794) (describing why he was voting against the unapportioned carriage tax later at issue in *Hylton*).

74. *See, e.g., The Federalist No. 36,* at 220 (Alexander Hamilton) (Clinton Rossiter ed., New York: Mentor Books, 1961).

75. Johnson, *Purging:* p. 1725.

76. 2 Max Farrand ed., *The Records of the Federal Convention of 1787* (New Haven: Yale University Press, 1937): p. 350 (Aug. 20, 1787); *see, e.g., Union Electric,* 363 F.3d at 1297 (quoting King).

77. Morrow, *Income Tax:* p. 398.

78. Keith L. Dougherty, *Collective Action Under the Articles of Confederation* (New York: Cambridge University Press, 2001): p. 151.

79. 2 Elliot, *Debates:* p. 36 (Jan. 17, 1788).

80. 2 Elliot, *Debates:* p. 57 (Jan. 21, 1788).

81. *See The Federalist No. 21,* at 141.

82. 3 Elliot, *Debates:* p. 300 (June 12, 1788).

83. Letter from James Madison to George Thompson (Jan. 29, 1789), *reprinted in* 11 The Papers of James Madison (Robert A. Rutland & Charles F. Hobson eds., Charlottesville: University Press of Virginia, 1977): pp. 433, 436.

84. *Hylton,* 3 U.S. (3 Dall.) at 174 (Chase, J.).

85. *Hylton,* 3 U.S. (3 Dall.) at 181.

86. *Hylton,* 3 U.S. (3 Dall.) at 174; *see also Hylton,* 3 U.S. (3 Dall.) at 181–82 (Iredell, J.).

87. Johnson, *Purging:* p. 1725.

88. Charles J. Bullock, "The Origin, Purpose and Effect of the Direct-Tax Clause of the Federal Constitution" (pt. 2), *Political Science Quarterly* 15 (1900): 452.

89. Edwin R. A. Seligman, *The Income Tax* (New York: Macmillan, 1914) (1911): p. 552.

90. Seligman, *Income Tax:* p. 559.

91. Ackerman, *Taxation:* p. 58; *see also* Ackerman, *Taxation:* p. 31; Johnson, *Purging:* pp. 1724–25, 1734.

92. 2 Farrand, *Records:* p. 106 n.* (July 24, 1787).

93. Morris apparently did not want apportionment for direct taxation to survive; he "meant it as a bridge to assist over a certain gulph; having passed the gulph the bridge may be removed." 2 Farrand, *Records:* p. 106 (July 24, 1787) (footnote omitted). It survived nonetheless.

94. *The Federalist No. 54,* at 336 (James Madison) (Clinton Rossiter ed., New York: Mentor Books, 1961).

95. *The Federalist No. 54,* at 340–41.

96. *See* Consider Arms et al., "Reasons for Dissent," *Hampshire Gazette* (Apr. 9, 1788), *reprinted in* 4 Storing, *Complete:* pp. 255, 256.

97. *Hylton,* 3 U.S. (3 Dall.) at 181 (Iredell, J.).

98. Johnson, *Purging:* p. 1726.

99. *Lee v. Weisman,* 505 U.S. at 616 n.3 (Souter, J., concurring).

100. Johnson, *Barbie Dolls:* p. 832. Johnson uses the "tax killer" argument in support of the proposition that the apportionment rule should be ignored.

101. *See* Act of Aug. 5, 1861, Ch. 45, 12 Stat. 292; Act of Mar. 5, 1816, Ch. 24, 3 Stat. 255; Act of Feb. 27, 1815, Ch. 60, 3 Stat. 216; Act of Jan. 9, 1815, Ch. 21, 3 Stat. 164; Act of Aug. 2, 1813, Ch. 37, 3 Stat. 53; Act of July 14, 1798, Ch. 75, 1 Stat. 597.

102. James Wilson, *October 1787 Speech:* p. 106.

103. Socius, "Some Thoughts on the Fears Which many Appear to Entertain About the Federal Constitution," *Carlisle Gazette* (Nov. 14, 1787), *reprinted in Friends:* pp. 164, 166.

104. Roy Douglas, *Taxation in Britain Since 1660* (New York: St. Martin's Press, 1999): p. 4.

105. Daniel N. Shaviro, "Psychic Income Revisited: Response to Professors Johnson and Dodge," *Tax Law Review* 45 (1990): 707, 711 n.17.

106. *South Carolina v. Baker,* 485 U.S. at 524.

107. *Graves,* 306 U.S. at 480, quoted in *South Carolina v. Baker,* 485 U.S. at 520. In Union Electric Co. v. United States (2004), the Federal Circuit cited New York v. Graves (1937) in support of the proposition that the Court "seemed to disapprove of the reasoning

that an income tax on proceeds from the use of land was equivalent to a tax on the land itself." *Union Electric,* 363 F.3d at 1299 n.8.

108. *See* Home Mut. Ins. Co. v. Commissioner, 639 F.2d 333, 350 n.3 (7th Cir. 1980) (per curiam) (en banc) (suggesting that *Graves* effectively overruled *Pollock,* "thereby making the Sixteenth Amendment superfluous").

109. *Union Electric,* 363 F.3d at 1299 (footnote omitted).

110. Ackerman, *Taxation:* p. 55.

111. Ackerman, *Taxation:* p. 3.

112. *See* Johnson, *Purging:* p. 1733; Ackerman, *Taxation:* pp. 33–39; Erik M. Jensen, "The Taxing Power, the Sixteenth Amendment, and the Meaning of 'Incomes,'" *Arizona State Law Journal* 33 (2001): 1057, 1117–20.

113. *See* Johnson, *Purging:* pp. 1731–33.

114. *See South Dakota v. Dole,* 483 U.S. at 207 n.2 ("The level of deference to the congressional decision is such that the Court has more recently questioned whether 'general welfare' is a judicially enforceable restriction at all." (citing *Buckley v. Valeo,* 424 U.S. at 90–91); *Hawaii Housing Authority v. Midkiff,* 467 U.S. at 239 ("When the legislature has spoken [in defining 'public use'], the public interest has been declared in terms well-nigh conclusive." (quoting *Berman v. Parker,* 348 U.S. at 31)).

115. Victor Thuronyi, "The Concept of Income," *Tax Law Review* 46 (1990): 45, 53.

116. Thuronyi, *Concept:* p. 61.

117. Thuronyi, *Concept:* p. 101 (footnote omitted).

118. Marjorie E. Kornhauser, "The Constitutional Meaning of Income and the Income Taxation of Gifts," *Connecticut Law Review* 25 (1992): 1, 24.

119. Lawrence Zelenak, "Radical Tax Reform, the Constitution, and the Conscientious Legislator," *Columbia Law Review* 99 (1999): 833, 838.

120. *See* Jensen, *Taxing Power:* p. 1119.

121. U.S. Const. Amend. XVI.

122. Johnson, *Purging:* p. 1733 (quoting S.J.R. 25, 61st Cong., 1st Sess., 44 Cong. Rec. 1568 (Apr. 28, 1909)).

123. Johnson, *Purging:* p. 1733.

124. *See* Jensen, *Taxing Power:* p. 1120.

125. *Obear-Nester Glass Co.,* 217 F.2d at 58.

126. The requirement that compensation be paid for a taking constrains the legislature from defining "public use" in an excessively broad way. It serves the "role of surrogate assurance of public purpose." Laurence H. Tribe, *American Constitutional Law* (2d ed., Mineola: Foundation Press, 1988): p. 590.

127. *See, e.g.,* Ackerman, *Taxation:* pp. 42–46.

128. Income Tax Law of 1913, ch. 16, § II.B, 38 Stat. 167.

129. *Macomber,* 252 U.S. at 202.

130. *Eisner v. Towne,* 242 F. at 704 (emphasis added), quoted in *Macomber,* 252 U.S. at 202.

131. Revenue Act of 1916, Ch. 463, § 2(a), 39 Stat. 757.

132. *Macomber,* 252 U.S. at 203.

133. *Macomber,* 252 U.S. at 205.

134. *Macomber,* 252 U.S. at 206 (emphasis added).

135. *Macomber,* 252 U.S. at 206 (emphasis added).

136. *Macomber,* 252 U.S. at 207 (quoting *Stratton's Independence, Ltd. v. Howbert,* 231 U.S. at 415; *Doyle v. Mitchell Bros. Co.,* 247 U.S. at 185).

137. *Macomber,* 252 U.S. at 203.

138. *Macomber,* 252 U.S. at 214–15.

139. *Macomber,* 252 U.S. at 220–21. Or *Macomber* might have been viewed as having had a choice of stock or cash, also taxable. *Cf.* I.R.C. § 305(b)(1).

140. *Glenshaw Glass,* 348 U.S. at 429–30.

141. *Macomber,* 252 U.S. at 219–20 (Holmes, J., dissenting).

142. Fiss, *History:* p. 100.

143. Ackerman, *Taxation:* pp. 45–46.

144. *Macomber,* 252 U.S. at 220 (Holmes, J., dissenting) (quoting Bishop v. State, 149 Ind. at 230).

145. *Macomber,* 252 U.S. at 220.

146. *Macomber* should never have been understood to exempt everything to which the label "stock dividend" might have been attached from income taxation. *See* Koshland v. Helvering (1936). In two cases decided the next year, United States v. Phellis (1921), and Rockefeller v. United States (1921), the Court held that the receipt of stock dividends which changed shareholders' respective interests in assets and earnings and profits was a taxable event. The rationale for not taxing Macomber, that her interest remained unchanged, did not apply to those cases.

147. *See Weiss,* 265 U.S. at 253. Since the Court had collapsed constitutional and statutory analysis in *Macomber,* it might be possible to see *Weiss* as a statutory interpretation case. But McReynolds' references to the Amendment confirm *Weiss*'s constitutional basis. (Nevertheless, struggling to understand reorganizations, the Court soon limited *Weiss* and *Macomber* to cases where the "business enterprise actually conducted remained exactly the same." *Marr v. United States,* 268 U.S. at 540. And in *Cottage Savings Ass'n v. Commissioner,* 499 U.S. at 563–64, the Court discussed *Weiss* and *Marr* with no mention of the Constitution.)

148. *Cuba R.R.,* 268 U.S. at 632.

149. *Cuba R.R.,* 268 U.S. at 633.

150. *Cuba R.R.,* 268 U.S. at 631–32.

151. *James,* 366 U.S. at 248–49 (Whittaker, J., dissenting) (quoting *Cuba R.R.,* 268 U.S. at 631–32).

152. *James,* 366 U.S. at 248 n.1.

153. *Burk-Waggoner Oil,* 269 U.S. at 114.

154. *Taft v. Bowers,* 278 U.S. at 481.

155. *Independent Life,* 292 U.S. at 379.

156. *Bowers v. Kerbaugh-Empire Co.,* 271 U.S. at 174.

157. *Merchants' Loan & Trust Co. v. Smietanka,* 255 U.S. at 519.

158. For 1913, the tax applied only to "net income accruing from March first to December thirty-first." Income Tax Law of 1913, Ch. 16, § II.D, 38 Stat. 168. Congress did not try to tax distributions from pre-1913 earnings. *See* Revenue Act of 1916, Ch. 463, § 2(a), 39 Stat. 756, 757 (defining "dividends" as distributions "out of earnings or profits accrued since March first, nineteen hundred and thirteen"); I.R.C. § 316(a) (defining "dividends" as "distributions . . . out of earnings and profits accumulated after February 28, 1913"). Nor did it try to tax pre-1913 appreciation. *See* Revenue Act of 1918, Ch. 18, § 202(a)(1), 40 Stat. 1060 (providing for "property acquired before March 1, 1913, the fair market value of such property as of that date" would be basis); *see also* I.R.C. § 301(c)(3)(B) (exempting non-dividend distributions exceeding basis to extent distribution is "out of increase in value

accrued before March 1, 1913"); I.R.C. § 1015(c) (treating basis of property acquired by gift before 1921 as value at time of acquisition).

159. *See* The Income Tax: Opinions of Hon. John K. Shields, Hon. Cordell Hull, and Thurlow M. Gordon on the Proposed Income-Tax Provision of the Pending Tariff Bill, S. Doc. No. 63–171 (1913).

160. *See Macomber,* 252 U.S. at 203–04.

161. Michael J. Graetz, *The Decline (and Fall?) of the Income Tax* (New York: W. W. Norton & Co., 1997): p. 285.

162. *Union Electric,* 363 F.3d at 1302 n.11.

163. *Bruun,* 309 U.S. at 468–69.

164. *Griffiths,* 318 U.S. at 372 (citing I.R.C. § 115, 53 Stat. 1, 47 (1940)).

165. *See Griffiths,* 318 U.S. at 375 ("The Court in [Koshland v. Helvering (1936), holding taxable a distribution of common stock on preferred stock] in effect limited *Eisner v. Macomber* to the kind of dividend there dealt with.").

166. *Griffiths,* 318 U.S. at 404 (Douglas, J., dissenting).

167. *See, e.g.,* Ackerman, *Taxation:* p. 52.

168. *Glenshaw Glass,* 348 U.S. at 431.

169. *Cottage Savings,* 499 U.S. at 562.

170. *Cottage Savings,* 499 U.S. at 563.

171. *Cottage Savings,* 499 U.S. at 559 (quoting *Helvering v. Horst,* 311 U.S. at 116).

172. Cottage Savings sold participation interests in blocks of low-interest mortgages and purchased economically identical interests in other blocks. It successfully argued the sale was a taxable "disposition of property," I.R.C. § 1001(a), so it could recognize a loss. The government argued there was no disposition because, after the dust had settled, Cottage Savings' economic position was unchanged. Much of the discussion in the case focused on whether the two blocks "differ[ed] materially either in kind or in extent." Treas. Reg. § 1.1001–1; *see Cottage Savings,* 499 U.S. at 560–67.

173. Leon Gabinet & Ronald J. Coffey, "The Implications of the Economic Concept of Income for Corporation-Shareholder Income Tax Systems," *Case Western Reserve Law Review* 27 (1977): 895, 919.

174. *Macomber,* 255 U.S. at 519; *see also Bowers v. Kerbaugh-Empire Co.,* 271 U.S. at 174 ("It was not the purpose or effect of that Amendment to bring any new subject within the taxing power.").

175. *Macomber,* 252 U.S. at 220 (Holmes, J., dissenting) (quoting *Bishop v. State,* 149 Ind. at 230).

176. *Taft,* 278 U.S. at 481.

177. *Cuba R.R.,* 268 U.S. at 631–32.

178. *Independent Life,* 292 U.S. at 381.

179. *See Penn Mut. Indem. Co. v. Commissioner,* 277 F.2d at 20. In some cases, unapportioned gross receipts taxes have been held to be excises on the right to engage in business in a particular form and, therefore, not subject to apportionment. *See, e.g.,* Spreckels Sugar Ref. Co. v. McClain (1904) (upholding tax measured by gross receipts on persons engaged in refining petroleum or sugar, or controlling pipeline to transport oil or other products); Pac. Ins. Co. v. Soule (1868) (upholding tax on insurance company gross premiums).

180. *Cf. Doyle v. Mitchell Bros.,* 247 U.S. at 185 ("In order to determine whether there has been gain or loss, and the amount of the gain, if any, we must withdraw from the gross

proceeds an amount sufficient to restore the capital value that existed at the commencement of the period under consideration.").

181. *Independent Life,* 292 U.S. at 381 (emphasis added).

182. Seligman, *Income Tax:* p. 19.

183. Income Tax Law of 1913, ch. 16, § II.A.1, 38 Stat. 166.

184. *See* William D. Andrews, *Basic Federal Income Taxation* (5th ed., Gaithersburg: Aspen Law & Business, 1999): p. 22.

185. *Sanford & Brooks,* 282 U.S. at 361.

186. *Sanford & Brooks,* 282 U.S. at 364.

187. *See* Brownlee, *Federal:* p. 45.

188. *Sanford & Brooks,* 282 U.S. at 364–65.

189. *Sanford & Brooks,* 282 U.S. at 365 (emphasis added).

190. *Sanford & Brooks,* 282 U.S. at 365; *see also Sanford & Brooks,* 282 U.S. at 363.

191. *See* Act of Aug. 5, 1861, Ch. 45, 12 Stat. 292; Act of Mar. 5, 1816, Ch. 24, 3 Stat. 255; Act of Feb. 27, 1815, Ch. 60, 3 Stat. 216; Act of Jan. 9, 1815, Ch. 21, 3 Stat. 164; Act of Aug. 2, 1813, Ch. 37, 3 Stat. 53; Act of July 14, 1798, Ch. 75, 1 Stat. 597.

192. *See* Robert A. Becker, *Revolution, Reform, and the Politics of American Taxation, 1763–1783* (Baton Rouge: Louisiana State University Press, 1980): p. 49.

193. *The Federalist No. 36,* at 223.

194. "Essays by a Farmer," *Maryland Gazette* (Mar. 18, 1788), *reprinted in* 5 Storing, *Complete:* pp. 35–36.

195. The term *poll tax,* as used here, is synonymous with capitation tax. It does not refer to a tax that must be paid in order to vote—the more common modern usage.

196. "The Address and Reasons of Dissent of the Minority of the Convention of Pennsylvania to Their Constituents," *Pennsylvania Packet & Daily Advertiser* (Dec. 18, 1787), *reprinted in* 3 Storing, *Complete:* pp. 145, 162.

197. *See* Fiss, *History:* p. 92.

198. Furthermore, even with the counting rules gone today, determining who ought to be counted, and taken into account, in the apportionment formula is not obvious.

199. *See* Adam Smith, *The Wealth of Nations* (Edward Cannan ed., New York: Random House, 1937) (1776): pp. 818–21.

200. Smith, *Wealth:* p. 819.

201. *See Hylton,* 3 U.S. (3 Dall.) at 175 (Chase, J.), 3 U.S. (3 Dall.) at 183 (Iredell, J.); 3 U.S. (3 Dall.) at 177 (Paterson, J.).

202. *See* Act of Aug. 5, 1861, Ch. 45, 12 Stat. 292; Act of Mar. 5, 1816, Ch. 24, 3 Stat. 255; Act of Feb. 27, 1815, Ch. 60, 3 Stat. 216; Act of Jan. 9, 1815, Ch. 21, 3 Stat. 164; Act of Aug. 2, 1813, Ch. 37, 3 Stat. 53; Act of July 14, 1798, Ch. 75, 1 Stat. 597.

203. *See, e.g., Springer v. United States,* 102 U.S. at 602 ("*[D]irect taxes,* within the meaning of the Constitution, are only capitation taxes, as expressed in that instrument, and taxes on real estate. . . ."); *Scholey v. Rew,* 90 U.S. (23 Wall.) at 348 (characterizing estate tax on real estate as excise on passage of value, as distinguished from tax on ownership of real estate, which would have been direct); *Veazie Bank v. Fenno,* 75 U.S. (8 Wall.) at 543 (noting that direct taxes imposed to that time had all been on real estate, and that "personal property, contracts, occupations, and the like, have never been regarded by Congress as proper subjects of direct tax").

204. *Pollock,* 157 U.S. at 558.

205. For purposes of this analysis, "avoidability" must be understood in a reasonable way. If all taxes were treated as avoidable because of a limited role for taxpayer choice,

nothing would be left of *direct taxes*, and the term was intended to have effect. Suicide takes care of capitation tax obligations; one does not pay income tax if one avoids income; and one does not pay a real-estate tax if one acquires no real property. But the "should-I-kill-myself?" or "should-I-have-income?" or "should-I-own-property?" decisions are different from the choice inherent in the archetypical indirect tax: Do I buy this particular product and pay the associated tax?

206. *Knowlton,* 178 U.S. at 81–82 (quoted in *Union Electric,* 363 F.3d at 1305). The *Union Electric* court also cited New York Trust Co. v. Eisner (1921), following *Knowlton,* for the proposition that lack of avoidability does not automatically require treating a tax as direct. *See New York Trust,* 256 U.S. at 349.

207. *Bromley,* 280 U.S. at 136 (citations omitted); *see Bromley,* 280 U.S. at 137 (noting "persistence" of distinction between taxing an owner because he is an owner, regardless of use of property, and taxing based on particular use).

208. *Independent Life,* 292 U.S. at 378. A tax on the imputed income associated with real estate ownership (income that has not been realized) would presumably be subject to this rule.

209. *See, e.g.,* Ackerman, *Taxation:* pp. 56–58; Bruce A. Ackerman & Anne Alstott, *The Stakeholder Society* (New Haven: Yale University Press, 1999). Professor Ackerman basically argues that the constitutional revolutions of the twentieth century, particularly during the New Deal, rendered the original understanding of what constituted a direct tax irrelevant. *See* Ackerman, *Taxation:* p. 3. At bottom, his position is a restatement of the idea that the national taxing power is plenary in character, or at least that the power became plenary with the development of modern conceptions of government. Ackerman's position is difficult to refute because it rests more on his perceptions of the *Zeitgeist* than it does on specific authority, and necessarily so. The status of taxes under the Direct-Tax Clauses has not been a hotly litigated issue for years.

210. Professor Johnson has also argued that wealth taxes should not be treated as direct because of a "more general intent" of the founders. Calvin H. Johnson, "Apportionment of Direct Taxes: The Foul-Up in the Core of the Constitution," *William & Mary Bill of Rights Journal* 7 (1998): 1, 70. That is, had the founders thought more carefully about what they were doing, they would have seen that it made no sense to subject real-estate taxes to the apportionment rule. Whatever the merits of this logic, the founders did, to a man, see real-estate taxes as direct. With no doubt whatsoever about what the founders thought on this point, it is not clear why we should even think about looking for a "more general intent."

211. *See* Johnson, *Purging:* pp. 1728–29.

212. *See* Johnson, *Purging:* p. 1733.

213. H.R. Rep. No. 53–276, at 3 (1894) (emphasis added).

214. *See, e.g.,* 26 Cong. Rec. 6634 (June 21, 1894) (statement of Senator Peffer).

215. Some said apportionment had outlived its usefulness, *see, e.g.,* 44 Cong. Rec. 4392 (July 12, 1909) (statement of Representative Clark), but with cases from *Hylton* to *Pollock* on the books, it was hard to imagine an unapportioned tax on real property surviving judicial review.

216. It is not apparent now either, for that matter.

217. In fact, some have thrown all caution to the winds and have argued that, because *any* tax is likely to be paid out of income, it should be characterized as a tax on incomes. That position, however, is not one the drafters and ratifiers of the Sixteenth Amendment would have been comfortable with.

218. Deborah H. Schenk, "Saving the Income Tax with a Wealth Tax," *Tax Law Review* 53 (2000): 423, 441.

219. Schenk, *Saving:* p. 442.

220. Schenk, *Saving:* p. 442.

221. *Union Electric,* 363 F.3d at 1304.

222. *The Federalist No. 21,* at 143.

223. *See The Federalist No. 21,* at 142–43 ("It is a signal advantage of taxes on articles of consumption that they contain in their own nature a security against excess.").

224. 1 Farrand: p. 592 (July 12, 1787).

225. Thomas M. Cooley, *A Treatise on the Law of Taxation, Including the Law of Local Assessments* (Chicago: Callaghan & Co., 1876): p. 5 (footnote omitted)

226. Cf. David P. Currie, *The Constitution in the Supreme Court: The First Hundred Years, 1789–1888* (Chicago: University of Chicago Press, 1985): p. 37 ("Under [Adam] Smith's definition, . . . a tax on income is precisely what is meant by a direct tax.").

227. *See* Robert E. Hall & Alvin Rabushka, *The Flat Tax* (2d ed., Stanford: Hoover Institution Press, 1995); Robert E. Hall & Alvin Rabushka, "The Flat Tax: A Simple, Progressive Consumption Tax," in *Frontiers of Tax Reform* (Michael J. Boskin ed., Stanford: Hoover Institution Press, 1996): p. 27.

228. *See* Murray Weidenbaum, "The Nunn-Domenici USA Tax: Analysis and Comparisons," in Boskin, *Frontiers:* p. 54; Laurence S. Seidman, *The USA Tax: A Progressive Consumption Tax* (Cambridge: MIT Press, 1997).

229. The term *direct-consumption tax* is not derived from constitutional law, of course, but the founders' understanding of direct taxation and the understanding of contemporaneous economic thinkers were not dissimilar.

230. *See, e.g.*, Zelenak, *Radical:* p. 838

231. Marjorie E. Kornhauser, "The Rise of Rhetoric in Tax Reform Debate: An Example," *Tulane Law Review* 70 (1996): 2345, 2347.

232. Marjorie E. Kornhauser, "What Do Women Want: Feminism and the Progressive Income Tax," *American University Law Review* 47 (1997): 151, 152 (footnotes omitted).

233. Thuronyi, *Concept:* pp. 99–100 (emphasis added) (footnotes omitted).

234. Congress could enact an income tax while labeling it as something else: "It is not necessary to uphold the validity of [a] tax . . . that the tax itself bear an accurate label." *Penn Mut. Indem. Co. v. Commissioner,* 277 F.2d at 20. But the direct-consumption taxes are not income taxes as Amendment ratifiers understood such taxes. Some writers have used terms like "cash flow personal income tax" to describe a direct-consumption tax, *see, e.g.,* William D. Andrews, "A Consumption-Type or Cash Flow Personal Income Tax," *Harvard Law Review* 87 (1974): 1113, but that was for purposes of comparing an expenditure tax with the existing income tax.

235. *See, e.g.,* Zelenak, *Radical.*

236. *Hvoslef,* 237 U.S. at 13.

237. *Marbury,* 5 U.S. (1 Cranch) at 179.

238. *IBM,* 517 U.S. at 845.

239. *IBM,* 517 U.S. at 861.

240. *Fairbank,* 181 U.S. at 290.

241. *Fairbank,* 181 U.S. at 292.

242. I.R.C. § 4371(1).

243. *IBM,* 517 U.S. at 863 (Kennedy, J., dissenting).

244. Act of July 6, 1797, Ch. 11, § 1, 1 Stat. 527.

245. *See* Act of June 13, 1898, Ch. 448, 30 Stat. 448, 461.

246. *Thames & Mersey,* 237 U.S. at 25.
247. *Thames & Mersey,* 237 U.S. at 26.
248. *IBM,* 517 U.S. at 854.
249. *See IBM,* 517 U.S. at 851.
250. *IBM,* 517 U.S. at 859.
251. *Brown v. Maryland,* 25 U.S. (12 Wheat.) at 445.
252. *See IBM,* 517 U.S. at 857.
253. *IBM,* 517 U.S. at 863.
254. "Leading Cases: Export Clause," *Harvard Law Review* 110 (1996): 196, 200–01.
255. *Thames & Mersey,* 237 U.S. at 26.
256. I.R.C. §§ 4461(a), 4462(a)(2).
257. I.R.C. § 4462(a)(3)(A).
258. *U.S. Shoe,* 523 U.S. at 362.
259. I.R.C. § 4462(f)(1), (2).
260. *U.S. Shoe,* 523 U.S. at 363.
261. *U.S. Shoe,* 523 U.S. at 370 (quoting *Pace v. Burgess,* 92 U.S. at 376).
262. *Pace,* 92 U.S. at 375–76.
263. *Pace,* 92 U.S. at 376.
264. *U.S. Shoe,* 523 U.S. at 370 (quoting *Pace,* 92 U.S. at 376).
265. U.S. Const. Art. I, § 8, cl. 1.
266. U.S. Const. Art. I, § 8, cl. 1.
267. U.S. Const. Art. I, § 9, cl. 5.
268. U.S. Const. Art. I, § 9, cl. 1.
269. U.S. Const. Art. I, § 10, cl. 2.
270. U.S. Const. Art. I, § 2, cl. 3; U.S. Const. Art. I, § 9, cl. 4.
271. *Pace,* 92 U.S. at 375.
272. Act of July 20, 1868, Ch. 186, § 74, 15 Stat. 125, 157.
273. *Pace,* 92 U.S. at 375 (quoted in *U.S. Shoe,* 523 U.S. at 369).
274. *Pace,* 92 U.S. at 376.
275. Claire R. Kelly & Daniela Amzel, "Does the Commerce Clause Eclipse the Export Clause? Making Sense of *United States v. United States Shoe Corp.,*" *Minnesota Law Review* 84 (1999): 129, 161.
276. *See, e.g., Packet Co. v. St. Louis,* 100 U.S. at 427–28 (holding that municipal corporation could "charg[e] and collect[] from those using its wharves and facilities, such reasonable fees as will fairly remunerate it for the use of its property," despite the Import-Export Clause's prohibition on states' levying "Duties on . . . Exports" without congressional consent).
277. Kelly & Amzel, *Commerce:* p. 161.
278. *See, e.g., IBM,* 517 U.S. at 846.
279. *Pace,* 92 U.S. at 376 (emphasis added).
280. *See, e.g.,* United States v. Sperry Corp. (1989) (holding that 1½% *ad valorem* fee on awards certified by Iran–U.S. Claims Tribunal was user fee, not so excessive as to violate Takings Clause).
281. *U.S. Shoe,* 523 U.S. at 368.
282. *IBM,* 517 U.S. at 846.
283. Act of October 3, 1913, Ch. 16, § II, 38 Stat. 166, 172.
284. *W. E. Peck & Co.,* 247 U.S. at 174–75.

285. *IBM,* 517 U.S. at 846.
286. *Cornell,* 192 U.S. at 427.
287. *Brown,* 25 U.S. (12 Wheat.) at 445.
288. 2 Story, *Commentaries* § 1012, at 471.
289. *See* Act of July 6, 1797, Ch. 11, § 1, 1 Stat. 527.
290. Act of June 13, 1898, Ch. 448, 30 Stat. 448, 451, 459.
291. Act of June 13, 1898, Ch. 448, 30 Stat. 459.
292. *Fairbank,* 181 U.S. at 295.
293. *Almy,* 65 U.S. (24 How.) at 174.
294. *Fairbank,* 181 U.S. at 315 (Harlan, J., dissenting).
295. *Fairbank,* 181 U.S. at 312.
296. *Thames & Mersey,* 237 U.S. at 26.
297. *Thames & Mersey,* 237 U.S. at 25.
298. Act of June 13, 1898, Ch. 448, § 6, 30 Stat. 448, 451, 460.
299. *See* Act of July 6, 1797, Ch. 448, § 1, 1 Stat. 527, 528 (imposing one-dollar tax on "any charter-party").
300. *Hvoslef,* 237 U.S. at 17.
301. *Hvoslef,* 237 U.S. at 13.
302. *Hvoslef,* 237 U.S. at 13.
303. *IBM,* 517 U.S. at 846.
304. *IBM,* 517 U.S. at 848 (citing Pace v. Burgess (1876); Turpin v. Burgess (1886); and Cornell v. Coyne (1904)).
305. Act of June 6, 1896, Ch. 337, § 9, 29 Stat. 253.
306. *Cornell,* 192 U.S. at 427.
307. *See* Act of July 20, 1868, Ch. 186, § 74, 15 Stat. 125, 157.
308. *See* Act of August 8, 1882, Ch. 468, 22 Stat. 372.
309. *Turpin,* 117 U.S. at 505.
310. *Turpin,* 117 U.S. at 506.
311. *Turpin,* 117 U.S. at 507.
312. *Turpin,* 117 U.S. at 507.
313. Act of July 20, 1868, Ch. 186, § 74, 15 Stat. 125, 157.
314. *See IBM,* 517 U.S. at 848.
315. War Revenue Act of October 3, 1917, Ch. 63, § 600(f), 40 Stat. 300, 316.
316. *Spalding,* 262 U.S. at 69.
317. *Spalding,* 262 U.S. at 69.
318. *Spalding,* 262 U.S. at 68.
319. *Spalding,* 262 U.S. at 70.
320. *Spalding,* 262 U.S. at 70.
321. *Spalding,* 262 U.S. at 70.
322. *U.S. Shoe,* 523 U.S. at 368.
323. *Brown v. Maryland,* 25 U.S. (12 Wheat.) at 445.
324. *IBM,* 517 U.S. at 851.
325. *U.S. Shoe,* 523 U.S. at 368.
326. *Department of Revenue of Wash. v. Association of Wash. Stevedoring Cos.,* 435 U.S. at 757.
327. *U.S. Shoe,* 523 U.S. at 368.
328. *IBM,* 517 U.S. at 851.

329. Act of July 6, 1797, Ch. 11, § 1, 1 Stat. 527.

330. 1 Stat. at 528.

331. *Fairbank,* 181 U.S. at 295.

332. As is discussed in Chapter 10, however, the Supreme Court has generally deferred to Congress's characterization of a purported levy as a tax, at least as long as some minimal revenue is raised.

333. *Cf.* Veazie Bank v. Fenno (1869) (upholding tax on state bank notes, although purpose of tax was to drive notes out of existence; government had power to regulate currency, so that "tax" at issue might have been valid even if not characterized as tax).

334. *See* 1 St. George Tucker, *Blackstone's Commentaries* (Philadelphia: W. Y. Birch & A. Small, 1803): app. p. 246, *quoted in* 2 Story, *Commentaries* § 1051.

335. See 1 Tucker, *Blackstone's Commentaries:* app. p. 247.

336. *See* 2 Story, *Commentaries* § 1051.

337. 2 Farrand, *Records:* p. 377 (Aug. 22, 1787).

338. *See* 2 Farrand, *Records:* p. 412 (Aug. 25, 1787).

339. 2 Farrand, *Records:* p. 392 (Aug. 23, 1787).

340. *See* 2 Farrand, *Records:* p. 47 (July 18, 1787).

341. 2 Farrand, *Records:* pp. 168, 182.

342. "Essays of Brutus. VIII" (Jan. 10, 1788), *reprinted in* 2 Storing, *Complete:* p. 405.

343. 2 Story, *Commentaries* § 1051.

344. 2 Farrand, *Records:* p. 303 (Aug. 16, 1787).

345. 2 Farrand, *Records:* p. 309 (Aug. 16, 1787).

346. James Madison, "The Bank Bill," House of Representatives (Feb. 2, 1791), *reprinted in* 13 *The Papers of James Madison* (Charles F. Hobson & Robert A. Rutland eds., Charlottesville: University Press of Virginia, 1981): pp. 372, 376.

347. 2 Farrand, *Records:* p. 310 (Aug. 16, 1787).

348. 2 Farrand, *Records:* p. 309 (Aug. 16, 1787).

349. 2 Farrand, *Records:* pp. 309–10 (Aug. 16, 1787).

350. 2 Farrand, *Records:* p. 309 (Aug. 16, 1787).

351. 2 Farrand, *Records:* p. 310 (Aug. 16, 1787).

352. 2 Farrand, *Records:* p. 309 (Aug. 16, 1787).

353. 2 Farrand, *Records:* p. 310 (Aug. 16, 1787).

354. Luther Martin, "Mr. Martin's Information to the General Assembly of the State of Maryland" (1788), in 2 Storing, *Complete:* pp. 27, 56–57.

355. 2 Farrand, *Records:* p. 310 n.* (Aug. 16, 1787).

356. Knox v. Lee (The Legal Tender Cases) (1872); Hepburn v. Griswold (1870).

357. 1 Farrand, *Records:* p. 233 (June 13, 1787).

358. 1 Farrand, *Records:* p. 543 (July 6, 1787).

359. *The Federalist No. 58,* at 359 (James Madison) (Clinton Rossiter ed., New York: Mentor Books, 1961).

360. *The William,* 28 F. Cas. at 621.

361. 2 Elliot, *Debates:* p. 452 (Dec. 3, 1787).

362. 2 Farrand, *Records:* p. 416 (Aug. 25, 1787).

363. 2 Farrand, *Records:* p. 417 (Aug. 25, 1787).

364. 2 Farrand, *Records:* p. 416 (Aug. 25, 1787).

365. 2 Farrand, *Records:* p. 417 (Aug. 25, 1787).

366. 2 Farrand, *Records:* p. 417 (Aug. 25, 1787) (emphasis added).

367. 2 Farrand, *Records:* p. 417 (Aug. 25, 1787).

368. *See* Joel S. Newman, "Slave Tax as Sin Tax: 18th and 19th Century Perspectives," *Tax Notes* 101 (2003): pp. 1019, 1022.

369. *South Carolina v. Baker,* 485 U.S. at 523 (quoting *United States v. New Mexico,* 455 U.S. at 735).

370. *Day,* 78 U.S. at 122–23.

371. *Day,* 78 U.S. at 126.

372. *Day,* 78 U.S. at 127.

373. *Gerhardt,* 304 U.S. at 416.

374. *Gerhardt,* 304 U.S. at 417.

375. *Gerhardt,* 304 U.S. at 425–27 (Black, J., concurring).

376. *Graves,* 306 U.S. at 484–87.

377. *Graves,* 306 U.S. at 480.

378. *Graves,* 306 U.S. at 483.

379. *Graves,* 306 U.S. at 490 (Frankfurter, J., concurring).

380. *Graves,* 306 U.S. at 489.

381. *South Carolina v. Baker,* 485 U.S. at 520.

382. *Railroad Co.,* 84 U.S. at 327.

383. *South Carolina v. Baker,* 485 U.S. at 523 (quoting *United States v. New Mexico,* 455 U.S. at 735).

384. *South Carolina v. Baker,* 485 U.S. at 524–25.

385. *South Carolina v. Baker,* 485 U.S. at 522.

386. *McCulloch,* 17 U.S. (4 Wheat.) at 316, 436.

387. *South Carolina v. Baker,* 485 U.S. at 523 (quoting *United States v. New Mexico,* 455 U.S. at 735).

388. *South Carolina v. Baker,* 485 U.S. at 523.

389. 1 Boris I. Bittker & Lawrence Lokken, *Federal Taxation of Income, Estates and Gifts* (3d. ed., New York: Warren Gorham & Lamont, 2000): ¶ 1.2.8, § 1–43.

390. 1 Bittker & Lokken, *Federal Taxation:* ¶ 1.2.8, § 1–43 (quoting I.R.C. § 511 (a) (2) (B)).

391. *See, e.g., South Carolina v. United States,* 199 U.S. at 461; *Ambrosini v. United States,* 187 U.S. at 3.

392. *Massachusetts,* 435 U.S. at 456.

393. *Massachusetts,* 435 U.S. at 459–60.

394. *Garcia,* 469 U.S. at 554.

395. Ellen P. Aprill, "Excluding the Income of State and Local Governments: The Need for Congressional Action," *Georgia Law Review* 26 (1992): 421, 454–55.

396. *Massachusetts,* 435 U.S. at 463.

397. *McCray,* 195 U.S. at 58 (quoting *Spencer v. Merchant,* 125 U.S. at 355).

398. *Sonzinsky,* 300 U.S. at 512.

399. *Sonzinsky,* 300 U.S. at 513.

400. *Kahriger,* 345 U.S. at 28.

401. *Kahriger,* 345 U.S. at 38.

402. *See also* Minor v. United States (1969).

403. *See also* Leary v. United States (1969).

404. *See also* United States v. Knox (1969).

405. *Child Labor Tax Case,* 259 U.S. at 36.

406. *A. Magnano Co.*, 292 U.S. at 44.

407. *Carlton,* 512 U.S. at 32.

408. *Carlton,* 512 U.S. at 31–32 (quoting *Pension Benefit Guaranty Corp. v. R. A. Gray & Co.,* 467 U.S. at 729).

409. Eric Kades, "Drawing the Line Between Taxes and Takings: The Continuous Burdens Principle, and Its Broader Application," *Northwestern University Law Review* 97 (2002): 189.

410. Kades, *Drawing:* p. 190.

411. Ackerman, *Taxation:* p. 3.

412. *See* Calvin R. Massey, "Takings and Progressive Rate Taxation," *Harvard Journal of Law and Public Policy* 20 (1996): 85, 104.

413. *See* Walter J. Blum & Harry Kalven, Jr., *The Anatomy of Justice in Taxation* (Univ. of Chicago Law School, Occasional Papers, 1973): p. 4.

414. *See* Richard A. Epstein, *Takings: Private Property and the Power of Eminent Domain* (Cambridge: Harvard University Press, 1985): pp. 297–300.

415. Epstein, *Takings:* p. 282.

416. Kades, *Drawing:* p. 206.

417. *Griffin,* 4 N.Y. 420.

418. Thomas M. Cooley, *The Law of Taxation* (4th ed., Clark A. Nichols ed., Chicago: Callaghan & Co., 1924): pp. 102–03.

419. *Hatter,* 532 U.S. at 567.

420. *Will,* 449 U.S. at 217–18.

421. 3 Story, *Commentaries* § 1622, at 490.

422. *The Federalist No. 79,* at 472 (Alexander Hamilton) (Clinton Rossiter ed., New York: Mentor Books, 1961).

423. Letter from R.B. Taney to Hon. S.P. Chase (Feb. 16, 1863), *reprinted in* 157 U.S. 701 (1895).

424. 13 Op. Att'y Gen. 161 (1869).

425. *See Wayne v. United States,* 26 Ct. Cl. at 290.

426. *See* Income Tax Law of 1913, Ch. 16, § II.B., 38 Stat. 114, 168.

427. Act of February 24, 1919, Ch. 18, § 213(a), 40 Stat. 1057, 1065.

428. *Miles,* 268 U.S. at 508.

429. *Miles,* 268 U.S. at 508–09.

430. Ch. 209, § 22(a), 47 Stat. 169, 178, *reenacted by* Revenue Act of 1936, Ch. 690, § 22(a), 49 Stat. 1648, 1657.

431. *O'Malley,* 307 U.S. at 282.

432. *O'Malley,* 307 U.S. at 282–83.

433. *Will,* 449 U.S. at 227.

434. Pub. L. No. 97–248, Tit. II, Subtit. E, Pt. III, § 278, 96 Stat. 324, 559–63.

435. Pub. L. No. 98–21, § 101(b)(1), 97 Stat. 65, 69.

436. *Hatter,* 532 U.S. at 567.

437. *Hatter,* 532 U.S. at 560 (quoting *O'Malley,* 307 U.S. at 282).

438. Nevertheless, in several appropriation acts in the mid- and late 1990s, Congress blocked otherwise automatic, annual adjustments in judicial salary, which had been provided for in the Ethics Reform Act of 1989, Pub. L. No. 101–194, 103 Stat. 1716. Although the congressional actions were suspect under *Will,* the Supreme Court refused to hear a case brought by several judges who had been sitting when the Ethics Reform Act was

enacted. Justice Breyer wrote a vigorous dissent to the denial of *certiorari,* in which two other justices joined. *See* Williams v. United States (2002).

439. *Hatter,* 532 U.S. at 571 (citations omitted).

440. *Hatter,* 532 U.S. at 577 (citations omitted).

441. *Hatter,* 532 U.S. at 586 (citation omitted).

442. *Will,* 449 U.S. at 220–21 (citing *Evans v. Gore,* 253 U.S. at 253; 1 James Kent, *Commentaries on American Law* (New York: O. Halsted, 1826): p. 276).

443. *New York v. United States,* 505 U.S. at 210 (Stevens, J., dissenting).

444. *The Federalist No. 36,* at 220–21.

445. *The Federalist No. 44,* at 292 (James Madison) (Clinton Rossiter ed., New York: Mentor Books, 1961).

446. 6 *Annals of Congress:* 2636, 2699 (Dec. 14, 1796) (reprinting *Wolcott Report*); *see* Currie, *Constitution in Congress:* p. 225.

447. *Wolcott Report:* p. 2699.

448. *See* 6 *Annals of Congress:* 1882 (Jan. 16, 1797).

449. 2 *Abridgement of the Debates of Congress, from 1789 to 1856,* at 265 (May 5, 1798); *see* Act of July 14, 1798, 1 Stat. 597.

450. 5 *Annals of Congress:* 793 (Mar. 17, 1796); 5 *Annals of Congress:* 856 (Apr. 4, 1796).

451. Currie, *Constitution in Congress:* pp. 225–26 (footnote omitted).

452. Act of Aug. 2, 1813, 3 Stat. 53, 71, § 6.

453. Act of Aug. 2, 1813, 3 Stat. 53, 71, § 7.

454. *Pollock,* 158 U.S. at 620–21.

455. *See generally* Jack N. Rakove, *Original Meanings: Politics and Ideas in the Making of the Constitution* (New York: Knopf, 1996).

456. *See* Frederick Schauer, "Easy Cases," *Southern California Law Review* 58 (1985): 399, 404.

457. Rakove, *Original:* p. 179.

458. *Bromley v. McCaughn,* 280 U.S. at 137 (citing *Nicols v. Ames,* 173 U.S. at 515).

459. Edward J. McCaffery, "Tax's Empire," *Georgetown Law Journal* 85 (1996): 71, 126.

460. Ratner, *Taxation:* p. 19.

461. *Pollock,* 158 U.S. at 632.

462. *See generally* Henry Paul Monaghan, "Stare Decisis and Constitutional Adjudication," *Columbia Law Review* 88 (1988): 723.

463. Monaghan, *Stare Decisis:* p. 744.

464. *Pollock,* 157 U.S. at 641 (White, J., dissenting).

465. *Pollock,* 157 U.S. at 642.

Bibliographic Essay

Taxation is central to American government—indeed, to any government—but literature focusing on the taxing power under the Constitution is sparse. Although that situation might seem counterintuitive, it really should not be surprising. With some important exceptions, historians have generally shied away from a subject that can be very dry and technical. And, working with the conventional understanding that the Constitution imposes few constraints on the taxing power, legal academics have also devoted relatively little effort to constitutional issues associated with taxation. If everyone assumes that Congress can do what it likes in taxation, what is there to write about?

Although the literature is less expansive than one might like, there are nevertheless many interesting works on constitutional issues in taxation waiting to be explored. This essay notes some of the major ones.

HISTORICAL OVERVIEWS

A very useful, accessible history of American taxation is W. Elliot Brownlee, *Federal Taxation in America: A Short History* (Cambridge: Cambridge University Press, 1996).

And one can find much of interest, encompassing the vast scope of American tax history, in Randolph E. Paul, *Taxation in the United States* (Boston: Little Brown, 1954); and Sidney Ratner, *Taxation and Democracy in America* (New York: John Wiley & Sons, 1967). Paul's work was that of a prominent lawyer, rather than a trained historian, and that gives the book a valuable perspective.

I have not tried to sort out the best of the more general works on American history, but such works occasionally devote space to constitutional issues in taxation. The controversies surrounding Hylton v. United States (1796) and Pollock v. Farmers' Loan & Trust Co. (1895) (and the resultant push for the Sixteenth Amendment) were subjects of great public interest. It is hard to imagine a historical work on the United States in the 1890s not making at least passing reference to the income tax and *Pollock.*

For an overview of the taxing power in the late nineteenth century, before *Pollock* and the Sixteenth Amendment, the indispensable source is Thomas M. Cooley, *A Treatise on the Law of Taxation* (Chicago: Callaghan and Co., 1876). Cooley's work is not limited to national taxation, but it is invaluable in what it does say about the nineteenth-century understanding of national constitutional issues. What Thomas Cooley thought about these issues is a good indication of what informed, late nineteenth-century commentators generally thought—or would have thought after perusing *Cooley on Taxation.*

THE FOUNDING PERIOD

The critical materials in trying to understand the founders' conceptions of taxation are the same sources one would use in trying to understand the founders' conception of any subject: the various records of debates in the Constitutional Convention (the most valuable collection remains Max Farrand, *The Records of the Federal Convention of 1787* (New Haven: Yale University Press, 1937)); the reports of debates in state ratification conventions (the still preeminent collection is that of Jonathan Elliot, *The Debates in the Several State Constitutions on the Adoption of the Federal Constitution* (Philadelphia: J. B. Lippincott Co., 1836)); the *Federalist Papers* (available in several solid editions); and Herbert J. Storing's superb collection of anti-federalist literature, *The Complete Anti-Federalist* (Chicago: University of Chicago Press, 1981). *The Founders' Constitution* (Chicago: University of Chicago Press, 1987), a five-volume collection of original materials compiled by Philip B. Kurland and Ralph Lerner, provides an indispensable entryway into several collections of primary sources, as well as other materials that one might not otherwise think of consulting. (The world is a better place now that *The Founders' Constitution* is available online and in an inexpensive paperback edition from the Liberty Fund.)

Joseph Story's *Commentaries on the Constitution of the United States* (Boston: Hilliard, Gray & Co., 1833) is rich in its exposition of original understanding. The *Commentaries* were written after the founding period, of course, but at a time when founding debates were still part of the memory of many Americans.

Several monographs about the founding period and taxation have been especially helpful in my work:

Robert A. Becker, *Revolution, Reform, and the Politics of American Taxation, 1763–1783* (Louisiana State University Press, 1980)

Roger H. Brown, *Redeeming the Republic: Federalists, Taxation, and the Origins of the Constitution* (Baltimore: Johns Hopkins University Press, 1993)

E. James Ferguson, *The Power of the Purse: A History of American Public Finance, 1776–1790* (Chapel Hill: University of North Carolina Press, 1961)

Dall W. Forsythe, *Taxation and Political Change in the Young Nation 1781–1833* (New York: Columbia University Press, 1977)

And David P. Currie's volumes about the brand new Congress and the brand new Supreme Court are extraordinary compilations of important information and high-level intellectual musings about many issues, including taxation:

David P. Currie, *The Constitution in Congress: The Federalist Period, 1789–1801* (Chicago, University of Chicago Press, 1997)

David P. Currie, *The Constitution in Congress: The Jeffersonians, 1801–1829* (Chicago, University of Chicago Press, 2001)

David P. Currie, *The Constitution in the Supreme Court: The First Hundred Years, 1789–1888* (Chicago: University of Chicago Press, 1985)

THE MOVE TO THE INCOME TAX

There was a great deal of contemporaneous writing about the Supreme Court's decision in Pollock v. Farmers' Loan & Trust Co. (1895) and the subsequent move to amend the Constitution. Some of that material is cited in the endnotes to Chapters 4 and 7.

Useful discussion of *Pollock* can be found in David P. Currie, *The Constitution in the Supreme Court: The Second Century, 1888–1986* (Chicago: University of Chicago Press, 1990), and Owen M. Fiss, *History of the Supreme Court of the United States: Troubled Beginnings of the Modern State, 1888–1910* (New York: Macmillan, 1993).

Quite a few books, and parts of books, have been written about the development of the modern income tax. The following have been particularly helpful in my work (and the Brownlee, Paul, and Ratner books cited above are relevant here as well):

Roy G. Blakey & Gladys C. Blakey, *The Federal Income Tax* (New York: Longmans, Green & Co., 1940)
John D. Buenker, *The Income Tax and the Progressive Era* (New York: Garland, 1985)
Louis Eisenstein, *The Ideologies of Taxation* (New York: Ronald Press, 1961)
Michael J. Graetz, *The Decline (and Fall?) of the Income Tax* (New York: W. W. Norton & Co., 1997)
David E. Kyvig, *Explicit & Authentic Acts: Amending the U.S. Constitution, 1776–1995* (Lawrence: University Press of Kansas, 1996)
Sheldon D. Pollack, *The Failure of U.S. Tax Policy* (University Park: Penn State Press, 1996)
Edwin R. A. Seligman, *The Income Tax* (New York: Macmillan, 1914)
Robert Stanley, *Dimensions of Law in the Service of Order: Origins of the Federal Income Tax, 1861–1913* (New York: Oxford University Press, 1993)
Stephen R. Weisman, *The Great Tax Wars* (New York: Simon & Schuster, 2002)
John F. Witte, *The Politics and Development of the Federal Income Tax* (Madison: University of Wisconsin Press, 1985)

Seligman's work is of particular historical interest because, as one of the leading economists of his time, Seligman was an active participant in the events leading to the Sixteenth Amendment and the first post-Amendment income tax legislation.

My own article, "The Taxing Power, the Sixteenth Amendment, and the Meaning of 'Incomes,'" *Arizona State Law Journal* 33 (2001): 1057, deals with the history of the Sixteenth Amendment in detail, as does Marjorie E. Kornhauser's "The Constitutional Meaning of Income and the Taxation of Gifts," *Connecticut Law Review* 25 (1992): 1.

PARTICULAR ISSUES

Most of the particular constitutional provisions and doctrines discussed in this book have also been the subject of serious scholarship.

The Uniformity Clause

The one unquestionably indispensable work on this clause is Nelson Lund, "The Uniformity Clause," *University of Chicago Law Review* 51 (1984): 1193. Do not be put off by the fact that the piece was a student note; this is a first-rate piece of work.

The Direct-Tax Clauses, the Sixteenth Amendment, and the Income Tax

On the understanding of the Direct-Tax Clauses, and whether the Sixteenth Amendment was even necessary to make an unapportioned income tax possible, a fair amount has been written recently—reflecting some heated disagreements. I have supplied some of the heat in these debates, and have been burned as well. Some of the more significant articles follow:

Bruce Ackerman, "Taxation and the Constitution," *Columbia Law Review* 99 (1999): 1

Erik M. Jensen, "The Apportionment of 'Direct Taxes': Are Consumption Taxes Constitutional?" *Columbia Law Review* 97 (1997): 2334

Erik M. Jensen, "Taxation and the Constitution: How to Read the Direct-Tax Clauses," *Journal of Law and Politics* 15 (1999): 689

Erik M. Jensen, "The Taxing Power, the Sixteenth Amendment, and the Meaning of 'Incomes,'" *Arizona State Law Journal* 33 (2001): 1057

Erik M. Jensen, "The Constitution Matters in Taxation," *Tax Notes* 100 (2003): 821; "Jensen's Response to Johnson's Response to Jensen's Response to Johnson's Response to Jensen (Or Is It the Other Way Around?)," *Tax Notes* 100 (2003): 841

Calvin H. Johnson, "Apportionment of Direct Taxes: The Foul-Up in the Core of the Constitution," *William & Mary Bill of Rights Journal* 7 (1998): 1

Calvin H. Johnson, "Purging Out *Pollock*: The Constitutionality of Federal Wealth or Sales Taxes," *Tax Notes* 97 (2002): 1723

Calvin H. Johnson, "Barbie Dolls in the Archeological Dig: Professor Johnson Responds," *Tax Notes* 100 (2003): 832

Yet another exchange between Professor Calvin Johnson and me—on the meaning of the Direct-Tax Clauses and the Sixteenth Amendment—is scheduled to appear in *Constitutional Commentary*.

Export Clause

The Export Clause has had amazingly little written about it, considering that it was critical to the formation of the Constitution and that it has remained important enough to occupy Supreme Court time twice in the 1990s. I immodestly think the key article is now Erik M. Jensen, "The Export Clause," *Florida Tax Review* 6 (2003): 1. But readers should look as well at the more expansive conception of the Clause outlined in Claire R. Kelly & Daniela Amzel, "Does the Commerce Clause Eclipse the Export Clause? Making Sense of *United States v. United States Shoe Corp.*," *Minnesota Law Review* 84 (1999): 129.

Taxation and Takings

As the text indicates, the relationship between the taxing and takings powers is likely to be of more significance in academic debate than it is in real-world controversies. No matter. Richard A. Epstein makes the case for treating takings doctrine seriously as a limitation on the taxing power in *Takings: Private Property and the Power of Eminent Domain* (Cambridge: Harvard University Press, 1985). The key recent article describing the state of the debate is Eric Kades, "Drawing the Line Between Taxes and Takings: The Continuous

Burdens Principle, and Its Broader Application," *Northwestern University Law Review* 97 (2002): 189.

The Compensation Clause and Taxation

The decision in Hatter v. United States (2001) did not make the relationship between the taxing power and the Compensation Clause into a hot topic for cocktail conversation, but the issues are actually quite interesting. Two relevant articles are Jonathan L. Entin & Erik M. Jensen, "Taxation, Compensation, and Judicial Independence: *Hatter v. United States*," *Tax Notes* 90 (2001): 1541; and Jonathan L. Entin & Erik M. Jensen, "*United States v. Hatter* and the Taxation of Federal Judges," *Tax Notes* 92 (2001): 673.

Requisitions

Whether Congress has retained the power to issue requisitions to the states is actually an important constitutional question. It is important not because Congress will ever again try to do such a thing, but the continuing vitality of requisitions is relevant in trying to understand the extent to which Congress might commandeer state governments to serve federal purposes. On that issue, see Erik M. Jensen & Jonathan L. Entin, "Commandeering, the Tenth Amendment, and the Federal Requisition Power: *New York v. United States* Revisited," *Constitutional Commentary* 15 (1998): 353.

Table of Cases

A

Alabama v. King & Boozer, 314 U.S. 1 (1941)
Almy v. California, 65 U.S. (24 How.) 169 (1860)
Ambrosini v. United States, 187 U.S. 1 (1902)

B

Bailey v. Drexel Furniture Co. (*See Child Labor Tax Case*)
Berman v. Parker, 348 U.S. 26 (1954)
Bishop v. State, 149 Ind. 223 (1898)
Bowers v. Kerbaugh-Empire Co., 271 U.S. 170 (1926)
Bromley v. McCaughn, 280 U.S. 124 (1929)
Brown v. Maryland, 25 U.S. (12 Wheat.) 419 (1827)
Brushaber v. Union Pacific RR, 240 U.S. 1 (1916)
Bruun, Helvering v., 309 U.S. 461 (1940)
Buckley v. Valeo, 424 U.S. 1 (1976)
Burk-Waggoner Oil Ass'n v. Hopkins, 269 U.S. 110 (1925)

C

Carlton, United States v., 512 U.S. 26 (1994)
Child Labor Tax Case, 259 U.S. 20 (1922)
Cook v. Pennsylvania, 97 U.S. 566 (1878)
Cornell v. Coyne, 192 U.S. 418 (1904)
Cottage Savings Association v. Commissioner, 499 U.S. 554 (1991)

D

Day, Collector v., 78 U.S. 113 (1870)
Department of Revenue of Washington v. Association of Washington Stevedoring Cos., 435 U.S. 734 (1978)
Dobbins v. Commissioners of Erie County, 41 U.S. (16 Pet.) 435 (1842)
Doremus, United States v., 249 U.S. 86 (1919)
Doyle v. Mitchell Brothers Co., 247 U.S. 179 (1918)

E

Edwards v. Cuba RR, 268 U.S. 628 (1925)
Evans v. Gore, 253 U.S. 245 (1920)

F

Fairbank v. United States, 181 U.S. 283 (1901)
Flint v. Stone Tracy Co., 220 U.S. 107 (1911)

G

Garcia v. San Antonio Metropolitan Transit Authority, 469 U.S. 528 (1985)
Gerhardt, Helvering v., 304 U.S. 405 (1938)
Glenshaw Glass, Commissioner v., 348 U.S. 426 (1955)
Graves v. New York, 306 U.S. 466 (1939)
Griffin v. Mayor of Brooklyn, 4 N.Y. 419 (1851)
Griffiths, Helvering v., 318 U.S. 371 (1943)
Grosso v. United States, 390 U.S. 62 (1968)

H

Hammer v. Dagenhart, 247 U.S. 251 (1918)
Hatter v. United States, 532 U.S. 557 (2001)
Hawaii Housing Authority v. Midkiff, 467 U.S. 229 (1984)
Head Money Cases, 178 U.S. 41 (1900)
Hepburn v. Griswold, 75 U.S. (8 Wall.) 603 (1870)
Home Mutual Insurance Co. v. Commissioner, 639 F.2d 333 (7th Cir. 1980)
Horst, Helvering v., 311 U.S. 112 (1940)
Hvoslef, United States v., 237 U.S. 1 (1915)
Hyde v. Continental Trust Co., 157 U.S. 654 (1895)
Hylton v. United States, 3 U.S. (3 Dall.) 171 (1796)

I

Independent Life Insurance Co., Helvering v., 292 U.S. 371 (1934)
International Business Machines Corp., United States v., 517 U.S. 843 (1996)

J

James v. Drago Contracting Co., 302 U.S. 134 (1937)
James v. United States, 366 U.S. 213 (1961)

K

Kahriger, United States v., 345 U.S. 22 (1953)
Knowlton v. Moore, 178 U.S. 41 (1900)
Knox v. Lee (The Legal Tender Cases), 79 U.S. (12 Wall.) 457 (1872)
Knox, United States v., 396 U.S. 77 (1969)
Koshland v. Helvering, 298 U.S. 441 (1936)

L

Leary v. United States, 395 U.S. 6 (1969)
Lee v. Weisman, 505 U.S. 577 (1992)

Leloup v. Port of Mobile, 127 U.S. 640 (1888)
Lopez, United States v., 514 U.S. 549 (1995)

M

Macomber, Eisner v., 252 U.S. 189 (1920)
A. Magnano Co. v. Hamilton, 292 U.S. 40 (1934)
Marbury v. Madison, 5 U.S. (1 Cranch) 137 (1803)
Marchetti v. United States, 390 U.S. 39 (1968)
Marr v. United States, 268 U.S. 536 (1925)
Massachusetts v. United States, 435 U.S. 444 (1978)
McCray v. United States, 195 U.S. 27 (1903)
McCulloch v. Maryland, 17 U.S. (4 Wheat.) 316 (1819)
Merchants' Loan & Trust Co. v. Smietanka, 255 U.S. 509 (1921)
Miles v. Graham, 268 U.S. 501 (1925)
Minor v. United States, 396 U.S. 87 (1969)
Mountain Producers Corp., Helvering v., 303 U.S. 306 (1938)
Munoz-Flores, United States v., 495 U.S. 385 (1990)

N

New Mexico, United States v., 455 U.S. 720 (1982)
New York v. Graves, 300 U.S. 308 (1937)
New York v. United States, 505 U.S. 144 (1992)
New York Trust Co. v. Eisner, 256 U.S. 345 (1921)
Nicols v. Ames, 173 U.S. 509 (1899)

O

Obear-Nester Glass Co., Commissioner v., 217 F.2d 56 (7th Cir. 1954)
Oklahoma Tax Commission v. Texas Co., 336 U.S. 342 (1949)
O'Malley v. Woodrough, 307 U.S. 277 (1939)

P

Pace v. Burgess, 92 U.S. 372 (1876)
Pacific Insurance Co. v. Soule, 74 U.S. (7 Wall.) 433 (1868)
Packet Co. v. St. Louis, 100 U.S. 423 (1879)
Patton v. Brady, 184 U.S. 608 (1902)
W. E. Peck & Co. v. Lowe, 247 U.S. 165 (1918)
Penn Mutual Indemnity Co. v. Commissioner, 277 F.2d 16 (3d Cir. 1960)
Pension Benefit Guaranty Corp. v. R. A. Gray & Co., 467 U.S. 717 (1984)
Perry v. United States, 294 U.S. 330 (1935)
Phellis, United States v., 257 U.S. 156 (1921)
Philadelphia Steamship Co. v. Pennsylvania, 122 U.S. 326 (1887)
Pollock v. Farmers' Loan & Trust Co., 157 U.S. 429 (1895), 158 U.S. 601 (1895)
Printz v. United States, 521 U.S. 898 (1997)
Ptasysnki v. United States, 462 U.S. 74 (1983)

R

Railroad Co., United States v., 84 U.S. 322 (1872)

Regional Rail Reorganization Act Cases, 419 U.S. 102 (1974)
Rockefeller v. United States, 257 U.S. 176 (1921)

S

Sanchez, United States v., 340 U.S. 42 (1950)
Sanford & Brooks Co., Burnet v., 282 U.S. 359 (1931)
Scholey v. Rew, 90 U.S. (23 Wall.) 331, 348 (1875)
Seminole Tribe v. Florida, 517 U.S. 609 (1996)
Sonzinsky v. United States, 300 U.S. 506 (1937)
South Carolina v. Baker, 485 U.S. 505 (1988)
South Carolina v. United States, 199 U.S. 437 (1905)
South Dakota v. Dole, 483 U.S. 203 (1987)
A. G. Spalding & Brothers v. Edwards, 262 U.S. 66 (1923)
Spencer v. Merchant, 300 U.S. 506 (1937)
Sperry Corp., United States v., 493 U.S. 52 (1989)
Spreckels Sugar Refining Co. v. McClain, 192 U.S. 397 (1904)
Springer v. United States, 102 U.S. 586 (1881)
Stanton v. Baltic Mining Co., 240 U.S. 103 (1916)
Stratton's Independence, Ltd. v. Howbert, 231 U.S. 399 (1913)

T

Taft v. Bowers, 278 U.S. 470 (1929)
Thames & Mersey Marine Insurance Co. v. United States, 237 U.S. 19 (1915)
Towne v. Eisner, 245 U.S. 418 (1918)
Towne, Eisner v., 242 F. 702 (S.D.N.Y. 1917)
Turpin v. Burgess, 117 U.S. 504 (1886)

U

Union Electric Co. v. United States, 363 F.3d 1292 (Fed. Cir. 2004)
United States Shoe Corp., United States v., 523 U.S. 360 (1998)

V

Veazie Bank v. Fenno, 75 U.S. (8 Wall.) 533 (1869)

W

Wayne v. United States, 26 Ct. Cl. 274 (1891)
Weiss v. Stearn, 265 U.S. 242 (1924)
Will, United States v., 449 U.S. 200 (1980)
The William, United States v., 28 F. Cas. 614 (D. Mass. 1808)
Williams v. United States, 535 U.S. 911 (2002)

Index

ABOUT THE AUTHOR

ERIK M. JENSEN is the David L. Brennan Professor of Law at Case Western Reserve University in Cleveland, Ohio, where he has been teaching for more than twenty years. He has also taught at the Cornell Law School. Formerly a practicing tax lawyer, Jensen has written widely on tax issues in academic law reviews and other journals. In recent years he has focused his work on constitutional issues affecting taxation.